Conversations with
Beth Henley

Literary Conversations Series
Monika Gehlawat
General Editor

Conversations with Beth Henley

Edited by Jackson R. Bryer and
Mary C. Hartig

University Press of Mississippi / Jackson

The University Press of Mississippi is the scholarly publishing agency of
the Mississippi Institutions of Higher Learning: Alcorn State University,
Delta State University, Jackson State University, Mississippi State University,
Mississippi University for Women, Mississippi Valley State University,
University of Mississippi, and University of Southern Mississippi.

www.upress.state.ms.us

The University Press of Mississippi is a member
of the Association of University Presses.

First printing 2023
∞

Library of Congress Cataloging-in-Publication Data

Names: Bryer, Jackson R., editor. | Hartig, Mary C., editor.
Title: Conversations with Beth Henley / Jackson R. Bryer, Mary C. Hartig.
Other titles: Literary conversations series.
Description: Jackson : University Press of Mississippi, 2023. | Series: Literary
    conversations series | Includes index.
Identifiers: LCCN 2022057664 (print) | LCCN 2022057665 (ebook) |
    ISBN 9781496844293 (hardback) | ISBN 9781496844309 (paperback) |
    ISBN 9781496844316 (epub) | ISBN 9781496844323 (epub) |
    ISBN 9781496844330 (pdf) | ISBN 9781496844347 (pdf)
Subjects: LCSH: Henley, Beth—Interviews. | Dramatists, American—
    Interviews. | Playwriting.
Classification: LCC PS3558.E4962 Z55 2023 (print) | LCC PS3558.E4962 (ebook) |
    DDC 812/.54—dc23/eng/20230131
LC record available at https://lccn.loc.gov/2022057664
LC ebook record available at https://lccn.loc.gov/2022057665

British Library Cataloging-in-Publication Data available

Works by Beth Henley

Am I Blue. New York: Dramatists Play Service, 1982.

Crimes of the Heart. New York: Viking Press/Penguin Books, 1982; New York: Dramatists Play Service, 1982.

The Wake of Jamie Foster. New York: Dramatists Play Service, 1983.

"Hymn in the Attic" in *24 Hours—PM.* New York: Dramatists Play Service, 1983. 49–53.

The Miss Firecracker Contest. New York: Dramatists Play Service, 1985; Garden City, NY: Nelson Doubleday, 1985.

The Lucky Spot. New York: Dramatists Play Service, 1987.

Abundance. New York: Dramatists Play Service, 1991.

The Debutante Ball. With art by Lynn Green Root. Jackson: University Press of Mississippi, 1991.

Four Plays [*The Wake of Jamie Foster, The Miss Firecracker Contest, The Lucky Spot, Abundance*]. Portsmouth, NH/London: Heinemann/Methuen, 1992.

Monologues for Women. Rancho Mirage, CA: Dramaline Productions, 1992.

The Impossible Marriage. Garden City, NY: Stage & Screen, 1998; New York: Dramatists Play Service, 1999.

Collected Plays Volume I: 1980–1989 [*Crimes of the Heart, Am I Blue, The Wake of Jamie Foster, The Miss Firecracker Contest, The Lucky Spot, The Debutante Ball*]. Lyme, NH: Smith and Kraus, 2000.

Collected Plays Volume II: 1990–1999 [*Abundance, Signature, Control Freaks, Revelers, L-Play, Impossible Marriage*]. Lyme, NH: Smith and Kraus, 2000.

Three Plays [*Control Freaks, L-Play, Sisters of the Winter Madrigal*]. New York: Dramatists Play Service, 2002.

Revelers. New York: Dramatists Play Service, 2002.

Signature. New York: Dramatists Play Service, 2002.

Ridiculous Fraud. New York: Dramatists Play Service, 2007.

"Report on Motherhood" in *Motherhood Out Loud.* New York: Dramatists Play Service, 2012. 45–47.

The Jacksonian. New York: Dramatists Play Service, 2014; Evanston, IL: Northwestern University Press, 2015.

Laugh. Hanover, NH: Smith and Kraus, 2015; New York: Dramatists Play Service, 2016.

"Resemblance Between a Violin Case and a Coffin" in *Desire.* New York: Dramatists Play Service, 2017. 7–23.

Contents

Introduction   xi

Chronology   xix

Beth Henley   3
John Griffin Jones / 1981

Beth Henley   20
Elizabeth Mullener / 1981

Beth Henley Talks about Her Way of Writing Plays   26
Hilary DeVries / 1983

Life after the Pulitzer   29
Linda Sherbert / 1984

Beth Henley   33
Kathleen Betsko / 1984

Mississippi Playwright Downplays Her Success   45
Leslie R. Myers / 1985

Beth Henley   49
Beverly Walker / 1986

The Eccentric Genius of *Crimes of the Heart*   51
Margy Rochlin / 1987

Beth Henley   55
Kevin Sessums / 1987

Beth Henley   59
  Cynthia Wimmer-Moul / 1991

Beth Henley Takes the Director's Chair for *Control Freaks*   79
  Hedy Weiss / 1992

Beth Henley   83
  Mary Dellasega / 1993

Beth Henley: Signature of a Nonstop Playwright   93
  V. Cullum Rogers / 1995

Playing Dollhouse on a Huge Scale:
An Interview with Beth Henley   96
  Bonnie Lyons / 1997

The Mellowing of Miss Firecracker   110
  Pamela Renner / 1998

Stage-Struck in Screen City   114
  Don Shirley / 1999

Beth Henley   118
  Alexis Greene / 1999

Expressing "The Misery and Confusion Truthfully":
An Interview with Beth Henley   136
  Jackson R. Bryer / 2002

An Interview with Beth Henley   151
  Dan O'Brien / 2011

Ridiculous Fraud and *The Jacksonian*—Beth Henley's New Plays
about the South: An Interview   155
  Verna A. Foster / 2012

Beth Henley Returns to New York and Her Southern Roots with
Gothic Black Comedy *The Jacksonian*   167
  TheaterMania / 2013

The Long Journey Home: An Interview with the Playwright about Her Play *The Jacksonian*   170
   Robert Falls / 2014

An Interview with Beth Henley   175
   Karen Carpenter / 2017

In Conversation with Theresa Rebeck and Beth Henley   199
   Theresa Rebeck / 2019

KP Live ABCs: Beth Henley!!!!!!!!   205
   Samantha Barrios and Sam Gianfala / 2020

Index   217

Introduction

Beth Henley's fame came suddenly when in 1981, shortly before her twenty-ninth birthday, she won the Pulitzer Prize for *Crimes of the Heart*, a play that also won the New York Drama Critics' Circle Award. She was, at the time, the first woman to receive the Pulitzer for drama in twenty-three years and the first woman to receive the Drama Critics' Circle Award in twenty-one years. It was her first professionally produced play and her first full-length play. Since then, Henley has been a working playwright and screenwriter, as well as—since 2005—a professor at Loyola Marymount University in Los Angeles, where she teaches playwriting. Los Angeles has been her home since 1976.

Born in 1952 and raised in Jackson, Mississippi, Henley also spent a significant amount of her girlhood in her parents' hometowns, Hazlehurst and Brookhaven, Mississippi, the settings for two of her most famous plays, *Crimes of the Heart* and *The Miss Firecracker Contest*. Henley's roots in the South are only slightly deeper than her roots in theater. As the child of a community theater actress, Henley read lines with her mother and attended rehearsals and performances. Lydy Becker Henley (later Caldwell) frequently appeared at the Jackson Little Theatre and later New Stage Theatre in Jackson, starring as Laura Wingfield in *The Glass Menagerie* and Blanche DuBois in *A Streetcar Named Desire*, among many other roles. There were always Samuel French acting editions lying around the house, and Henley "got into the habit of picking them up" (Dellasega 1993).

In her youth, Henley herself acted occasionally at New Stage. Her interest in theater continued in college, where, as an undergraduate at Southern Methodist University, she majored in acting. It was also at SMU that she wrote her first play, *Am I Blue*, for a sophomore playwriting class. After graduation, she stayed in Dallas, supporting herself by working various day jobs: famously, filing at the Alpo dog food company and, less famously, teaching at a children's theater. About the children's theater instruction, she—with typical appreciation for absurdity—told Jackson R. Bryer in 2002, "I taught badly because I was into nihilism at the time." That year, 1975, she also wrote the book for a musical, *Parade*, with music and lyrics by her friends Mark Hardwick and Stephen Tobolowsky.

During the summer of 1976, after one year of graduate school in acting in Illinois, she worked as part of the original acting company of the Great American People Show at the New Salem State Park theater in Petersburg, Illinois. The 1976 acting company not only premiered but had also collaborated—under the direction of University of Illinois theater professor John Ahart—on the creation of *Your Obedient Servant, A. Lincoln* (1976), a play that was performed annually and was the centerpiece of GAPS from 1976 until 1993 (it was revived in 1995). The play was influenced by Brecht and was, with its use of the Civil War letters of ordinary people, a precursor to the Ken Burns Civil War documentary that would captivate the nation in 1990.

After dropping out of graduate school, Henley moved to Los Angeles to pursue an acting career. Once in California, she again needed to take up what for her were intolerable day jobs; but her creative output—apart from auditioning—included a screenplay, "The Moonwatcher" (eventually made under the title *Nobody's Fool* and released in 1986), and the play that would change everything, *Crimes of the Heart*. In 1981, Henley called those early years in L.A. her "years of destitution" (Jones).

The success of *Crimes of the Heart* at the Actors Theatre of Louisville in 1979 led finally to its great success in New York. Henley's 1981 Pulitzer Prize win brought with it credibility in the theater and film worlds. She sold the rights to *Crimes of the Heart* to the movies, realized she could make a living as a writer, and was able to get productions mounted of plays she had already been working on as well as of future work. Ultimately, the early Pulitzer win gave her the "freedom to write things [she] cared about" (Lyons 1997) for years to come. But the Pulitzer win was not entirely pleasurable at the time: Sounding like one of her own characters, Henley told Elizabeth Mullener in 1981 how she felt shortly after winning: "About three days later, the telephone was still ringing so much I couldn't stand to be in the house, and all these dead flowers were around and I was hung over. . . . [I]t was making me miserable." In 1984, while admitting to Kathleen Betsko that there was a thrill to winning, she believed there was a price to be paid as well: "I think the fate of *The Wake of Jamey Foster* is part of the cost of winning. They just make sure you don't get overwhelmed by it. They want you to feel like it's not a big deal. 'They' meaning the fates, not necessarily the critics."

But the failure of *The Wake of Jamey Foster*, which closed ten days after its opening night, was freeing, too: "[A]fter *The Wake*, I had a chance not to be so humble anymore and to stop being so careful not to be conceited when everybody was telling me how wonderful *Crimes* was. When people tell you you're a shit, then you can be brazen. That was the nice part of the failure" (Sessums 1987). The other useful aspect of failure to Henley is that "failure [is] information" from which one can learn moving forward (Barrios and Gianfala 2020).

Henley's screenplay for *Crimes of the Heart* was nominated for an Academy Award. In addition to *Nobody's Fool*, her other screenplays include *Miss Firecracker* (1989) and *It Must Be Love* (2004), as well as the cowritten *True Stories* (1986) and *A Family Tree* (1987). Others that were never made into films allowed her to pursue what she has called her "expensive hobby": writing plays. Henley's plays (followed by the year of first full production) are *Am I Blue* (1973), *Parade* (the book of a musical, 1975), *Crimes of the Heart* (1979), *The Miss Firecracker Contest* (1980), *The Wake of Jamey Foster* (1982), *Hymn in the Attic*, part of *24 Hours—PM* (1982), *The Debutante Ball* (1985), *The Lucky Spot* (1986), *Abundance* (1989), *Control Freaks* (1992), *Signature* (1995), *L-Play* (1996), *Revelers* (1996), *Impossible Marriage* (1998), *Family Week* (2000), *Sisters of the Winter Madrigal* (2001; written in the 1970s), *Exposed* (2003), *Ridiculous Fraud* (2006), *Report on Motherhood*, part of *Motherhood Out Loud* (2010), *The Jacksonian* (2012), *Laugh* (2015), *Resemblance Between a Violin Case and a Coffin*, part of *Desire* (2015), and *Lightning (or The Unbuttoning)* (2019). In 2021, Henley completed a new play for the stage, *Downstairs Neighbor*, which has not yet been produced. Also during the COVID-19 pandemic, she wrote a short Zoom play, *Give Me Fever*.

Much has influenced Henley's writing for the stage, not least her study and experience of acting. At SMU, she studied theater history, not only reading plays but also studying the art and dance of various periods. Acting brought with it an enhanced appreciation of language: "[E]ven if you had a tiny part [in a Shakespeare play] you would hear that poetry over and over again, the structure of it" (Wimmer-Moul 1991). Also, being onstage enriched her understanding of the logistics of a production as well as "what's fun to do onstage": "It's fun to throw glitter. It's fun to walk out in a hat with a big plume. So you write those things" (Rogers 1995). Beyond a knowledge of theater history, an absorption of great language, and an understanding of staging, Henley's acting background has also infused her writing of characters: "I write each character . . . as if I had to perform them, and I really want to know" what their secrets and dreams and fears are (Wimmer-Moul 1991).

When asked in various interviews about her influences and favorites among other writers, Henley named, among others, playwrights Chekhov,

Shakespeare, O'Neill, Williams, Beckett, Mamet, Shepard, Ibsen, and Hellman, as well as novelists Cather, Styron, Dostoyevsky, Welty, and Richard Ford. She was also "influenced by Reynolds Price and John Kennedy Toole from getting to work so closely trying to adapt their books into screenplays" (Wimmer-Moul 1991). Frequently, Henley singled out Chekhov as a major influence, telling John Griffin Jones in 1981, early in her career, that she "like[s] how he doesn't judge people as much as just shows them in [their] comic and tragic parts." She credited Chekhov's influence for her understanding of the importance of "track[ing] the characters' throughline[s]" and said, "[I] try to understand, even if it makes no rational sense whatsoever, what is compelling them to behave the way they do" (Dellasega 1993). She cited Chekhov's genius in his creation of Lopakhin, for whom buying the cherry orchard is at once "the greatest moment of his life and the most despairing moment" (Lyons 1997). It was Chekhov who revealed to her "how things could be simultaneously tragic and comic" (Bryer 2002). Indeed, this notion imbues all of her work. She has always been "attracted to split images. The grotesque combined with the innocent . . . a kitten with a swollen head" (Betsko 1984). Henley herself embodies these contradictions: a pessimist, "always" thinking about dying (Betsko 1984), even about suicide (Sessums 1987), and an optimist, exalted by the human capacity to "seek love and kindness even though we are filled with dark, bloody, primitive urges" (Betsko 1984). We see in her plays time and again that Henley finds the humor in tragedy and the ugliness beside beauty. There have been times when Henley was accused of looking down on her characters, but, on the contrary, she has tremendous empathy for most of them: "I do feel sorry for human beings, because they start off wanting things simply and innocently and truthfully, and getting through life can be so treacherous" (Greene 1999).

Her native South has itself been a major influence on Henley's writing: the storytelling ("People there are more loquacious and just brimming with stories" [Lyons 1997]), the language ("I like to write about the South because you can get away with making things more poetic" [Jones1981]), the long arm of the South's defeat, which informs some of her characters ("You may be beaten and defeated, but your spirit cannot be conquered. The South has gall to still be able to say we have our pride, but as a human characteristic it is admirable" [Walker 1986]). The more pernicious aspects of southern history, too, have left their mark. In September of 2002, she spoke to Bryer of the necessity of being "able to see two sides of the coin to survive because it is a racist society and yet you're being raised by racists. So what are you going to do? There are these people who are feeding you, but they're chauvinist and racist. You kind of have to get a little perspective. . . . You kind of have to go 'This is a little more complicated.'" Ten years later, we see in *The Jacksonian*—more emphatically than in her other plays—the effects of the South's racist past on her writing. *The Jacksonian* deals with the insidiousness of racism—its corrosive effect on the racists themselves, as well as on their targets—and is perhaps her masterpiece. In 2012, speaking to Verna Foster about the play, Henley said, "I was interested in . . . how evil bleeds into the lives of all people who exist in apartheid. What it does to people who would be maybe good people in other situations. . . . The corruption and violence are in the air you breathe."

But *The Jacksonian* is not just an indictment of the Jim Crow South; it is far more personal. Henley did not discuss in the later interviews—nor was she evidently asked about—her mother's brutal murder during a pre-dawn home invasion on October 24, 2002. The murderer was soon apprehended in Lydy Caldwell's car, which he had stolen. In 1999, when asked by Alexis Greene if she wanted to be like her mother when she was growing up, Henley had said, "She was such a goddess to me. . . . I just wanted to worship her, watch her put on her makeup. Talk to her. Adore her. And I still do." The devastation she must have felt after her mother's death cannot be overstated. Henley's experience at the time of and after the murder surely informs her characterization of the daughter Rosy in *The Jacksonian* as well as the elliptical structure of the play: She told Karen Carpenter while discussing the writing of the play, "I wanted it to be, in a way, from Rosy's, the daughter's, point of view after she's seen her mother dead, basically trying to psychically hold time back, to change it. . . . [C]ould we stop time. It's how time slows down when you're in shock, and time spins, and time quakes." Rosy is "trying to will that this didn't happen, that her mother isn't murdered if she can just will time" (Foster 2012). Also influencing the play were Henley's own parents' divorce and the death of her sister's childhood teacher, who was shot while helping her KKK boyfriend commit a racially motivated violent criminal act. Yet even in *The Jacksonian*, there is humor—albeit dark humor.

Violent images come to Henley unbidden, but so does her tendency to write funny: "I always feel so emotional and miserable when I'm working, like I'm writing something tragic. Then everything manages to come out funny . . . and I'm glad." She gets this sensibility in part from her family, whose habit "was to see the humor or the ironic point of view in the midst of tragedy" (Betsko 1984). The tragicomic is Henley's territory—at that Chekhovian intersection that characterizes her work and, in her view, a good deal of human experience. Henley wants to understand "the banality of evil," saying that to do so, she must find it within herself (Wimmer-Moul), but do not assume that there is no delight in her; indeed, she is often fun and funny in conversation.

Henley spoke about her writing process to several of the interviewers. She fills notebooks with bits of dialogue, ideas for possible scenes, and images; "getting to page one is quite a mess and takes, for me, the most time and is the hardest" (Bryer 2002). When she is working on a play, she thinks about her characters constantly. As she told Kevin Sessums in 1987, "I'm heartsick when I don't have a play that I'm working on, 'cause I don't know what to think about when I'm in the shower or in the grocery line." When a play does not rise solely from her imagination and requires research, Henley is an avid and absorbed researcher; she spent years researching the nineteenth-century American West for *Abundance* and considerable time researching the Depression era for *The Lucky Spot*.

Her process of revision, as with many playwrights, is often shaped by seeing the work rehearsed and performed in previews by talented actors. The "most glorious thing about working in the collaborative art" of drama is when a playwright sometimes has actors "who are better than your play" or "a director that sees things in the play that you didn't envision and knows how to heighten them and move the rhythm of it" (Bryer 2002). And as the playwright, hearing the play repeatedly in rehearsal gives her a "sense of what the rhythm of the lines is" (Bryer 2002).

Comparing writing for the movies to writing for the theater, Henley noted that not only does she retain more control over what she writes for the stage, but unlike films, plays are "alive and changeable. Every production incorporates the qualities of a whole new set of actors, so the play never becomes stagnant. . . . I'm hooked on the sheer challenge of theater" (Weiss 1992). And the singular voice? Where does that come from? The answer lies perhaps in what she told Greene when asked whom she writes for. Her answer: "Gosh. Myself. Period. When I write plays."

In keeping with the conventions of the Literary Conversations Series, reprinted interviews are uncut and arranged chronologically by the date each interview was conducted rather than by its publication date. We have silently corrected typographical errors, regularized titles into italics, and have made other editing changes for consistency.

Our greatest debt of gratitude is to Beth Henley, who supported this project at all stages. In addition to the interviewers and editors who gave us permission to print or reprint interviews, we wish to thank Kristofer Jon Reed, Melanie Rio, Elizabeth Bryer, Leland Person, Elizabeth Swain, Traugott Lawler, and, from the University Press of Mississippi, Mary Heath.

MCH

JRB

Chronology

1952   May 8: Elizabeth Becker Henley is born in Jackson, Mississippi, to Charles Boyce Henley, a lawyer and later a state legislator, and Elizabeth Josephine "Lydy" Becker Henley, an actress. Henley is the second of the couple's four daughters.

1958–66   Henley attends St. Andrews Day School, Duling Elementary School, and Bailey Junior High School in Jackson, Mississippi. She spends a significant amount of time in Hazlehurst and Brookhaven, Mississippi, visiting relatives with her family.

1970   Henley graduates from Murrah High School, Jackson, Mississippi.

1970–74   Henley attends Southern Methodist University in Dallas, Texas, graduating with a BFA in theater, specializing in acting. Sophomore year: Henley writes her first play, the one-act *Am I Blue*, in a playwriting class. Senior year: After Henley has done some rewrites, *Am I Blue* is staged at SMU under the pseudonym "Amy Peach." (It will be revived by Circle Repertory Company in New York, opening with one-acts by Lanford Wilson and John Bishop on January 10, 1982, under the collective title *Confluence*.)

1974–75   Summer 1974–Summer 1975: After graduating from SMU, Henley, while working at various jobs (file clerk, Santa photographer, children's theater teacher), writes the book for the musical *Parade*, with music by Mark Hardwick and lyrics by Stephen Tobolowsky; it is performed by SMU students before Henley leaves Dallas for graduate school in Illinois.

1975–76   Fall 1975–Spring 1976: Henley attends a single year of a graduate acting program at University of Illinois Urbana-Champaign, where she both studies acting and teaches it to undergraduates.

1976   Summer: Henley is a member of the inaugural acting company of the Great American People Show at the New Salem State Park theater in Petersburg, Illinois. The inaugural company creates and premieres—under the direction of University of Illinois theater professor John Ahart—*Your Obedient Servant, A. Lincoln*

(1976), a play that for nearly two decades will remain the center-piece of GAPS. While doing *Your Obedient Servant, A. Lincoln,* Henley also completes a draft of her one-act play *Sisters of the Winter Madrigal.* Autumn: Henley leaves Illinois and moves to Los Angeles.

1977   Henley writes a screenplay, "The Moonwatcher," while audition-ing for acting jobs and working various "day" jobs in L.A. ("The Moonwatcher" will become the film *Nobody's Fool,* released in 1986.) Henley also reworks *Sisters of the Winter Madrigal* but is unable to get it staged until 2001.

1978   Henley writes *Crimes of the Heart,* intending to "do it as a show-case" with friends (Henley would have played Babe). June 30: Henley's father, Charles Boyce Henley, dies.

1979   February 3: *Crimes of the Heart* premieres under the direction of Jon Jory at the Actors Theatre of Louisville and is co-winner of first place at ATL's Festival of New American Plays.

1980   March: *The Miss Firecracker Contest* premieres at the Victory Theatre in Burbank, California, directed by Maria Gobetti. Decem-ber 9: After runs at a few regional theaters around the country in 1979 and 1980, *Crimes of the Heart* opens Off-Broadway at the Manhattan Theatre Club, directed by Melvin Bernhardt.

1981   April: *Crimes of the Heart* wins the Pulitzer Prize before having had a Broadway production. June: *Crimes of the Heart* wins the New York Drama Critics' Circle Award. Summer: Henley plays the Bag Lady in Frederick Bailey's farce *No Scratch* at the Odyssey Theatre in L.A. November 4: *Crimes of the Heart* has its Broad-way premiere at the John Golden Theatre, directed by Melvin Bernhardt (and will run until February 13, 1983).

1982   January 1: *The Wake of Jamey Foster* premieres at Hartford Stage in Connecticut, directed by Ulu Grosbard. June 6: *Crimes of the Heart* is a nominee for Best Play at the 36th Annual Tony Awards. October 14: *The Wake of Jamey Foster* opens on Broadway at the Eugene O'Neill Theatre and runs only until October 23. Novem-ber: *Hymn in the Attic,* a brief play by Henley and part of an anthol-ogy presentation titled *24 Hours—PM,* is produced at the Back Alley Theatre in Van Nuys, California.

1983   Henley acts in the film *Swing Shift* (released in 1984), playing the role of the Bible Pusher.

1984   March: Henley plays the part of Wiler Wiener in *Two Idiots in*

Hollywood by Stephen Tobolowsky at Theatre/Theater in Los Angeles. May 1: After several productions around the country, *The Miss Firecracker Contest* opens at the Manhattan Theatre Club under the direction of Stephen Tobolowsky.

1985   April 9: *The Debutante Ball* premieres at South Coast Repertory, directed by Stephen Tobolowsky. (A Manhattan Theatre Club production will open in April 1988, directed by Norman René.)

1986   July 30: *The Lucky Spot* premieres at the Williamstown Theatre Festival, Massachusetts, directed by Norman René. (A Manhattan Theatre Club production, under the direction of Stephen Tobolowsky, will open in April 1987.) October: *True Stories*, a film written by Henley, Stephen Tobolowsky, and David Byrne (who directs and stars), is released. November: The film *Nobody's Fool* (screenplay originally titled "The Moonwatcher") is released. December: The film version of *Crimes of the Heart* is released; Henley's screenplay, adapted from her play, will be nominated for an Academy Award.

1987   October 18: *A Family Tree*, written in 1985 with Budge Threlkeld— the first episode in a comedy anthology called *Trying Times*—airs on PBS. This half-hour teleplay stars Rosanna Arquette and David Byrne and is directed by Jonathan Demme. (The PBS series' original title was *Survival Guide*.)

1989   January: Henley is a member of the Dramatic Jury at the Sundance Film Festival. April 21: *Abundance* premieres at South Coast Repertory, directed by Ron Lagomarsino. (*Abundance* will open under Lagomarsino's direction at the Manhattan Theatre Club in October 1990.) Also in 1989, the film *Miss Firecracker* is released; the screenplay by Henley is based on her play *The Miss Firecracker Contest*.

1990   Summer: *Signature* is given a workshop production under the direction of Thomas Schlamme at the Powerhouse Theater at Vassar, as part of the Vassar College and New York Stage and Film summer workshop series in Poughkeepsie.

1991   Henley completes an adaptation of her play *The Lucky Spot* for the screen at the request of British director Lewis Gilbert, who has seen a production of the play in London, but the film is never made.

1992   September 20: *Control Freaks*, with Henley directing, premieres at Center Theater in Chicago; the play has been workshopped by the Center Theater Ensemble.

1993   July 16: *Control Freaks* opens at the Met Theatre in Hollywood in a production directed by Henley and starring Bill Pullman, Holly Hunter, and Carol Kane.

1995   March 29: *Signature* premieres at Charlotte (NC) Repertory Theatre, directed by Steve Umberger. July: Henley gives birth to her son, Patrick Henley.

1996   January: L.A. Theatre Works records an audio production of *Crimes of the Heart*. February: A reading of *L-Play*, a benefit for Los Angeles's Met Theatre, stars James Gammon, Ed Harris, Holly Hunter, Amy Madigan, Bill Pullman, and Alfre Woodard. August 21: *L-Play*, directed by Eric Hill, premieres at the Berkshire Theatre Festival. September 7: *Revelers* premieres at Center Theater, Chicago, directed by Dan La Morte; the play has been workshopped by the Center Theater Ensemble.

1997   January: L.A. Theatre Works records an audio production of *The Lucky Spot*. July: L.A. Theatre Works records an audio production of *Abundance*.

1998   October 15: *Impossible Marriage*, directed by Stephen Wadsworth, premieres at Roundabout Theatre Company in New York City. Also in 1998, Henley is honored for Distinguished Achievement in the Art of Playwriting by the American Theatre Wing.

2000   April 10: *Family Week* opens Off-Broadway at the Century Center for the Performing Arts in New York City, Ulu Grosbard directing. Also in 2000, Henley receives the Richard Wright Literary Excellence Award from the Natchez Literary and Cinema Celebration.

2001   July 14: The one-act *Sisters of the Winter Madrigal*, written in 1976 and revised in 1977, premieres on a double bill with Frederick Bailey's one-act farce *Dirty Ugly People and Their Stupid Meaningless Lives* at the Los Angeles Theatre Center; Frederick Bailey directs.

2002   October 24: Henley's mother, Lydy Becker Caldwell, age seventy-four, is murdered in her home by a burglar.

2003   July 18: *Exposed* premieres, in a workshop presentation, at the Powerhouse Theater at Vassar in Poughkeepsie, New York, co-produced by Vassar and New York Stage and Film, directed by David Esbjornson.

2004   February 15: *It Must Be Love*, Henley's television screenplay, an adaptation of a short story by Nancy Whitmore, is released.

2005   Henley becomes Professor of Theatre Arts at Loyola Marymount University in Los Angeles (where she still teaches playwriting at the time of the publication of this book).

2006   May 12: *Ridiculous Fraud* premieres at McCarter Theatre in Princeton, New Jersey, under the direction of Lisa Peterson.

2007   Henley is a New York Stage and Film Honoree.

2009   June 26: Henley's sister, Leonette "Lyn" Elizabeth Rogers, dies of throat cancer.

2010   March 3: *Report on Motherhood*, Henley's part of *Motherhood Out Loud*, scenes and monologues by fourteen playwrights, opens at Hartford Stage. (*Motherhood* will open Off-Broadway at Primary Stages on October 4, 2011.) Also in 2010, Henley is given the Association for Theatre in Higher Education (ATHE) Ellen Stewart Career Achievement in Professional Theatre Award.

2012   February 15: *The Jacksonian* premieres at the Geffen Playhouse in Los Angeles, directed by Robert Falls, starring Ed Harris, Glenne Headly, Amy Madigan, and Bill Pullman. (A production by The New Group with the same actors—only the role of Rosy is recast—and with Falls again directing will open at the Acorn Theatre in New York City on November 7, 2013.)

2013   April: Henley is awarded the Cleanth Brooks Medal for Lifetime Achievement at the 17th Biennial Celebration of Southern Literature in Chattanooga, Tennessee.

2014   July 18: *Laugh* begins a workshop production under the direction of David Schweizer at the Powerhouse Theater at Vassar as part of the Vassar College and New York Stage and Film summer workshop series.

2015   March 11: *Laugh* premieres at Studio Theatre in Washington, D.C. The premiere is directed by David Schweizer, as was the workshop production at Vassar. September 10: *The Resemblance Between a Violin Case and a Coffin*, an adaptation of a Tennessee Williams short story of the same name, premieres as part of an evening of six one-act plays by six playwrights directed by Michael Wilson; all are adapted from short stories by Williams and are collectively titled *Desire*. (The works have been commissioned by New York's Acting Company and are performed at 59E59 Theaters in New York City. *Desire* has been workshopped over the summer at Powerhouse Theater, Vassar, in the festival of new works [June 26–Aug 2, 2015], co-produced by Vassar and New York Stage and Film.)

2017   April 19–22: Henley is the honoree at the 36th annual William Inge Theater Festival at Independence Community College in Independence, Kansas, where she is presented with the William Inge Award for Distinguished Achievement in American Theater.

2019   July 18: *Lightning (or The Unbuttoning)* premieres at the Powerhouse Theater at Vassar, Poughkeepsie, New York, co-produced by Vassar and New York Stage and Film and directed by Mark Brokaw.

2020–22 August 27, 2020: A reading of *The Jacksonian* with much of the original cast is live-streamed on thenewgroup.org website as a benefit for Race Forward, a racial justice organization. During this COVID-19 pandemic period, Henley completes a new stage play, *Downstairs Neighbor*, as well as a short Zoom play, *Give Me Fever*. She also writes an original screenplay called "Miss Macy" to star Jean Smart, which Amblin Pictures is tentatively scheduled to start producing in summer 2022, as well as a revision of a screenplay, "Barbette," that is to star Ed Harris for Magnolia Mae Films. Throughout this period, Henley continues to teach at Loyola Marymount University via Zoom, and eventually, when students return to campus, in person under COVID-19 safety protocols. May 7, 2022: A full production of *Exposed*, which had been workshopped at the Powerhouse Theater at Vassar in 2003, premieres at the Black Box Performing Arts Center in Englewood, New Jersey, and runs until June 5.

Conversations with
Beth Henley

Beth Henley

John Griffin Jones / 1981

From *Mississippi Writers Talking* by John Griffin Jones (Jackson: University Press of Mississippi, 1982), 169–90. Copyright © 1982 by University Press of Mississippi. Reprinted by permission of University Press of Mississippi. John Griffin Jones is the editor of *Mississippi Writers Talking II* (1983) and coeditor of *Lines Were Drawn: Remembering Court-Ordered Integration at a Mississippi High School* (2016).

March 10, 1981

This interview was conducted about a month before Beth won the Pulitzer Prize for her play *Crimes of the Heart*. At the time of our meeting, the play had been accepted for the 1981 Broadway season having just completed a successful five-week run Off-Broadway in December 1980 and January 1981. Our mothers are friends of long standing, and it was through their combined efforts that I secured the scripts of *Crimes of the Heart* and *The Miss Firecracker Contest*, and then was able to interview Beth during one of her brief visits to her childhood home in Jackson. At twenty-eight, she was not inured to the interview process. She sat in a high-backed chair with one leg under her and spoke in an open and unselfconscious way. On the Monday night in April when we got the news that Beth had been awarded the Pulitzer Prize there was great excitement and rejoicing in our home.

John Griffin Jones: This is John Jones with the Mississippi Department of Archives and History, and I'm about to interview Beth Henley. We are at Beth's mother's house. This is where you grew up?

Beth Henley: Well, after the fourth grade I moved here.

Jones: Right. It's a house on Avondale in Jackson, Mississippi. Today is Tuesday, March 10, 1981. As I told you before we cut the tape recorder on, Beth, I just wanted to get some basic biographical data first, if you could tell me something about your early life, when and where you were born, your schooling, and things like that.

Henley: I was born in Jackson on May 8, 1952. I went to St. Andrew's Day School for the first through the third grade, and then I went to Duling Elementary School, and then I went to Bailey Junior High School.

Jones: Did you?

Henley: Yes, did you go there?

Jones: Yes.

Henley: I went to Murrah [High School]. That's all in Mississippi. Then I went to SMU in Dallas for four years. Then I did one year of graduate work at the University of Illinois.

Jones: In what?

Henley: In acting.

Jones: Theater arts, yes. Did you act all through high school? Were you in the Murrah players, or whatever?

Henley: No. I wasn't even in the Thespians. I'm surprised. When I look back now, most of my friends were in the Thespians, but I never was.

Jones: When did you get interested in it?

Henley: Well, I did some plays at New Stage. I went to a class that they had there. I can't remember if I was actually in a play there. Yes, I was. Oh, gosh. What's that one I did with John Maxwell?

C. C. Geno: I can't remember.

Henley: *Stop the World.*

Jones: Let me mention this: With Beth and me are Chrissy Wilson from the Department, and C. C. Geno, Beth's sister. You did this play when you were in college?

Henley: In high school.

Geno: And you were in *Summer and Smoke* when you were little.

Henley: Right. I did *Summer and Smoke* when I was in the fifth grade.

Jones: We'll talk more about that. Are your family roots in Hazlehurst and Brookhaven, the settings of *Crimes of the Heart* and *Miss Firecracker*?

Henley: Right. My mother's family is from Brookhaven and my father's family is from Hazlehurst.

Jones: I see. You still have family there now?

Henley: Yes, in both places. My grandmother still lives in Hazlehurst, and some of my cousins and an uncle, my father's brother and his wife. And then in Brookhaven, my mother's mother and some great-uncles and aunts and cousins, and an uncle lives there.

Jones: That's interesting. And you would visit there a lot when you were growing up, spend summers there and things?

Henley: We'd go down there a lot on the weekends, go down for the holidays.

Jones: So you went to SMU for four years?

Henley: Right.

Jones: I have some newspaper clippings written about you, and in those articles I read that that was where you took your first playwriting course.

Henley: Yes.

Jones: Your last year?

Henley: No, it was my second year.

Jones: I'm interested to get you to describe by what process you finally decided to sit down and write. Had you been thinking about it your whole life?

Henley: No. I wanted to write, I think, when I was in junior high school, but then I started reading books and I said, "No way. I could never write." It was just too hard. I wasn't even that hot in English, in grammar and spelling and stuff. Then I took a playwriting course just like you take theater history or lighting design. It was something I thought would be fun. You had to write a play to pass, so I wrote that play.

Jones: What play?

Henley: *Am I Blue* is the name of it. It's a one-act.

Jones: And that was your first try?

Henley: Well, in the sixth grade I wrote a play that we tried to produce. Other than that, I was in a creative writing course in junior high school, and I remember having to read my story in front of the class. I said, "But I'm not finished," and they said, "Ah, go on and read it anyway, 'cause nobody's written anything anyway." So I got up to read and I was about halfway finished and it wasn't sounding like I wanted it to sound like. I smashed it up and threw it in the trash and ran out of the class crying. Like I thought I was really going to get in trouble, but the teacher felt so sorry for me she didn't say anything.

Jones: So that was your first production.

Henley: Yes, in that creative writing class.

Jones: Was *Am I Blue* ever staged?

Henley: Yes. My senior year—I'd written it my sophomore year—my senior year they were doing Rick Bailey's play called *Badlands* at the time, I think he's changed it to *The Bridgehead*, and they needed a companion piece to go on the bill with it. Jill Peters was a director there, and she was looking through all the old one-acts that had been written and she found mine. She said, "This is the most together play I've come across, so why don't we do it?" So I did a few rewrites on it and they did it to fill out the evening.

Jones: Hmm. Have you ever or have you yet tried prose or poetry? Is playwriting your only creative concern?

Henley: No, I haven't tried them yet. I don't know if I could do them. I used to write some poetry when I was a freshman. We'd all sit down and see who could write the grossest poetry, weird poems. But that's all I did. I did that when I was a freshman. I still don't have good grammar for putting like a whole novel or whole story together. I can just write dialogue.

Jones: Do you think that's something you'd like to try? Certainly you have the ear and the eye.

Henley: To write like a novel or something?

Jones: To write prose.

Henley: I might try that. It would be a relief because once you finished it and somebody published it you wouldn't have to worry about it anymore. With a play that's where your problems just begin.

Jones: Yes. Tell me, after *Am I Blue* came, *Crimes of the Heart* was your next one?

Henley: Well, I wrote the book for a musical my first year after I was out of SMU. A friend of mine who's a really talented musician wanted to write a musical, and said, "I really like that play you wrote, so why don't you write the book for this?" So I said okay. I was working at horrible jobs all the next year after I graduated. So I wrote the book for the musical at that time, and the students did it right before I left for Illinois. It was fun because I had never been around musicians that much. It was a 1940s musical called *Parade*. It was a real exciting thing to do.

Jones: What is the book?

Henley: The book. That's just the dialogue. There's a composer and a lyricist. Somebody writes the music, somebody writes the lyrics to the music, and I wrote the lines the people actually say in between the songs.

Jones: Oh, yes. Tell me something about the genesis of *Crimes of the Heart*.

Henley: Okay. I was out in Los Angeles. I was trying to act. It was so hard trying to get a job out there. I had an acting agent, but she'd never call you up and I'd sit at home all day long. She was reduced to working at the Broadway Department Store and making calls on her lunch hour. I was working with a group of actors out there, among them Rick Bailey, the playwright, and I thought I'd just write a play with parts for people around our age and we can do it as a showcase out there. I thought I may as well do something while I was sitting out there. I'd written a screenplay when I first got out there, so I was kind of in the habit of writing.

Jones: What happened to the screenplay?

Henley: The screenplay is called "The Moonwatcher." It takes place in Illinois, which is from when I worked there, and it's about a girl who's kind of at a crisis in her life. She's been jilted by the boy that she's in love with. She's going to have his baby but he marries somebody else and she has to give up her baby. Now she's all confused. Now, just before I left Los Angeles to go to Dallas, there was a lady who'd read the screenplay and she really liked it and is interested in it, so I'm glad it didn't just die. I thought it was kind of dead. I don't know if anything will happen to it.

Jones: What's the difference in writing a screenplay and writing a play?

Henley: I don't know. That screenplay was really just one of those gifts, you know, just came to me image after image. It seems it was a lot easier to write than any play I ever wrote because you can just say something very quickly and very vividly and move on to something else. I really enjoyed writing it, but it's just so impossible. For two years after I wrote that I couldn't get anybody to read it, much less consider producing it—you know, millions of dollars. With a play you can feasibly do it on your own. At the time that was a consideration. I wanted something that could be done.

Jones: What years are we talking about when you were in L.A. and looking for work?

Henley: Okay. I left Illinois the fall of 1976 and moved to Los Angeles. Let's see. My play, *Crimes of the Heart*, wasn't done in Louisville until 1979, so that's that many years of destitution.

Jones: Goodness. What were you doing out there during this time, besides writing?

Henley: Working at temporary jobs that I hated, trying to avoid work.

Jones: Did you ever get any work as an actress?

Henley: No, I didn't, come to think of it. I worked in a workshop, but I never got any work.

Jones: Out there with some people that you knew from SMU or from Illinois?

Henley: Yes, some people from Texas, some people who were at SMU ahead of me were out there.

Jones: When did you—I'm asking too many chronological questions. It's like a history test. We'll talk about the other in a minute. When did you decide to sit down and write *Crimes of the Heart*?

Henley: Let's see. I wrote that in seventy . . . Daddy died in 1978. That was right before I finished it. I wrote it in 1978.

Jones: How long did it take you?

Henley: It only took me three months to write the first draft. I had to do a lot of rewrites on it, a rewrite every production. I had to do one rewrite before it went to Louisville, and then one during rehearsals at Louisville, and then for all the other productions I've worked on it.

Jones: Were these full-fledged rewrites or just cutting?

Henley: Just mainly cutting. Like the major cut I've done is cut Uncle Watson out. I don't know if you have a script with Uncle Watson in it. I had to cut him out for the New York production. That's just like a page and a half really. But, no, the characters have remained the same. The end is what I've had to work on. It's really pretty much intact. I've added some and subtracted some.

Jones: Did it hurt your feelings when they asked you to cut your play?

Henley: No. I was overly eager at first, because I was so happy to be having it done. I was just a slave to trying to please them. I was just the opposite. Now I'm not so much.

Jones: Now you have your own opinions about it.

Henley: Right.

Jones: Will you tell me why you sat down and wrote it, what inspired you?

Henley: You mean the idea?

Jones: Well, yes.

Henley: I kind of had two different ideas. One was based on my grandfather, my father's father, [who] had gotten lost in the woods in Hazlehurst. They called up. I didn't go home. I was in Dallas at the time. For three days he was lost in the woods. They had picnic tables out there, and helicopters. In the Copiah County paper they had like, "Thirty-foot snake found in the search for W. S. Henley!" And they had paratroopers. . . .

Geno: The National Guard.

Henley: The National Guard. The governor came down. It was just a huge deal. People were out on horseback, people were out on foot.

Geno: The Coca-Cola people came in their trucks and advertised free Cokes.

Henley: Did you go down there?

Geno: Yes.

Henley: Anyway, my grandfather was just walking through the woods, and according to him was never lost. He knew where he was: Copiah County. He found this little shack. He got to this little shack, and these people brought him into town and they got to a gas station where some people were saying, "They're gonna find that old man, but he'll be dead." And he said, "No they are not! Here I am alive!" So he returned alive after three days. So I thought that would be a good idea for a play: a family crisis bringing everybody back home. It was too close or something, anyway I couldn't get a lead on writing a play about my grandfather getting lost in the woods. I had that idea: a family and everybody gets back home. Also I heard this story about Walter Cronkite was sitting up on the front porch of these rich people's house in the South, and this little Black kid came up and said he wanted ice cream, and the man came down and socked him in the face and said, "Don't you ever come around to this front door again." That made such an impression on him. I thought, "God, I'd like to kill somebody for just being cruel like that to some innocent person." So that kind of gave me the idea of Zackery beating up on Willie Jay. I thought it would be interesting to write about a character who tries to kill somebody, but you'd be in their corner rather than in against them. So I kind of combined those two ideas. I guess that's what started it.

Jones: You said you were hesitant to write about your grandfather being lost in the woods in Copiah County because it is too close to you. My question is how much of your writing is bits and pieces of what you have heard, your memory, and how much is imagination?

Henley: I don't know if I could say a percentage.

Jones: No.

Henley: But some of the things I might not have heard from my family but have heard from other people in Texas or even in New York that I transposed down to the South, to Mississippi, or even in Los Angeles because that's where I live now. But a lot of them are from stories I've really heard, more in *Miss Firecracker* than *Crimes of the Heart*. I totally made that up about being hung with the cat. I never knew anyone who would shoot their husband because they didn't like their looks, and then go fix lemonade. I made all that up.

Jones: I know that's kind of a nebulous question. Chrissy and I were talking about that on the way over here. Are there things as a writer that you won't touch, that are too close? Do you feel that as a writer you are able to deal with any emotion of anybody, you can use any family history, that everything is open to you because you're an artist? Or are you shy about talking about certain things?

Henley: I think I would prefer to disguise certain things, you know, instead of . . . I've put some things in my plays and I wondered how people would react. Usually they don't even remember saying them or doing them or something like that. For some reason I don't like to get too factual, because it's too confining. It's easier for me to deal with that area of fiction where you're not stifled by having to adhere to "I'm going to write this story to really show how my father was, or my grandmother was."

Jones: Right.

Henley: I don't think I really answered your question. I guess if it's something really good I don't feel that bad about putting it in, you know. I'll just stick it in there. I don't think I've hurt anybody's feelings so far. People always like to read themselves into your work. When it was about three sisters my sisters assumed it was going to be about them and our lives and everything. They were kind of surprised when they saw it: "That's nothing like me!"

Jones: Right. How has your family treated your success as a playwright? Do they like your work?

Henley: Oh, they love it. My mother has come up for practically all my productions. C. C. came up to New York with her husband. My mother and her new husband came up to New York. My father was the only one who didn't like it. He died before I ever made any money. I hadn't done anything and he was like, "What are you doing? You should go back to secretarial school and learn to type faster."

Jones: Yes. Your father was a Mississippi state senator, Charles Henley.

Henley: Right. Charles Henley.

Jones: And he died in 1978?

Henley: Right.

Jones: Before *Crimes of the Heart*.

Henley: Right.

Jones: I want to ask you something just to get your reaction to it. We don't necessarily have to include this in the transcript. My mother was talking with your mom about your success, and they were kidding like they do, and your mom was saying that your new play, *The Wake* [*of Jamey Foster*], was based on the death of your father and the fact that his family took a long time to bury him, which was a matter of great pain for her. They were joking, you know. Was—did you write it based on your experiences at that time?

Henley: It's not based on any actual experience that I had at that time, except for the experience. It was definitely based on that. We were thinking then, "Gosh, this would make a great play." It was so interminable! All the family was together, and there was all this tension and all these raw emotions. That makes for a good play, I think. You know, people have an excuse to drink and an excuse to scream and an excuse to act their fullest. I thought that would be a real good idea for a play. There's not tons of similarities— I would say there are no similarities between the actual thing here. It was much grimmer than my play. My play's a real comedy. Here it was just really a drag. Maybe if you were in the play you'd look at it as a drag. I don't know.

Jones: And the guy in the play actually dies from getting kicked in the head by a mule.

Henley: A cow.

Jones: Right. Well, when you finished *Crimes of the Heart*, did you know you had something there? Had you read extensively in the plays that have come out over the last ten years and knew that yours was something new in the art?

Henley: I remember I was at T.R.W. in the parts department, back there after I'd written it. I had taken off from work to try to finish it; you know, temporary work. I thought, "Oh, God, I'll probably be doing this till I'm eighty." I didn't know. I mainly read old things. I missed a lot of reading when I was young, so I like to read more classical stuff. I don't read tons of contemporary plays. I didn't really know what the score was. I didn't even know they weren't doing three-act plays anymore. They told me, "They're not doing three-act plays anymore," and I went "They're not? Wow! Back when I was reading plays they were doing them." So I was real surprised that people liked it as much as they did.

Jones: You showed it to friends first. I know the story of your friend [Frederick Bailey] sending it to [Jon Jory at Actors Theatre of] Louisville to the 1979 competition. So what happened then? Did you immediately get an agent? What happened to it after it was recognized?

Henley: Well, we had a reading at my house. It was real fun and went well. Then a friend of mine who was at the reading, her agent was trying to start a literary department out in Los Angeles. My agent, Gilbert Parker, was coming in to visit. He didn't have any scripts to read, so my friend told her agent, "Well, give him this of my friend's. It's really good." So she gave it to her agent who gave it to Gilbert. This was before it was done in Louisville. I got in that night and there was a message on my phone machine to call him. I didn't even know who he was. I didn't know who his clients were. "Mark Medoff, now I know he's written something. Paul Zindel?" He thought I was brainless beyond belief. It was so embarrassing. He got off the phone and said, "How can she write such good plays and be so . . ." I don't know if he said, "ignorant." So then he was my agent. He's real nice. He's a good agent. He just liked it from reading it.

Jones: I've also read where you said you wrote the play with the intention of playing the part of Babe in a production of it. Any truth in that?

Henley: That was in the production we were going to do. They had that publicity that I was going to give myself a part. I was kind of embarrassed by that statement. But I did have in mind with the cast we were going to have that I would play Babe. Now I'm so old I probably couldn't play Lenny. That is true.

Jones: Let me ask you this: people that I've talked to have said that acting and writing [are] really much the same insofar as you're under the spotlight and if it's good it sticks, is remembered. Being an actress, do you think it was any easier for you to write?

Henley: Being an actress really helped me writing plays particularly. It is the same for me in a sense. You just get into a character, and what that character wants, what are their greatest dreams, their greatest fears, what would they feel at this moment or in this scene. As a writer I can play a fifty-three-year-old man, or I can play a tall brunette woman, you know, as many characters as you want. The pleasure of writing is when you write, and the hell of it is to go into rehearsals. With acting your creative work is in rehearsals. It's more immediate.

Jones: Yes. In the reviews I read some critic likened Babe to a character out of Flannery O'Connor, Meg to a, I believe he says, a benign Tennessee Williams, and then Lenny from Chekhov. Are those people you've read, and did you do that consciously?

Henley: I hadn't read Flannery O'Connor. Like, in my first review in Louisville they compared me to her. I hadn't read her. Now I love her. I think she's great. I had read Tennessee Williams and Chekhov, and I think they're great. Now, what did you ask me?

Jones: If you drew that parallel consciously, or if that tradition meant anything to you when you sat down to write?

Henley: Chekhov and Shakespeare, of course, are my favorite playwrights. Chekhov, I feel he influenced me more than anyone else, just with getting lots of people onstage. I don't do anything close to what he does with orchestration. That fascinates me. I also like how he doesn't judge people as much as just shows them in the comic and tragic parts of people. Everything's done with such ease, but it hits so deep. So I guess I've got to say he influenced me more than I guess anybody.

Jones: What about the literary tradition of Mississippi, certainly with fiction? A lot of the humor you use in the two plays I've read is taking that Southern Gothic heritage and turning it upside down, you know, with the mother who hangs her cat and then herself. Do you take that old southern eccentricity as something you are trying to satirize? Are you really conscious of that?

Henley: Well, I didn't consciously like say that I was going to be like Southern Gothic or grotesque. I just write things that are interesting to me. I guess maybe that's just inbred in the South. You hear people tell stories, and somehow they are always more vivid and violent than the stories people tell out in Los Angeles. It's always so mellow.

Jones: Right. Do you think you would have been a playwright had you grown up—there's really no way to answer that—say in California? Is your real inspiration here in Mississippi?

Henley: I don't think I'd be writing the same type of plays, but I'm not saying California is devoid of inspiration. The poet Charles Bukowski writes very well about Los Angeles. The South just suits me better.

Jones: Can you write when you're here in Mississippi?

Henley: No. I can't even breathe. I get hay fever every time I come here.

Jones: You really can't write?

Henley: I can take a few notes or something like that, but there is no way I could sit down and write in my parents' house. It's so in-and-out, you know, and there's too much going on to sit down and write.

Jones: When you come to Mississippi do you go to Brookhaven and Hazlehurst and visit the people?

Henley: I go to Hazlehurst all the time. I was there Sunday. But I don't go to Brookhaven as often.

Jones: I wanted to get you to describe what inspires your characters, your characterizations. Is it the small southern town that interests you so? Is it something else?

Henley: I don't know, because Jackson's not really that small a southern town. It's the one I grew up in. It's not a large metropolis. I think it's that in a small southern town there's not that much to detract from looking at characters. If you live in Los Angeles there's just so much going on that you can't write about it. But here things are small and southern and insular, and you get a bird's-eye view of people's emotions. I don't know if that's a good answer.

Jones: It is. Will you always return to Mississippi in your writing?

Henley: I'm really not sure. My next play takes place in the South, in Jackson, if I ever get to writing on it. But I'm not sure if I'll ever be able to write about Los Angeles, or if that will interest me. I just don't know. I like to write about the South because you can get away with making things more poetic. The style can just be stronger. If I could figure it out I'm sure I could do it with any place, but I haven't.

Jones: You've been in New York for a while. Does the cultural world still think things southern are neat?

Henley: I haven't really spent a lot of time in New York because my play [*Crimes of the Heart*] only ran [Off-Broadway at the Manhattan Theatre Club] five weeks. I was there for the rehearsals and for a few days. There were no lines of people dying to find out about me by any means. I'm not really sure about New York because I was there for only a short time.

Jones: Your play [*Crimes*] is going to run on Broadway next season?

Henley: Right. In the fall.

Jones: Let me get you to talk to this too: John Simon said that the only fear he had was that your play *Crimes of the Heart* came from a stockpile of youthful memories, and that there was a chance—I know you remember his saying that—and that there was a chance that you would not be able to come up to what that play is ever again. What do you think about that?

Henley: Well, I was just glad I'd finished those two other plays by that time so I didn't panic and be in total distress. I don't think *Crimes of the Heart* was as autobiographical as he was implying. It's true I'm from Mississippi, and I have two sisters, but my mother isn't dead with suicide, my sister hasn't shot her husband, you know, my sister doesn't have a missing ovary. All the characters were imaginary. I guess it is biographical in the sense that they were sisters and they are from Mississippi.

Jones: He also said, or others have said, that it is a play about adversity being triumphed over by unity and a family coming together. I've read where you said that, and then said, "I guess that's the theme of the play, that's what they tell me." Was the play defined for you by the critics?

Henley: A lot of it really was. It's much easier for me to talk about it after reading my reviews. It was like, "Oh, I see, that's what it's about," because I don't think very thematically. I think more in terms of character and story. I don't necessarily know whether I'm writing it to any end, you know, to any theme. Like, I just found out vaguely what the theme to *The Wake* might be after we had the reading. I said, "I think I may know what this play's about." See, I didn't know when I was writing it, and watching it made it much more simple.

Jones: Yes. That's one of the reasons I was anxious to talk with you, especially after reading your quote about the theme of *Crimes of the Heart*. Many of the artists today are so concerned with art for art's sake, you know, having the right lingo when talking about "their art," that it's really great to be able to talk with someone young like you who has maybe not learned all the ropes, and maybe whose art is more spontaneous and real than the rest. You know what I mean? Is that helpful to what you are trying to do? I don't know how to make a question out of it.

Henley: Well, I think it's helpful not to be confined by anything at the start, you know, "This is what my play's going to be about." Well, maybe that's not what your play's going to be about, maybe you don't have the vaguest idea, maybe your characters want it to be about something else. Also, I don't like the idea of a playwright sitting there saying, "This is what my play's about," because then everybody says, "Well, if the playwright says this is what it's about then this is what it's got to be about." People can have different viewpoints about it. It can mean different things to different people. If you have it in black and white that that's what you're thinking about, you might not think that's what it's about if you read it ten years from now. So I really wouldn't like to write down what I think about the theme of my play.

Jones: What about *The Miss Firecracker Contest*, did that come quickly?

Henley: No, that was hard to write. I was doing a lot of traveling then. Before, I didn't have anything to distract me at all. When I was writing *Crimes* there was no pressure, you know. This was harder to write because I was having to go here and there. And *The Wake* was even harder. That's too bad.

Jones: You were writing *Miss Firecracker* during the Louisville time, or was it before that?

Henley: No, right when I got back from Louisville I started working on it. I worked for television that summer, so I had to do that for three months. Then in the meantime there had been a production in California of *Crimes*, and then there was a production in the fall of *Crimes* that I had to go to. That was in St. Louis. Gosh. Then I got to work on *Miss Firecracker*. Then I finished it, I think.

Jones: Was the Jackson New Stage production of it [*Miss Firecracker*] the first?

Henley: The second. It was done in Los Angeles at a ninety-seat showcase theater, the Victory Theatre.

Jones: And where is it now?

Henley: It's in Dallas.

Jones: Right. So it came harder than *Crimes*, and *The Wake* was harder still?

Henley: Right. The next one will be impossible. Actually it's not as hard, it's just getting the time and getting your mind in the place of the play. When I get to work on another play my mind goes to work on that play. Then I have to get back and read over all my notes, and that's real boring but I have to do it so my mind will be on the play.

Jones: Did you have something, Chrissy?

Wilson: Yes. I just wanted to ask if you think New Yorkers can appreciate your plays as well as southerners.

Henley: Oh, gosh. I think southerners would have the edge generally speaking, but I think New Yorkers can enjoy the play. They have, but I do think maybe southerners have an edge.

Wilson: You said earlier that your characters are not based on your family but maybe a caricature or exaggeration of many southern families. When New Yorkers go to your play, do you think they think all southern families are like that, or do you think a lot of southern families are really like that?

Henley: I think a lot of southern families are really like that. I heard people in the audience of *Crimes* say, "You know, my sister's just like that. That reminds me just of my sisters." They can relate to it like that. But I don't know.

Wilson: Better than New Yorkers can.

Henley: No, that *is* people from New York.

Wilson: They all think that.

Henley: Yes.

Jones: I've read where you said your next play will be about two old friends that meet in the restroom of the Stardust Ballroom during an Iggy Pop concert. That's your California play.

Henley: Yes. I've been trying to work that out in my brain.

Jones: Don't have anything down about it yet?

Henley: I have a few notes on it. I think that would be fun to write about. I could write about that, if I could just find the right tone to do it so it wouldn't be commenting on it or taking it lightly. You know, I'd like to make it real.

Jones: You would take it seriously?

Henley: Yes. You know, I've got to get to where I can understand the people enough to take them seriously and not make fun of them, figure out why they are doing that.

Jones: Why they are at an Iggy Pop concert with green hair.

Henley: Yes, why people become punkers.

Jones: I'd like to read that.

Henley: Yes.

Jones: Is that pretty much sweeping California? I know Steve, your boyfriend, is involved with a punk rock band.

Henley: Right. I don't know if he calls it punk rock, but I do. It's really a rock-and-roll band, the L.A. Slugs.

Jones: A good punk name.

Henley: Yes. They're real good.

Jones: Is he out there now?

Henley: No, he's here.

Jones: Yes, I've been seeing somebody wandering around. I thought that might be him.

Henley: Yes.

Jones: What about your success? I know it's changing your life, but is it changing the things you want to do? Will playwriting replace acting as your ambition?

Henley: Well, I would like to be able to do both. Like, I'm going to work in a play when I get back out to L.A. [*No Scratch*, a farce in which she played a bag lady]. Writing is probably—it just gives you so much more freedom, because you can sit down there and you can create all this stuff and you don't have to worry about somebody writing a part that's right for you, casting other people that are good in it. You need so much to really make things work artistically as an actor. I mean, just getting cast at all is a miracle, much less in a part that you give a damn about. So I would like to write and just act in situations that I know would have some importance to me, rather than just beating my brains out to get a commercial.

Wilson: Beth, could you compare your satisfaction with the production here of *Miss Firecracker* and the Broadway production?

Henley: Well, they're two different plays. [Of the two, only *Crimes of the Heart* had been done in New York at that point.]

Wilson: Yes, but I meant just as far as the quality of the production.

Henley: Well, I'll tell you, I was more satisfied with my production here with *Miss Firecracker* than I was with the one [of *Crimes of the Heart*] in New York. It's surprising. I really think it has a lot to do with having southern actors in a play. It's such an edge they have to get an understanding of these people that I just didn't see in the New York production—it was very Yankee stoic in many ways, instead of just bursting with the passion of these people. I didn't like that at all. I worked to change it, and it did improve. I just think on the whole that down here was much more fun. The show was more my vision than it actually ended up being in New York. The structure was all fine in New York. It just lacked some of the blood.

Jones: Is it hard as a playwright working with directors to get your vision across?

Henley: It's real hard. It really is.

Jones: You being young and female I was wondering if you'd gotten any condescension.

Henley: Oh, yes! I think anyone would get condescension from directors. So many of them are so insecure. I never realized it, but their jobs are really in jeopardy all the time. The producers can fire them. It's harder to get a job as a director than as an actor. They've got all sorts of responsibilities. I've had generally good relations with the directors. But if you get on their bad side then you better forget it. They won't listen to anything you say, because they don't have to. I never have had power enough to get a director fired, because usually the director is more of a name than me, or is the producer. I try to get along with them and hopefully be with the director long enough so that we'll have a similar vision of the play.

Wilson: Do you have a say in the casting?

Henley: In New York I did. I did here as a matter of fact.

Jones: What are you going to have to do about the Broadway production [of *Crimes of the Heart*], are you cutting it again?

Henley: I'm making just a few changes. Probably people who saw it wouldn't even notice them.

Jones: Are you going up there for the casting? Or have they done that?

Henley: They haven't cast it. They are trying to get the same three women who did it at the Manhattan Theatre [Club], which would be good because they really are a good ensemble. I mean, regardless of what I said before, they worked well together. And they got good reviews, and nobody wants to tamper with success, especially if the producer really wants to go for the bucks. But they may have other engagements, and you can't book an actor this far in advance according to the rules of Equity. So, we'll have to wait and see if they will accept it again.

Jones: So, is L.A. your permanent home now?

Henley: Gosh, I still can't relate to it. I have a Mississippi driver's license, Texas license plates, and Illinois car insurance. I refuse to say L.A.'s my home. I can't believe it! But now I think I'd rather live in Los Angeles than New York, just because I have a house with a garden and a car you can drive. I don't know. I guess it is, for a while.

Jones: What about someone like Miss Welty who writes very movingly about us and lives down the road? Do you think you'll ever be able to do that?

Henley: I don't know. I may. Right now there's just too much I want to do besides just come back and live here. It would just be too quiet for me.

Jones: It's not too interesting right now to you.

Henley: No, that's not true. It is. I've just got friends in Los Angeles, and it would just be hard to leave. Steve works out there.

Jones: Well, you have anything else, Chrissy? C. C., you have anything else?

Geno: No.

Jones: This has been nice. I appreciate your having us over and talking with us. It's been really interesting.

Henley: God. How did it compare with all those other guys? They're probably really eloquent.

Jones: No, it's perfect. That's why I wanted to talk to you. You are the authentic thing, a real creative talent. Thanks again.

Beth Henley

Elizabeth Mullener / 1981

From *New Orleans Times-Picayune*, November 8, 1981, *Dixie*, pp. 7–8, 10, 12, 14.
Reprinted by permission of Capital City Press/Georges Media Group, and Baton Rouge, LA.
Elizabeth Mullener is the author of *War Stories: Remembering World War II* (2002).

It was her first visit home to Jackson since a Pulitzer Prize catapulted her from playwright to celebrity playwright last spring. She spoke at a ladies' charity luncheon, received congratulations from the governor of Mississippi, and talked about the problems of overnight success.

I got in by the skin of my teeth. The Kidney Foundation's annual shindig had been sold out for weeks, and nothing—not even the thirty-five dollars I had waiting in my wallet to pay for the ticket—could get me an invitation. Mrs. Bookhardt told me to call Mrs. Hunsaker and Mrs. Hunsaker told me to call Mrs. Brown and Mrs. Brown said the ladies would be only too delighted to have me, honey, and why didn't I come a little early and they'd take the final tally and see if they just couldn't find a place for me somewhere.

They did.

The sign out front said WELCOME HINDS CO. KIDNEY FOUNDA-TION / OYSTERS TEN CENTS / SUPPORT THE UNITED WAY. Inside, there were four hundred women—designated "patrons" by virtue of their thirty-five-dollar contributions to the Jackson, Mississippi, Kidney Founda-tion. It was a gala occasion, one of the highlights of Jackson's social season. "You have the opera, the symphony, the ballet, the art association, cancer, and this," explained one of the guests. "That's when everybody dresses up and goes out."

In the bar, they were serving Bloody Marys and screwdrivers and Mrs. Swayze, who plays the piano at the First Baptist Church, was giving her rendition of "Misty." Everybody there was anxious to see what chef Bobby Ginn had cooked up for the luncheon, all of them were anxious to see the fashions provided by Jackson's most exclusive shops, and, most important, all of them were anxious to see Beth Henley, the twenty-eight-year-old Jackson playwright who had recently won the Pulitzer Prize and who was this year's speaker.

Beth Henley, known in these parts as Jackson's own Beth Henley, is home for a visit. She is on her way from Los Angeles (where she is working on the film script of her play "Moonwatcher") to New York (where her play *Crimes of the Heart* will open on Broadway November 4). She is staying with her mother and her stepfather in their fashionable Belhaven home with a wide front lawn, big white columns, and an American flag out front. It's her first visit to Jackson since she won the Pulitzer Prize for drama last April, and that's why her mother's friends at the Kidney Foundation were particularly thrilled to have her as their honored guest.

Henley is an attractive woman in an uncontrived sort of way, genuinely modest and sweetly appealing. She talks in spurts—the words gushing out as if they were all attached to one another—and then gulps big breaths between sentences. She sits cross-legged on the plump sofa in her mother's den, her clothes wrinkled and her hair pulled back into an artless ponytail, popping Pepperidge Farm gingerbread men and laughing her shy, winning, slightly embarrassed laugh.

"My mother worked at the Jackson Little Theatre as an actress ever since I was a small child," she reminisces. "She'd take us there a lot because she didn't have anyplace else to take us and we'd get to sit in the theater and watch rehearsals. It was black and the lights would be up on the people onstage and they'd be saying wonderful things and moving around in exciting action and I fell in love with it then. It was like being out of the world or something.

"One night I remember I was in my room crying and crying and my mother came in and said, 'Honey, what's wrong?' And I said, 'I'm practicing to be Heidi for when the Little Theater does the production.' And she said, 'I don't think they're going to do that play because the grown-ups like to star themselves in parts.'

"I kept after her to try to get me into plays, but she decided to put me in a piano class. I was put on the plastic keys the very first day when all the other people were on regular keys and I was so embarrassed I gave it up. Then I went to ballet class but I gave that up, too. I told my mother it was because of my asthma, but actually it was my fat legs and lack of rhythm.

"When I was in the sixth grade, I wrote a musical comedy called 'Swing High, Swing Low.' We were going to do it in my garage and I cast it. But it was hard for me to *talk* to boys at that time, much less teach them how to sing and dance and act. So one day we decided to go swimming instead of continuing the rehearsals.

"After that my mother took me for an achievement test. They said I was tone-deaf, color blind, and had no real creative powers, but that I was kind of good in mathematics. I was devastated. So I decided to be popular in junior high school. I ended up in the ninth grade having orange hair and being a cheerleader, which was the pinnacle.

"But somehow, when I moved on to high school, I didn't fit in there as well and I tried writing again. I wrote a short story—I *kind of* wrote it. And then my mother signed me up for an acting class at the New Stage Theater.

"I always loved being in the theater. I love just sitting there. They could be rehearsing my play or anybody's play. I just enjoy it."

As much as she loved the theater, though, it came to Henley as a complete surprise that she could make a living at it.

"I was totally stunned," she says of her own success. "I was stunned that I could make a living in the first place. At anything. I just thought, oh Lord, I'll never earn a living in this world. No way. I just detested working. But then I couldn't *believe* that you could earn a living writing. I mean I didn't expect it. Not at all.

"I had thought about maybe I wanted to be a writer, but then I read some things and I didn't think I'd have much of a chance. I thought it was too hard. I was terrible in grammar and spelling. And I can't even write a paragraph. You should read my letters home. They're like a fifth-grader's. I don't know how to put sentences together. I even have trouble writing stage directions. I only know how to write dialogue.

"I still feel sometimes like I'm getting away with it. Like I'm not really a writer and somebody's going to find out someday. But I did get to where I really enjoy it. What I enjoy about it is that you can go anywhere in your mind that you want to and it's just like open spaces and totally up to your imagination and it's like an adventure.

"When I write a play, I just do it like acting. I get to know the characters real well and then it's like doing an improvisation. If I can get the first character to get the first line out, then the other one answers. If you know who the characters are and what the story is, then the dialogue just comes. I don't know the whole story before I start. I don't know the end of the play. That way you don't restrict yourself to all the ideas you had before the characters start talking. At least that's the way I do it."

The way she does it must work because Beth Henley has come a long way from her timid, hesitant, first attempts at theater in the garage.

She came first by way of Dallas, Tex. ("I chose SMU because they had an easy application to fill out. . . . I love the sunsets in Texas; they've got huge skies and it's gorgeous.") Then she went to graduate school at the University of Illinois. ("I dropped out. It's pretty ridiculous to get a master's degree in acting.") And finally, she went out to Los Angeles, where she lives now. ("I hate the smog in L.A. I hate the weather. I hate the crowds. But once you've got friends and a lifestyle, it's really hard to pick up and move.")

When she first went out to Los Angeles, Henley had trouble finding a job. So she wrote a screenplay. "But I couldn't get anybody to look at it," she says. "So I decided well, I'll write a play. Even I can do that."

Apparently, she was right. The play she wrote was *Crimes of the Heart*, the work that later brought her the Pulitzer Prize. A friend of hers, who had read the play and liked it, sent it off to the Actors Theatre in Louisville, Ky., a renowned regional repertory theater that sponsors what they call the Great American Playwriting Contest. Henley's play won the contest, and the Actors Theatre gave *Crimes of the Heart* its first production in 1979.

The rehearsal period was one of high anxiety for the playwright. "I just sat there and drank Cokes and ate cheeseburgers and chocolate cake and got fat and nervous," Henley says. "Sometimes people take your play and do it better than you imagine it, and then it's really like a high. But mainly, they don't do it like you want it. Sometimes you just want to kill actors if they're being indulgent and not doing it right. If they're making themselves more important than the part in the play. Or if they're making it real sloppily sentimental just to get the audience sympathy. But I always like to watch rehearsals anyway."

And then came opening night.

"I was out on the parking lot with my boyfriend," Henley says, "and I was crying. I saw all these people coming into the theater and it was snowing and I knew they had gotten babysitters and they had gotten all dressed up and they were coming to see this play and it was just terrible last night in dress rehearsal. And I said I just don't believe it. They're charging money to see something I wrote.

"But then we sat through the show and people were laughing. And every time somebody would laugh I'd think, oh God, and I was just glued to my chair. I was just amazed that people were enjoying it. It was thrilling. It was just the most astounding experience I've ever had."

Until April of 1981.

That's when Beth Henley walked into her apartment and found a strange message on her telephone-answering machine. It was from her agent's assistant and it said, "Beth, don't talk to anyone before you talk to Gilbert."

"I thought my agent had gotten me into some sort of scam," Henley says. "Then the phone rang and I picked it up and a guy said, 'This is the Associated Press,' and I thought oh no, they've caught me. And then he said, 'How do you feel about winning the Pulitzer Prize?' And I said, 'What?'

"About three days later, the telephone was still ringing so much I couldn't stand to be in the house, and all these dead flowers were around and I was hung over and it was like, I hate this. You know, it was making me miserable.

"From then on, people have been calling me, people I haven't seen in fifteen years. They want me to let them do a show at some theater in Oklahoma or something: 'Bring your new play here, I'd be a great director for it, don't you remember how good I directed that show in college?' I just hate that so much. I don't even answer my phone anymore.

"It just got to be overwhelming. I guess some people would have handled it better. But I'd been screaming and excited for days and saying oh yes, it's wonderful, I'm so happy. And it's like you just can't keep up that pace. It was just a lot of attention for me. I'm sure it would be nothing for Suzanne Somers."

Meanwhile, back at the Grand Ballroom of the Regency Inn, four hundred of Jackson's finest were enjoying themselves thoroughly. There were silk dresses in every color of the rainbow, a few shawls draped dramatically over one shoulder, a couple of wonderfully chic hats, and lots of antique jewelry.

And Beth Henley had them all in the palm of her hand.

"The play is pretty much honed down to the way I want it for Broadway," she told the audience full of her mother's friends. "I'll probably just sit there and say it's Bi-LUX-si, not Bi-LOCK-si, and stuff. They're good actresses, but they're all from the North and I think there are some things they really don't understand about the South. Some of the sense of humor and the ironies and the passions are lacking, but I'm not sure who will notice this in New York."

They loved every minute of it. They even gave her a standing ovation, and Gov. Winter announced that he was declaring this day Beth Henley Day. William Winter is handsome and savvy and bright, like all governors have to be these days. "Beth Henley," he said, "is another in a succession of Mississippi literary geniuses that this state, with its unique social patterns, seems endlessly capable of producing." Henley winced and squirmed in her seat and made faces at her sister across the table.

Everybody in the audience was chattering about Beth Henley and how adorable she looked and how wonderful it all was.

Ginny Marco, a former schoolmate, said, "You can tell people that have the ability to express themselves by either being an independent person or following the crowd. Beth would always do what she wanted to do. She wasn't *different*—I'm not saying that. I mean, she was in with the same crowd everybody was in with, the popular kids and stuff. But you could tell that she had her opinions about things and that someday she would *do something*."

Beth Henley Talks about Her Way of Writing Plays

Hilary DeVries / 1983

From *Christian Science Monitor*, October 26, 1983, *Arts & Leisure*, pp. 23, 26. © 1983 Christian Science Monitor. All rights reserved. Used under license. Hilary DeVries is the author of *After Midnight: The Life and Death of Brad Davis* (1997) and the novels *So 5 Minutes Ago* (2001) and *The Gift Bag Chronicles* (2005).

She looks like a college graduate in need of a job.

Small, thin, with a braid trailing down her back and stumping about in a rumpled cardigan, flannel skirt, and hiking boots, Beth Henley looks like anything but the prize-winning playwright that she is. She talks in a Mississippi molasses drawl only slightly tempered by her years in Los Angeles, and she still cringes with embarrassment about the publicity photographers who snap her picture during lunch.

"Oh, gosh, it's so embarrassing. People run up afterward and say, 'Who are you? Who are you?' I just tell them I hired that guy to take my picture while I eat."

This remark is typical of this southern-born actress-turned-playwright who is as much a crazy quilt of contradictions and oddball eccentricities as her Pulitzer Prize-winning play, *Crimes of the Heart*—an unusual but fetching tale of three slightly wacky Delta sisters reunited when one of them shoots her husband because "she didn't like his looks."

One critic termed the play "a collision between Chekhov and Carson McCullers." *New York Times* critic Mel Gussow said Miss Henley "finds humor even in violent acts."

"Well, there's a tension that sets up with danger," she tries to explain when asked about her unorthodox sense of humor. "Like in the old [*I Love*] *Lucy* shows. You know, you wonder, is she going to get caught in the candy factory or slip on the banana peel? It's tense but funny."

Curled up like a kitten here on the couch in the lounge of Boston's Shubert Theatre, Miss Henley is in town to launch the premiere touring production of *Crimes of the Heart*, which is still playing on Broadway. It was her first full-length play (she wrote a one-act during college), and in addition to the Pulitzer Prize, it won her a New York Drama Critics' Circle Award in 1981. She was twenty-seven at the time and the first woman to earn the Pulitzer Prize for drama since 1958. How does she feel about that?

"Oh, I don't know," she moans. "People always ask me that and I never come up with a good answer. Happy. Surprised. Good, I suppose." She concludes with a shrug and a tug on her braid.

Sitting with this playwright, who has been hailed by critics as part of a new and impressive generation of woman dramatists, one finds her more child than successful and wealthy playwright. *Crimes of the Heart* was sold to Hollywood for a reported $1 million, and Miss Henley now owns a house in the star-studded Los Angeles residential area of Laurel Canyon, a far cry from her southern upbringing as one of four daughters of a lawyer-father and actress-mother in Jackson, Mississippi.

But all that success pales in the face of the pixieish person sitting here. Completely at home in her baggy schoolgirl clothes and ponytail hair, she scrunches around the couch, scratches her leg, and squints and scowls her expressive face with abandon. She confides she likes doing Jane Fonda exercises, surfcasting, and going to David Bowie concerts. During a conversation she will lapse into different characters and voices—imitating people, making pouncing gestures with her hands, or pretending to play the piano—anything to drive home her points. It is not difficult to tell that she used to be an actress. "No, I still do acting," she corrects her questioner. "It keeps me in touch with my imagination."

That imagination, which percolates to the surface with such disarming regularity, is apparently what feeds the creative fires in this writer.

"Well, I just start with an idea of what I want to write about, like a funeral [*The Wake of Jamey Foster*], a beauty contest [*Miss Firecracker Contest*], or somebody in the family getting thrown in jail [*Crimes of the Heart*], and then I do a lot of thinking about the characters who are in the event and what happened to them before that. Then when I actually sit down to write the play it just comes real fast, almost like automatic writing."

She says that she does little reworking of her plays and that she tries to write every day—getting to her downtown Los Angeles office around noon, lying on the floor or a rose-colored chaise longue, and writing out her plays in longhand.

Since *Crimes of the Heart* debuted at the Actors Theatre of Louisville in 1979, Miss Henley churned out *The Wake of Jamey Foster*, which met a quick demise on Broadway earlier this year; an unproduced screenplay called "The Moon-watcher"; and her latest venture, *The Debutante Ball*, a play she says is not yet in production and is "even darker and more violent" than *Crimes*. "Those are just the images I get," she says; "they're not really a conscious choice."

Jon Jory, director of the Louisville theater where *Crimes* won the 1979 Great American Play Contest, says Miss Henley is more of a serious student of theater than she appears. "Theater history courses really meant something to her. She obviously loved Chekhov and really thought a lot about how those effects could be achieved."

Certainly her plays are peopled with characters whose bizarre bumpkinry is straight out of the Southern Gothic tradition. They tread a fine line between unbelievable caricature and poignant reality. One director said of her work, "It's because she writes for herself that her plays come out so true."

It's a sureness of vision that shines through the works of this woman who insists that she would "probably still be working in the parts department of TRW" if she hadn't stumbled into playwriting after a mild success with her one-act *Am I Blue*, written while still attending Southern Methodist University.

"She seems all glow and sparkle," says Mr. Jory, "but she is very firmly attached to her point of view. She's like a good piece of flint. You can strike sparks off her."

Those sparks are no more in evidence than when she is pressed about why women are just now gaining recognition in the creative fields. Suddenly the gawky little girl disappears, she sits up straight, and her voice is firm. "Well, picture not going to college. Picture tons of kids. No way to earn a livin' . . . not being able to vote. Think about that. People pretend that life is like the commercials. And it's not."

Life, she says, can be difficult, even terrifying, in its smallest moments. This is why she writes the way she does—chronicling the strange and often grotesque events of real life, but always tempering it with compassion and humor. As her character Lenny states in the concluding moments of *Crimes of the Heart*, "This . . . vision just sort of came into my mind . . . something about the three of us smiling and laughing together. . . . [I]t wasn't forever; it wasn't for every minute. Just this one moment and we were all laughing."

Life after the Pulitzer

Linda Sherbert / 1984

From the *Atlanta Journal*/the *Atlanta Constitution*, January 8, 1984, sec. H, pp. 1, 10. © 1984 The Atlanta Journal-Constitution. All rights reserved. Used under license. Linda Sherbert is a playwright and the former producing director of the 14th Street Playhouse in Atlanta.

Watching her play *Crimes of the Heart* open on Broadway in late 1981 could have been the ultimate heady experience for Mississippi-born playwright Beth Henley, then only twenty-nine years old.

Except that *Crimes* had won the 1981 Pulitzer Prize for drama the previous spring, making Beth Henley the first playwright to receive the coveted award prior to the play's Broadway debut. She also was the first woman to receive the prize in twenty-three years.

"I hadn't really even gotten to the stage in my career where I was dreaming about winning," confesses Ms. Henley, whose award-laden play will make its Atlanta premiere at the Alliance Theatre Wednesday night. "It was so from left field."

The Southern Gothic comedy about three adorably lunatic sisters in a small Mississippi town had dazzled the Pulitzer judges in a New York production at Off-Broadway's Manhattan Theatre Club. Then, a Hollywood producer made the fantasy complete by buying the movie rights for nearly $1 million. Not bad for the first full-length play she had ever written. Ever.

It is a tough act for the soft-spoken playwright to follow.

But Ms. Henley, now thirty-one, copes with Life After The Pulitzer with a good deal of humor—the same sort of absurdist whimsy found in her plays—and hard work, despite some ups and downs. Writing projects are stacked so high at her Los Angeles office that she has had to forsake her hoped-for visit to the Atlanta premiere.

Since Ms. Henley received her Pulitzer, playwright Marsha Norman, who once attended Agnes Scott College in Decatur, won the 1983 prize for

Broadway's *'night, Mother*. However, Ms. Henley does not believe these two awards signal the emergence of a new breed of southern women playwrights.

"There's a trend toward women doing a whole lot more of everything," she says during a telephone interview from her Los Angeles home. "Things have turned around."

Unlike many playwrights who spend their entire careers working toward a Pulitzer, Ms. Henley won what some consider the Super Bowl of playwriting as a rookie. To what can she aspire now?

"Well, keep up the payments on my house," she says, giggling at her earthbound, practical answer. "Keep working at something that I love instead of something I don't like."

That has been possible since the *Crimes* phenomenon. She also receives royalties from two later plays, *The Miss Firecracker Contest* and *The Wake of Jamey Foster*, both sporadically produced at small theaters around the country. *Miss Firecracker*, a comedy about a haywire beauty pageant, made its Atlanta debut last season at the Academy Theatre.

Meanwhile, Ms. Henley has been writing screenplays steadily, and another play is percolating in her imagination.

Last year she wrote the screenplay of *Crimes* for independent producer Burt Sugarman, who is best known for producing television's *The Midnight Special*. He owns the film rights but has not yet secured a commitment for production.

"The screenplay is in turnaround for a movie studio, and that means the people who were going to do it don't think they're going to do it anymore," she says, automatically explaining the Hollywoodese. "So the producer [Sugarman] is hoping another studio will pick it up."

In December, she began writing an as-yet-untitled screenplay for Sissy Spacek. "She's wanted to do comedy," Ms. Henley says in a mellifluous drawl remindful of Ms. Spacek's. "I had an idea, and he [an L.A. producer with a Spacek connection] liked it. So then we went out and met with her, and she liked it. So now I'm gonna just work on it. She's not bound to do it. She'll read it and see if she likes it."

When that project is completed within the next few months, she says, "I want to finish writing a Western—it's a play—and produce it. It will be a comedy. I've already started doing research."

Ms. Henley also is trying to get her first original screenplay, a comedy called "The Moonwatcher," made into a film. "It's hopefully gonna get done this summer," she says. "It's been hopefully gonna get done for the last two summers." Producers in Hollywood and New York are showing interest.

She has just begun writing for television. "I'm working on a script for a new PBS comedy series called *Survival Guide*," she says. "I'm co-writing the first half-hour episode [about modern life]. Mine's about how to survive your fiancé's relatives during the holidays."

Her mother, Lydy Henley Caldwell, is an actress and still lives in Jackson, Mississippi, where Ms. Henley grew up as the second-oldest of four sisters. (Jackson is home to Eudora Welty, a writer to whom the playwright is often compared.) The playwright's father, Charles Henley, a lawyer who served in both houses of the Mississippi legislature, died when she was twenty-six.

Ms. Henley majored in acting as a college student at Southern Methodist University in Dallas. She moved to Los Angeles in 1976 "because I wanted to act." She joined Actors' Equity, the professional union.

This past week, in between afternoon and late-night writing stints, she was to begin rehearsals of a play called *Two Idiots in Hollywood* at L.A.'s Theatre/Theater.

"I play Murray Franklin, a boy from New York," she says matter-of-factly. "Actually, I play a woman disguised as a man. But it's never really mentioned that I'm a woman. It's just like this woman had to become a man to get ahead." Like *Tootsie* in reverse? "Yes, except that it's like a real supporting part. It's a farce. It doesn't really matter what my voice sounds like."

She could afford the luxury of taking the small roles, partly because of money made from *Crimes*.

"The million dollars is a number that they say 'cause it's nice and round, but see, the thing is, I don't get a million dollars," she decides to explain. "The money was relative to how long the play ran in New York [more than fifteen months]. Also, the Broadway producers get 40 percent of it. My agent gets 10 percent. Louisville [the original producer, the Actors Theatre of Louisville, Ky.] gets five percent. My business manager gets five percent. So they kind of whittle it down pretty fast. Not to mention taxes. Not to mention we didn't get the whole million."

Although she says the publicity the Pulitzer brought her was far more valuable to her career than the thousand-dollar award that accompanies it ("I think I spent it on rent"), she does not allow herself to be overwhelmed by its glamour. "My [Pulitzer] certificate is still stored in a box at a friend's place from when I moved last July."

Her plays have inspired speculation about their autobiographical content. In *Crimes*, is the playwright most like ambitious middle sister Meg Magrath? (The independent-minded, twenty-seven-year-old character had left Mississippi for a Hollywood career and ended up, like Ms. Henley did for a while, working in a dog food factory.) Or siblings Babe or Lenny Magrath?

"I'm probably most like *all* of them," Ms. Henley says. "Different parts of me are different parts of them. Not any of them is all of me. I'm not all of any of them. But you know, I have the same feelings they all have."

Beth Henley

Kathleen Betsko / 1984

From *Interviews with Contemporary Women Playwrights*, edited by Kathleen Betsko and Rachel Koenig (New York: Beech Tree Books, 1987), 211–22. Copyright © 1987 by Kathleen Betsko and Rachel Koenig. Used by permission of HarperCollins Publishers. A champion for women playwrights, Kathleen Betsko, also known as Kathleen Betsko Yale, has written three produced plays, one of which, *Johnny Bull* (1981), she adapted for television.

Beth Henley was born and raised in Mississippi. She is the author of *Crimes of the Heart, The Miss Firecracker Contest,* and *The Wake of Jamey Foster.* Her plays have been produced extensively, on Broadway, in American regional theaters, and abroad. *Crimes of the Heart,* her first full-length play, won both the Pulitzer Prize in Drama and the New York Drama Critics' Circle Award for Best American Play in 1981, and was co-winner of the 1979 Great American Play Contest sponsored by the Actors Theatre of Louisville. She is at work on a new play entitled *The Debutante Ball.* Ms. Henley graduated from Southern Methodist University. She lives and works in Los Angeles.

Interviewer: Why are you living in Los Angeles when most of your fellow playwrights are in New York?

Beth Henley: Before I knew that I wanted to write, I wanted to act. It was either New York or Los Angeles. Some of my close friends were living in L.A., so I came out here. It was not a very calculated decision. The acting world was tough. I was on such a low level that I'd audition for anything in the paper. Right away they didn't like the way you looked or the way you talked. It was so much more difficult than writing.

Interviewer: Having been raised in the South, did you experience any culture shock when you first moved to Los Angeles?

Henley: It was like I'd crossed over to the moon! In the South, everything is staid. Everyone knows you. Out here, it's real transient. Nobody knows anybody, you're completely anonymous, and in a way I like that. I like going places and not running into several people I know. In Los Angeles, everybody's out for themselves. But everybody's trying, everybody's got these *dreams*—some of them pathetic and unreachable—but at least they do have hopes and aspirations. In the South, you just know what you're going to do and you do it. It gets to be very suffocating when I go back there.

Interviewer: What is a typical Beth Henley day like?

Henley: It depends. . . . Usually I get up late, piddle around my house, read the newspaper, have breakfast, and give my dog a bone . . . then I go to my office and work all day, till about five-thirty. Then Belita [Moreno], a friend, comes over to the office, and we do our Jane Fonda exercises. After that, I go out to dinner with friends (I hardly ever cook) or have people come over. I usually stay up pretty late at night, either reading or writing.

Interviewer: Tell us something about your creative process.

Henley: I write excessive notes, character charts, and outlines before I even start the dialogue. After the first draft, I usually don't need to do major rewrites, though I make a lot of minor changes and do some rewriting during rehearsals. I like to fix stuff that's not working. Though I used to write at night, I've taken to writing in the afternoons now that I have an office. I usually take my vitamins, pick up some lint on the floor, look out, look around, think about who I have to call, because I *hate* to make phone calls, I'm desperate about it. I always have to do *something* before I start writing. I don't think it's good to rush it. I do a certain amount of dialogue a day, which I reread the next day before I go on. I look over my notes. I always write out *What is this play all about? What are you writing? What does this mean? This sucks.* I've got all these notes on the floor. I have character charts and cross-references . . . all these rituals are really more complex than I can explain. I mainly just do this stuff to keep busy so my mind can be left alone to figure it out.

Interviewer: What is the rehearsal process like for you? How much input do you expect as a writer?

Henley: Equal to more input than the director on the script, and equal to less input into the production. If you work with someone you respect, you can always work things out.

Interviewer: Do you talk directly to the actors?

Henley: Generally I don't like to talk to the actors. I prefer to speak to the director—to give him notes—because actors seem to get really hurt when the playwright says something negative to them, much more so than when the director says things.

Interviewer: Do you sit through the entire rehearsal process?

Henley: If it's a first production of a play, I can't leave. I hate to get coffee or go to the bathroom. I love to sit there and watch, even if I'm just staring into space. I love to watch actors work and I love rehearsals. Watching the actors discover things is like watching a home run. I don't want to be out making phone calls or doing publicity.

Interviewer: When you feel the play isn't coming across the way you intended, will you push for what you want?

Henley: Oh, sure. I always push for what I want. Only on a couple of occasions have I had arguments with the director. Usually, I try to be more manipulative, you know, say, "This is just wonderful, but I've just got this little thought. . . ." I try not to get people on the defensive, I try not to say, "I *have* to have this idea," or "This thing really sucks, why don't you fix it?" I'd rather try to deal with specific problems.

Interviewer: How do you deal with opening night?

Henley: I sit in a bar across the street. . . . I'm talking about New York or London. . . . The thing is, it's a false night for the actors and for the playwright because the critics are there. I mean, I'm not going to sit in the theater with people who have notepads and are writing down criticisms of my plays. It makes me too sick. Besides, that's the great thing about being a playwright; you don't have to sit in the theater. I've sat in the theater and died a million deaths. So my advice is to leave. It saves you the misery and the terror.

Interviewer: Do you remember the first time you saw a production of one of your plays?

Henley: I remember I was real cavalier about it. I'd written *Am I Blue* as a sophomore in college [1972] and they pulled it out for production when I was a senior. I had my name down as Amy Peach.

Interviewer: You took a pseudonym?

Henley: Yeah. I remember I saw the play first in a preview. It wasn't very good and I was real embarrassed. But after a while, the show improved. I saw it later in Hartford [Hartford Stage Company, 1981] and then again in Dallas. I recall being moved by the play because it reflected so clearly who I was when I was eighteen. When I wrote *Am I Blue* I was so emotionally covered up that I didn't even realize what I was saying about myself or about life or loneliness, family situations. I just thought it was a kind of funny piece that I wrote to pass playwriting class. When I went back to it, I was so glad I'd written it down because I'll never be that innocent again . . . with that point of view, knowing nothing about life. At eighteen, I was simply terrified that I was a failure.

Interviewer: *Crimes of the Heart* [1979] is partially about sisterly love . . .

Henley: Oh, God. I have three sisters and the relationship with each is different. My littlest sister I've always just adored. My other two sisters were closer in age, so we always ganged up against each other. We had horrible, normal battles. . . . I don't know whether we loved each other more than most sisters, or whether we hated each other more than most. [*Laughter*] We're still into each other, we talk on the phone . . . we criticize the other sisters, things like "I think she should lose weight" or "I can't understand why she is with that idiot."

Interviewer: What was your family's response to all the Pulitzer publicity?

Henley: They were very surprised. On the negative side, I know my sister, C. C., felt pressured. She was in a dress shop and the woman who's done her alterations for years and years said, "C. C., I know you're just as smart as your sister, why don't you go out and get you one of those Pulitzer Prizes?" C. C. said she felt like Billy Carter. Mississippi is such a small place. It's much more significant there to have had a show on Broadway or a Pulitzer than it would be in, say, California. Out here, you have to be a major-major celebrity, like Farrah Fawcett, to feel like a big deal.

Interviewer: Did your father live to see you win the Pulitzer?

Henley: No. I'd written *Crimes of the Heart* and he had a stroke that summer. He'd read one of my earlier plays and didn't like it. It was a 1940s musical called *Parade*. He hated it because he'd been in World War II. He thought the work was completely abysmal and historically inaccurate. He didn't see me as a writer.

Interviewer: How do you think he would have felt about your success?

Henley: Oh, he would have loved it. He loved the limelight. He would have loved to come up and criticize my plays and tell me what needed to be fixed.

Interviewer: How did your hometown react?

Henley: My mother says people are always claiming that they recognize themselves in *Crimes of the Heart*, and I haven't even met them! They've met one of my sisters and think they've met me. The play was done in Mississippi this spring and it was a big hit. It's like something you wish in high school, being so shy, not really making good grades, not even being in Advanced English. Then you come back, and people are your friends, they are so nice to you and you think, "Who am I? Why are they nice to me now? What's different?" I understand what's different, but at the same time, there are parts of me that are intimidated or rebellious or just confused.

Interviewer: What was your own response to winning the Pulitzer Prize?

Henley: I felt so happy, it was just the moon. And it was really a surprise.

Interviewer: What are the negative points, if any, to winning?

Henley: Later on they make you pay for it. I think the fate of *The Wake of Jamey Foster* is part of the cost of winning. They just make sure you don't get overwhelmed by it, they want you to feel like it's not a big deal. "They" meaning the fates, not necessarily the critics. Winning the Pulitzer also put pressure, as I have said, on some of my family and friends and I didn't like that aspect of it at all. Mainly it was great because it got me a lot of money and a car, which I'd never had before. A bit of power.

Interviewer: Your mother is an actress.

Henley: Oh, yes. She acted in community theater. As a child I just loved going to the theater and sitting there in rehearsals, watching. I thought it was glamorous. She'd come out in this green dress and stand onstage and get kissed by a man. I thought it was the most wonderful thing for a mother to do.

Interviewer: In a *Time* magazine interview with Richard Corliss [February 8, 1982], you said that you are always afraid you're going to die before completing a play.

Henley: Oh, yes. I always think about death. I can't get through a day without thinking about it because it's my fate. When I'm working on a play, that's what helps drive me to finish it. Before I completed my new play, *The Debutante Ball*, I was going nuts because I had to go to the Hartford Stage Company for *The Wake of Jamey Foster* [January 1982], and I was working on the *Crimes of the Heart* screenplay. These responsibilities were taking me away from working on *The Debutante Ball*. I kept thinking, if I can at *least* get through these notes for the play, then maybe someone could finish it if I die.

Interviewer: Why do you write?

Henley: Writing always helps me not to feel so angry. I've written about ghastly, black feelings and thoughts that I've had. The hope is that if you can pin down these emotions and express them accurately, you will be somehow absolved. I like to write characters who do horrible things, but whom you can still like . . . because of their human needs and struggles.

Interviewer: You don't cover up the ugliness, do you?

Henley: I try to understand that ugliness is in everybody. I'm constantly in awe of the fact that we still seek love and kindness even though we are filled with dark, bloody, primitive urges and desires.

Interviewer: What is your fascination with the grotesque: swollen heads, dead and injured animals, burn victims, aborted babies, and suicides?

Henley: I've always been very attracted to split images. The grotesque combined with the innocent, a child walking with a cane, a kitten with a swollen head, a hunchback drinking a cup of fruit punch. Somehow these images are a metaphor for my view of life; they're colorful. Part of that is being brought up in the South; southerners always bring out the grisly details in any event. It's a fascination with the stages of decay people can live in on this earth . . . the imperfections. But I do feel that all my plays are extremely optimistic.

Interviewer: And what about all the animal imagery in the plays?

Henley: I hadn't ever realized there was animal imagery until my friend, playwright Frederick Bailey, pointed it out to me. I don't know what it means.

Interviewer: There is no intended symbolic value?

Henley: Well, humans are animals. We're mammals; I think we should stop pretending that we're not. In the set for *The Debutante Ball*, I've got a beautiful, lush upstairs sitting room and bathroom. I show all the things that people do in the bathroom before they go out to make themselves not animals, like shaving their legs, plucking their eyebrows, vomiting, pissing, perfume. . . . That is what is fascinating about people, their strange mixture of primitive instincts, intellect, and spiritual confusion.

Interviewer: Your plays are very funny. Would you discuss your ideas on comedy?

Henley: I always feel so emotional and miserable when I'm working, like I'm writing something tragic. Then everything manages to come out funny . . . and I'm glad.

Interviewer: So you don't set out to write a comedy?

Henley: No. Not at all. All these things that I feel inside are desperate and dark and unhappy. Or not *unhappy*, but searching. Then they come out funny. The way my family dealt with hardships was to see the humor or the ironic point of view in the midst of tragedy. And that's just how *my* mind works. I don't think the plays are hilarious, though I'm glad they're not somber because that could be real boring. My comedy comes out of the situation and the characters rather than in funny lines. However, I *do* understand about making the rhythm of the line a *comic* rhythm. I know I can take one word out, or put two words in and it will get a laugh.

Interviewer: Marshael plays the violin, though not very well, in *The Wake of Jamey Foster*. Babe, in *Crimes*, looks forward to improving her saxophone playing in jail. Are the musical instruments a metaphor for the creative impulse?

Henley: They must be. Growing up I never had a musical instrument because I didn't play. So for me, just to be around musical instruments means something special. Part of the reason I like to use musical instruments in my plays is so that they will be onstage, so that I can play around with them, pick them up when nobody is looking! They represent something beautiful, all this music and magic that I can't touch, can't grasp. I love saxophones and trumpets. The notes go so high, it's almost like the most exalted thing a human being can do, to play those wild high notes. It's like the musicians are straining, reaching for something beyond knowledge or the stars but they can't quite reach it.

Interviewer: When we hear the saxophone playing at the end of *Crimes of the Heart*, are we to believe that Babe is condemned to prison?

Henley: No. No. The saxophone is more of a freeing image. The sisters are able to have this wonderful moment, despite impending doom, despite the fact that everything isn't sorted out, straightened up, and made right. The idea is you've got to grab what you can, because when is life ever perfectly happy?

Interviewer: If you were to write a sequel, would Babe be in prison?

Henley: I've changed my mind on that a couple of times. I think Babe probably gets off. They get people off for all sorts of things in Mississippi.

Interviewer: The word *blue* seems to crop up frequently in your scripts—the color, as well as in reference to jazz and mood . . .

Henley: I like the blues, I like jazz . . . colors pop up a lot. It scares you when you start writing your plays and they're all somehow the same play; they're not the same, but you use the same troubles and perceptions. It must mean you haven't sorted anything out . . . you're still stuck with the same fucking problems year after year.

Interviewer: You were accused of writing another *Crimes of the Heart* when you wrote *The Wake of Jamey Foster*. Do you see them as the same story?

Henley: To me, they're different; they were dealing with different kinds of ghosts. I don't know . . . no one said, "Degas, don't paint any more ballerinas." I seem to have been driven to explore different southern families in different situations. *Miss Firecracker* and *The Debutante Ball* are also set in the South and they're about families, too. Maybe the plays are all variations on the same theme. I like dealing with similar characters. The Katty character in *The Wake of Jamey Foster* is something like Chick in *Crimes*. I was dissatisfied with the Chick character and I wanted to show the other side of her, to delve further. I have to write what is exciting to me and even if it may not seem very different to anybody else, it's exquisitely different to me—all glittering colors that I've seen but haven't dealt with fully before.

Interviewer: Which of the characters in your plays is most like yourself?

Henley: All of them are different facets of what I feel. I think everybody writes autobiographically. You can't say that anything in my plays has actually happened . . . well, that's not true . . . *The Wake*, I guess, is my most autobiographical play, as far as events. And *Debutante Ball* may be the most psychically autobiographical play I've written.

Interviewer: Tell us something about your new play, *The Debutante Ball.*

Henley: I just had a reading of it in my house. It was beautiful. I have some actors that I always use because they understand the tone of my writing. It's about the debutante and her mother, about mother-daughter love. About the fragility of love, how people need love so badly that the need literally cripples them in their struggle to attain it. They are no longer able to seek love in a pure way. Instead, strange distorted devices are used to attain this balm, this love that they now seem to need in druglike excesses.

Interviewer: Many of your characters are trying to break free of the labels that others have forced on them.

Henley: Yes, that's true. Particularly in *Miss Firecracker* and in *Crimes.* Both are about overcoming ghosts of the past and letting go of what other people have said you are, what they have told you to be. My other plays, *The Wake* and *The Debutante Ball*, are about what happens when you haven't overcome the shit . . . or have had more shit added on.

Interviewer: Why did most of the reviewers sensationalize the fact that Babe, in *Crimes of the Heart*, says she shot her husband because she "didn't like his looks." Didn't she have deeper motives? Hadn't Babe been physically and mentally abused by her husband for years?

Henley: The press like something that's quick and funny and catches your attention, a catchphrase. That's all I can figure out, or else they just didn't get the point.

Interviewer: Do you mind being called a "woman playwright"?

Henley: No.

Interviewer: Is there a female aesthetic in dramatic writing?

Henley: Probably in a general sense there is, just like there is a southern aesthetic or an animal aesthetic. But it all sounds too much like school to get me very excited.

Interviewer: Do you consider yourself a feminist?

Henley: Yes.

Interviewer: Do you think the critics, in their rush to pin a label on you, overlooked the fact that your work has a profound feminist message? Not one said you were a feminist, but several called you a "Southern Gothic" writer.

Henley: "Southern" won out over "feminist," I guess. . . .

Interviewer: Do you think this may have helped you escape some of the critical accusations often leveled at work with overtly feminist themes?

Henley: They're used to women writers from the South and so it's not such a big thing. There are so many women writers that are southern, I guess critics allow them the right to write what they want.

Interviewer: Do you think men's plays are critiqued differently from women's plays?

Henley: This is where my ignorance comes into play; I hate to read reviews. I have this hubris that always gets me in trouble if I ever read them. Like they sent me the reviews from the *Miss Firecracker* production in Chicago, a big package. I said, "I don't read reviews," and they said, "These are great. Read them." [*Ms. Henley screams.*] I pulled out the only horrible one. It said, "It's certain that she'll never write anything as good as *Crimes of the Heart.*"

Interviewer: I want to push you a bit on whether or not the work of male playwrights is evaluated differently.

Henley: Before *Crimes of the Heart* was a success, it was done in Louisville. I remember a review that said it was just "gossamer women" talking in the kitchen. And when *Miss Firecracker* was done out here, in California, they called it a petty play about a beauty contest. They wouldn't look for any of the deeper meaning or the spiritual levels in the play. Whereas if a man wrote a play about a baseball game, critics might be more inclined to find deep meanings about the Lost American Dream.

Interviewer: Critics have often condemned women's plays for being too wordy, for not having enough "action."

Henley: I know I go home to Mississippi and we *talk*. No TV, we just sit around the kitchen table and pick something to talk about. It's exciting, always amusing and dramatic. I love to listen to conversations, to sit and eavesdrop. It's just so interesting, people's lives and the little things that conversations show. That's why I like playwriting.

Interviewer: Language? Conversation?

Henley: Yes, and as a human being, I also find it fascinating to think about what the world is going to be like when people won't talk anymore. There are probably brilliant people, geniuses, alive today who don't even know how to say, "Hello, how do you do?" because their minds are absorbed with electronic images. I've been reading a book full of little bitty things from around the turn of the century in Wisconsin. Clippings from a newspaper in a small town: They use big words and twists of phrases that are poetic and much more literate than newspapers today. I'm astounded when I think of what a dive we've taken in such a short time.

Interviewer: Is *Miss Firecracker* an indictment of beauty contests?

Henley: It's a story about wanting to belong to the world. I didn't want to judge the contest. The contest is important to the character; winning it would make her feel like she is somebody. It's interesting to me what people do to make themselves special. It's exalting to me that they do these things.

Interviewer: Would you discuss the recurrence of barren women in your work?

Henley: In *The Wake of Jamey Foster* I wanted to capture an image of all the women, to present different images of women in their state of fertility: Marshael, who has had children; Katty, who wants to but can't; Collard, who'd had the abortion; and Pixrose, the virgin who dreams.

Interviewer: Is having children a present or future concern for you?

Henley: No, it makes me sad. I wish I were the type of person who wanted children, but I think I've got to admit I don't. I wish I could cook up a good spaghetti sauce, sling it out there on the table. But I'm not that type. My sisters have a lot of kids and I play with them and love to talk with them. They amuse me so, yet I know I have a fear of being tied down. My mother was. I know my fear is based on her being trapped in with all that talent she had, by kids and husband and the world. I purposely didn't take Home Economics; I didn't learn how to cook or sew or type. I finally had to teach myself to type. I'd refused to do things that would make me into something I didn't want to be. But it's sad, too, because you wonder and think that maybe you should commit yourself more to things. Something less completely selfish.

Interviewer: Somebody's got to write our plays.

Henley: Well, but now those assholes say everybody can write plays and have five kids and be gourmet cooks and all. Still, I've noticed that very few women writers throughout history had children. Because a kid's got to be more important than a fucking piece of paper. I know it could be so enriching to have a child. I am only speaking against it selfishly, in terms of writing. Sometimes I think, "Yeah . . . I could do all sorts of stuff . . . write during pregnancy. . . ." Then I think, "What are you doing? You'd be having this kid as a kind of experiment, and that's despicable." I couldn't inflict that on a little child.

Interviewer: Was it hard for you when *The Wake of Jamey Foster* closed so quickly [opened on Broadway, at the Eugene O'Neill Theatre, October 14, 1982, closed October 23, 1982], considering your previous success with *Crimes*?

Henley: Yes, very hard. But I don't think *Wake* was a flop artistically. And at the time it was running, it was exhilarating. I felt much happier after *The*

Wake opened than I did after *Crimes* opened. The day after *Crimes*, I was completely drained. I was stunned after *The Wake*, but as a woman from the South, I was ready for it. I thought, "You can overcome this! You can live with this! Fuck what everybody else thinks. You're alive!" When people praised *Crimes*, I felt like I had to be so self-effacing it wasn't any fun. I felt I had to say, "Ah . . . it's really nothing. I didn't mean to write that . . . I was really writing a grocery list." When you have a flop, you can fight. I must say I did love *The Wake*. I was exalted the whole week it ran after the reviews came out.

Interviewer: Is there still discrimination against women playwrights in the American theater?

Henley: Yes, I think there is. Simply because there are still a lot more men than women in charge of our theaters: producing, directing, managing, fundraising. That's where the power and the money are in this country. Men generally can't help but be more moved by a man's play because they relate to it in a personal way. Women are more used to identifying with men, because they're raised on it, they've got to be. Men aren't used to identifying with women. And all writing is creating or spinning dreams for other people so they won't have to bother doing it themselves. In terms of the people who make decisions about play production, the closer these dreams are to their version of themselves, the more chance they'll want to sit through a play or to find money to produce it.

Interviewer: Why don't we see more broadly political plays in America?

Henley: I can only speak for myself. . . . I like to write about people. The problems of just being here are more pressing and exciting to me than politics. Politics generally deals with the facades of our more desperate problems. I don't really feel like changing the world, I want to look at the world. That is fascinating and challenging enough—without saying, "I'm going to write a play to change this." And what is *this*? *This* is madness. So you change it? So you get a Republican in, so you get a Democrat in? You're still in hell. What is amazing to me is the existential madness that we—everyone—are born into. There's a sense of powerlessness in the world. I have a moratorium on watching the news since Reagan's been president. I know I am burying my head in the sand but I just can't bear it. It's all such a game, such big business. People lie and cheat and steal. My father was in Mississippi politics for a while and he understood that people buy votes. I'm cynical—that's the word—cynical about politics. So now I think, "Don't be rude to people in stores, don't litter, remember to send your grandmother flowers on her birthday, enjoy the trees, write what you write—that's all you can do—try to be kind from day to day." I can't go out there with a banner, it's not my personality.

Interviewer: Would you discuss the difference between writing for the stage and screenwriting?

Henley: I love writing for the screen. I like to zip from one image to another and the fact that you can go on and off the stage, have tons of characters, lots of scenes. One problem is that the writer doesn't have shit to say. They can take what you've written and change it any way they want. And another problem: I haven't been able to get a movie made yet. Also in the movies you have no control over casting. With a stage play you have the freedom to do your play and see it like you want. In Hollywood, they can fire your director, fire you, not do the movie, take the idea, which might be one of your only ideas—I don't have that many ideas that I can be throwing them off and selling them to movies. I've also written for TV. You go in with a committee of people and each one gets one of their own ideas in. It's like nailing them all together and trying to patchwork the thing. And it comes out brown dishwater: nonspecific, bland. I mean, they *work* at getting things bland for TV. Now I'm spoiled. I tell my agent I've got money from *Crimes of the Heart* coming in from the national tour, and I don't want to write for TV. Lots of times there *are* some good working situations, but I love having the control to just go anywhere in my mind. It's too great a freedom to give up just for money.

Mississippi Playwright Downplays Her Success

Leslie R. Myers / 1985

From the *Clarion-Ledger/Jackson Daily News*, July 21, 1985, sec. E, pp. 1–2.
© Leslie R. Myers–USA TODAY NETWORK. Reprinted by permission of IMAGN.

Pulitzer Prize-winning playwright Beth Henley likes to slip into her native Jackson without fanfare. She usually succeeds. The ruse works because her unassuming manner hasn't changed since she became Broadway's belle in 1980.

Henley looks exactly like her pictures, from most any era. But she managed to attend a recent party at her childhood haunt, New Stage Theatre, without prompting much recognition. The theater, where she was a young actress, even has produced three of her plays.

"Basically, when I come home, I don't usually feel like a big success," the traditionally shy Henley said. "I just see friends and family. No . . . I don't feel like a success."

"But it's nice to go down to my grandmothers' and be able to say, 'I have a job.' They don't have to say things like, 'Why don't you take typing?' It's nice that people don't have to worry about me now."

Nowadays, Henley has enough jobs for three people as a playwright, screenwriter, and part-time actress in Los Angeles.

Her latest project is working as the screenwriter for a motion picture version of *Crimes of the Heart*, her Pulitzer-winning play. Accomplished producer Dino De Laurentiis is heading up the project.

"But it's not fact this will be a movie," Henley stressed. "There's a real big IF," she said, explaining that the movie business has a lot of red tape. "If it goes completely according to schedule . . . it will be made in the spring. Who knows when it would be released?"

The *Crimes* project, along with a family reunion, was the purpose of her recent trip to Jackson.

Accompanying Henley was Bruce Beresford, who plans to direct the movie. He came to tour Mississippi for the first time.

In Jackson, Henley visited her mom, Lydy Becker Caldwell, and sisters.

"We also went to Hazlehurst, where the play [*Crimes*] is set, and talked to my grandmother," Henley said. "Then we went to Brookhaven for a family reunion with my [other] grandmother."

Beresford wanted to see some of the people and places that have influenced Henley's major plays.

Crimes in Hazlehurst was followed by *The Miss Firecracker Contest*, set in Brookhaven; *The Wake of Jamey Foster*, set in Canton; and *The Debutante Ball*, set in Hattiesburg.

Those plays have found varied success, but none has challenged the acclaim of *Crimes*.

Firecracker didn't set the nation on fire, but it has had a bright showing. Last season, it enjoyed a healthy run Off-Broadway in New York City. That production was directed by Stephen Tobolowsky, Henley's boyfriend of a dozen years. He also directed *Debutante Ball*'s premiere.

Although *The Wake* script made promising reading, it was panned by most critics when it hit the stage.

Debutante Ball—which had its world premiere in April near Los Angeles—has received mixed reviews, as well as some raves.

In the meantime, Henley also has written a few one-act plays and some screenplays.

"I've made a lot of money on screenplays, a lot more than on plays," she said, adding that none have been produced and released. "There are screenwriters who have been working here for years and who are living in Beverly Hills—who have never had a screenplay produced." She explained that screenwriters are paid before any production steps are taken.

Production, however, is about halfway completed on the Henley co-penned screenplay *The Survival Guide to Civilization*. It's a pilot script for a new public television comedy series.

Henley has sold the rights to "Strawberry," a screenplay about a Los Angeles comedian, which she wrote for actress Sissy Spacek.

She just sold the rights to an early screenplay, "Moonwatcher," which she started before *Crimes* and later rewrote.

Also in the works is another (still untitled) play, which she hopes to complete by fall. She still gets royalties from her other plays.

Although screenplays are a more lucrative business, they haven't won Henley's heart over stage plays.

"A screenplay is a lot more fun and a lot easier. But you have a lot less control artistically," she said of final production.

"I guess writing a play is more fulfilling because it's more difficult. And it is yours."

She said if the *Crimes* movie is produced, it probably won't be filmed in Mississippi.

The story is set in the interior of a house, so producer De Laurentiis probably would film it in his studio in North Carolina, she said.

(Italian-born De Laurentiis has produced such major motion pictures as *Firestarter, Ragtime, The Shootist, King Kong, Three Days of the Condor, Serpico,* and *Barbarella.*)

This week, Henley left Los Angeles to meet De Laurentiis in Australia, where he is filming another movie. She will consult with him about the *Crimes* screenplay, which she began writing about a month ago.

"This movie actually has been in the making since 1980. So I don't try to get my hopes up," she said. "If he likes the screenplay, he will do it. . . . So I work on it like it's going to work."

In 1980, the film rights to *Crimes* were purchased by an independent producer, who later sold the screen rights to United Artists. If De Laurentiis decides to produce the film, Henley said, he will buy the rights from United Artists.

Henley was said to have received $1 million when those screen rights first were sold. But she says mathematics, other costs, and the box office figures brought that total down considerably.

"It sounds like it was a million-dollar deal. But it was only *up to* $1 million," she said. "If *Crimes* had run ten years [on Broadway], then I'd have made $500,000," she said. "Then the Broadway producers would get 40 percent of the movie deal and your agent gets 10 percent."

Crimes' healthy Broadway run, however, only topped one year.

"So, I got a good deal, but I don't know exactly how much," she said. "And I'm getting more money to write the screenplay, but not that much."

By most any yardstick, however, Henley has become a success. But she hasn't forgotten what it's like to take odd jobs to support her writing or acting ambitions. Her California jobs after college include working in a dog food factory.

She still leads a basically average lifestyle, although she and Tobolowsky have a house with a pool and a hot tub.

"Now, when I go to the supermarket, I don't think: Will I get paper towels or Kleenex? I buy two towels and three Kleenex—and a nice bottle of wine.

I eat out at restaurants constantly," she said, trying to think of some extravagant addition to her lifestyle.

"I only travel, basically, when I'm working. But if I go home, I fly first class.

"When I was poor, it was not a big, big problem. And now that I have money, it's not a big problem," she said.

Henley's acting career has taken to a back burner, but she doesn't plan to abandon it. "I love to act. It means I get to work on projects with people I care about," she said. She sometimes performs in Tobolowsky's productions.

Her dreams aren't as big as some might expect. "I just want to be able to keep writing—without working at a straight job," she said.

Beth Henley

Beverly Walker / 1986

From *American Film* 12 (December 1986): 30–31. Copyright © 1986 by American Film Institute. Reprinted by permission. Beverly Walker is a Los Angeles-based film writer and the author of *Jack Nicholson: Anatomy of an Actor* (2014).

When Beth Henley's first produced play, *Crimes of the Heart*, was purchased by Hollywood in 1980 for a cool million dollars, the Mississippi-bred playwright knew she had completed a tortuous rite de passage: "I reckoned I wouldn't have to work in a dog-food factory anymore."

The movie version of *Crimes of the Heart*, starring Diane Keaton, Sissy Spacek, and Jessica Lange, follows two days in the lives of three unusual sisters. The oldest is a spinster with a shrunken ovary who is depressed about aging; the middle one has returned ignominiously to Mississippi, having been reduced to working in a dog-food factory when her singing career in Los Angeles faltered; the youngest is a naïf who has just shot her husband.

Henley's southern upbringing is undoubtedly the strongest single influence on her writing. She is most aware of "language . . . story-telling . . . conversation. In my house, people were more inclined to sit around the kitchen table and talk than to watch TV.

"There's something else, too, something I'm sure has to do with the South's defeat in the Civil War, which is that you should never take yourself too seriously. You may be beaten and defeated, but your spirit cannot be conquered. The South has gall to still be able to say we have our pride, but as a human characteristic it is admirable."

Currently, Henley has her name on two motion pictures and a segment of an innovative PBS comedy series. *Nobody's Fool* [formerly titled "The Moonwatcher"] was written in 1977, when an acting career was her primary goal and success still seemed far away. Rosanna Arquette plays the film's main character, a small-town girl who decides to leave for Los Angeles with Eric Roberts, a snazzy young set designer passing through. Maybe she'll become an actress, maybe not. The movie was directed by first-timer Evelyn Purcell, who optioned it in 1981, calling it "the most honest rendering of a girl growing up I'd ever read."

"It was full of anger when I first wrote it because I felt so young and powerless," Henley says. "I couldn't cope with the business side of acting, much less the rejection. Even sending résumés around was humiliating."

Henley's other 1986 project, the eagerly awaited *True Stories*, was haphazardly coauthored with David Byrne and Stephen Tobolowsky. "I'm very honored to have a credit, but all I really did was help David organize his ideas," Henley says. "Stephen and I went down to the Fort Worth-Dallas area to just drive around and look. Stephen and I subsequently wrote a long and baroque screenplay, from which David took what he needed."

Collaborators Byrne and Arquette both appear in a segment of PBS's *Survival Guide* that Henley coauthored in 1985 with comic Budge Threlkeld. "It was my first collaboration," she says. "Budge wanted to help me out of a depression I'd lapsed into after my play [*The Wake of Jamey Foster*] had bombed on Broadway. We wrote it on chocolate bars and vodka!" The half-hour show, directed by Jonathan Demme and based on producer Jon Denny's concept, is about a girl's first meeting with her future in-laws. "We open with a house in flames and Rosanna saying, 'But all I wanted was for them to like me.'"

This anecdote underscores a couple of striking Henley characteristics: a comically apocalyptic vision along with a penchant for working with longtime friends and colleagues. Indeed, she is like a den mother to a group of serious theater and film artists based in Los Angeles, many of them, like herself, graduates of Southern Methodist University.

Since *Crimes of the Heart* was launched onstage, Henley has written four plays that have all been produced. "I think I'm born for the theater," says Henley at this juncture of her career. "It's so alive. Audiences can pull it one way or another, and after the play you can go out and talk. On movies, everybody's like a monk—getting up early in the morning and putting in those long hours—and as the writer you don't know what you're doing there except waiting for the lunch wagon."

The Eccentric Genius of
Crimes of the Heart

Margy Rochlin / 1987

From *Ms.*, February 1987, pp. 12, 14. Reprinted by permission of Margy Rochlin. Margy Rochlin has been a journalist on radio and in print since the 1980s.

During one particularly rough, poverty-ridden patch of Beth Henley's life, she briefly had a fantasy that would forever after leave her with a twinge of guilt: it occurred to Henley that if an elderly relative of hers passed away she might inherit a valuable antique that she could sell to raise cash. "I love my family and I would die if they read this," says Henley. "But this shows how low I was."

Today, Henley could easily purchase anyone in her family a roomful of antiques to make up for the morbid wish. At thirty-four, she is the winner of the 1981 Pulitzer Prize for her play *Crimes of the Heart* (she sold the screen rights in a $1 million deal). And she has launched an impressive screenwriting career, scripting *True Stories* (coauthored with her boyfriend Stephen Tobolowsky and musician David Byrne), *Nobody's Fool*, and the new film version of *Crimes of the Heart.*

Henley's work has always been known for its comically idiosyncratic characters. For example, the close-knit, calamity-prone Magrath sisters from *Crimes of the Heart*: Lenny, the oldest, frets over their failing Old Granddaddy, the death by lightning bolt of her pet horse Billy Boy, and facing her thirtieth birthday as a spinster with a shrunken ovary; lustpot Meg, who took off for Hollywood to pursue a singing career, has returned demoralized and dispirited—instead of fame and fortune, she found a nervous breakdown; and the fluttery Babe, the youngest, who was having an affair with a fifteen-year-old Black kid, is out on bail for having shot her bully of a husband, Zackery. (Afterward, Babe trotted into the kitchen and quenched her thirst with three glasses of lemonade.)

It appears, however, that Henley has now become her own most charismatic and colorful creation. Insiders say that Rosanna Arquette's long-underweared, neo-bag lady look in *Nobody's Fool* was pure imitation Henley. Australian director Bruce Beresford soaked up the culture of the American South for the film *Crimes of the Heart* by spending several days at the Henley stronghold in Jackson, Mississippi.

Actress Sissy Spacek, who stars with Diane Keaton (Lenny) and Jessica Lange (Meg) in *Crimes*, confesses that any similarities between Henley and the fictitious Magrath sisters are hardly coincidental. While on location in North Carolina, says Spacek, she, Lange, and Keaton studied Henley's mannerisms and dress and incorporated them into their roles. For example, Jessica Lange twice performs one of Henley's nervous habits, snapping the plastic top off an aspirin bottle with her teeth. "We were all kind of taking things from Beth," says Spacek. "Like, I wore pajama tops all through the film. Beth is like somebody's little old aunt. We all just kept a beady eye on her."

Brown-haired and doe-eyed, Beth Henley sits in a straight-backed wooden chair in her Beverly Hills "office"—actually a tidy apartment furnished with a bordello-red satin chaise longue and a large antique table. She is trying to answer a question that has been put to her repeatedly over the last few months: does she consider herself a little, say, unusual? A petite five feet three inches tall, she is dressed in lavender knee socks, a light cotton seersucker shirt, and a baggy green sweater that nearly envelops her entire frame as she hunches over in thought. "Well," she says finally, in her soft southern drawl, "I *wish* I were an eccentric. My life is sooooo boring." The telephone suddenly rings. Picking it up, Beth chats with a friend about her new play, *The Lucky Spot.* As she talks, she launches into a bout of joint-popping stretching exercises: she balances flamingo-like on one Adidas-clad foot and, arching her back, sticks her other leg out behind her. The gesture is rather looney-looking, but totally unselfconscious; it's the act of someone who is either unconcerned with public opinion or has spent so much time by herself, she has forgotten that others are watching.

The second of four daughters, Henley says her goal as a teenager was simply "to not cause any trouble." Shy and withdrawn, she spent much of her days alone "reading, writing, listening to records, just biding my time. My parents were breaking up then," she remembers. "I wanted to please them; I didn't want to be more of a burden. So I tried to participate, be a part of things, but it just became more and more difficult."

At a high school where people were "overconcerned with football games and cheerleaders," Henley found herself disconcerted by the contrast between her life and "what was happening with the world. It was the Vietnam years—people were burning bras or setting themselves on fire in protest. There was excitement that I was totally missing."

But the worst part of her late adolescence, says Henley, was her own lack of ambition. "The boredom, the pain of having nothing to care about was overwhelming to me," she says. "I won this Gold Key for a picture I drew when I was in high school. It almost means more to me than the Pulitzer Prize. That's when I needed it badly, some sort of meager scrap of affirmation."

After high school, Henley studied acting at Southern Methodist University. A series of odd jobs followed graduation—working at a dog food factory, snapping photos of young children at Christmas. In 1976, she moved to Los Angeles in the hopes of becoming a working actress; instead she wrote her first screenplay, "The Moonwatcher," later retitled *Nobody's Fool*. "I would go to these sleazeball auditions and meet all these sleazeball people," she says. "But the hardness of this city helped me become a writer because it left me insane to do something creative. After all, I had the time." While still tinkering with *Nobody's Fool*, she wrote *Crimes of the Heart*, and subsequently won the Pulitzer. Besides her three film scripts, Henley has since had five plays produced—*The Wake of Jamey Foster*, *The Miss Firecracker Contest*, *The Debutante Ball*, and *Am I Blue*. Her new play, *The Lucky Spot*, first presented in Williamstown, Massachusetts, last summer, will be opening in the spring at the Manhattan Theatre Club. Actress Sissy Spacek is hoping to star in "Strawberry," a film script Henley wrote about an aspiring stand-up comedian in Los Angeles.

Though it's easy to draw parallels between Henley's life and her Mississippi-based plays, she claims her work is only "middling autobiographical. My sisters were very disappointed when they saw *Crimes*," she says as a point of fact. "They thought it would be about them." But she is acutely aware of how her imagination was stimulated by her southern upbringing. "Individuality or independence is applauded in the South much more so than other places," she explains. "There is a wildness in us that we are always trying to subdue. It's important to have the ability to tell stories and do outrageous things like throw steaks out your plate-glass window."

A debate has begun to rage over Henley's treatment of her exotic characters. Despite the obvious affection she accords them, some critics have carped that her portrayal of these citizens of small-town America is relentlessly contemptuous. "I think it offends some people that I don't cast a blind eye," she says. "It's about looking at these people and liking them for who they are. I don't talk down to them. To say that all small towns are quaint and darling would be like saying, 'All women are sweet, cute, and well-behaved.'"

On a side table in Beth Henley's office is a neat pile of Xeroxed film reviews that the studio has sent her. She admits to flipping through them briefly. "I glanced at this one," she says, holding out a particularly vicious dissection of *Nobody's Fool*. "Then I put this review over it." With the exception of the film title, the second account is printed entirely in Korean script. This witty bit of logic echoes the skewed but unrestrained optimism in her plays. Henley scrutinizes the article for a moment. "I think it's a rave," she decides.

Beth Henley

Kevin Sessums / 1987

From *Interview* 17 (February 1987): 85. Kevin Sessums is the author of the memoirs *Mississippi Sissy* (2007) and *I Left It on the Mountain* (2015).

When Beth Henley won the 1981 Pulitzer Prize for drama for *Crimes of the Heart*, she was the first woman in twenty-three years to be given the honor. Her other plays include *Am I Blue, The Miss Firecracker Contest, The Wake of Jamey Foster,* and *The Debutante Ball*. Her latest, *The Lucky Spot*, will be produced at Manhattan Theatre Club in the spring.

Recently, Henley turned her attention to motion pictures and television. She not only collaborated with David Byrne on *True Stories*, but also wrote the original screenplay for *Nobody's Fool* and the adaptation of her own *Crimes*. In June, PBS will air her *Trying Times*, directed by Jonathan Demme.

Beth and I grew up in Mississippi. Before we met in her suite at the Parker Meridien Hotel in New York, I was worried that all this show business success might have gone to her southern head. Not to worry. I knew I was in the presence of a died-in-the-cotton, cotillioned lady when she dialed up room service. "Hello, this is Miss Henley," she drawled. "I'd like to order some breakfast: a Co'-Cola and a glass of ice."

Kevin Sessums: You come from an interesting family. Your mother is a rather infamous local actress, and your father was a state senator for a number of years. Were you affected by his politics?

Beth Henley: I was very shy. We were taken around to politic for my father at a very early age, and I just loathed it. And I became cynical about politics because of it. But my mother loved it. When we'd go to a hick town, she'd say, "Beth, those shoes look a little too nice. Put some mud on 'em, girl." Or, "Okay, Beth, you've got a broken arm this summer. Play it up. Let's get the sympathy vote." You always knew it was showbiz.

KS: You were old enough in 1964 to be aware of the civil rights movement going on around you. Being the daughter of a Mississippi state senator had to have been a thrilling and troubling experience for a child then.

BH: It's odd—although my father was conservative, we would get threats from the KKK. They'd call us up on the phone. That was frightening. I remember when the synagogue was bombed. Then when the guy who was the head of the synagogue had his house bombed, I remember the windows breaking in our house 'cause we lived down the street from him. Oh, and my sister's fifth-grade teacher . . . did you hear about that? She was shot to death in a pair of hot pants when she was out with her lover trying to kill Black people or something. They ended up getting shot themselves. Maybe they were trying to plant a bomb; I can't quite remember. Anyway, my sister was devastated. It was one of her favorite teachers. And it wasn't so much that she was murdered, but that she was wearing *hot pants*.

KS: Would you ever write about politics in the South? So far you have only focused on families.

BH: I think I should. I was disenchanted with politics for so long. It would be fascinating if I could, though. I stayed fairly uninformed the whole time. I mean, I began to feel it didn't matter if this man won or that man won—they were still the same fools.

KS: I've got to ask you something. I heard this from an eyewitness, but you've got to corroborate it. When your father died, they brought him back to "Tara," as your house was known to some of us, because it was so big and had all those columns. Once there, they laid him out so people could come and pay their last respects. But it seemed sort of bare—no flowers were around his body or anything. So your mother—who was divorced from him by then—went to the refrigerator and got out a bunch of cold cuts and put them around the body. Made it into a buffet.

BH: That could have happened when I wasn't around, but I don't think so. That's a great story, though—and my mother probably started it to add to her legend. But they did bring his body back to the house and put the coffin out on the sun parlor, which was, in part, the inspiration for *The Wake of Jamey Foster*.

KS: That's the one play of yours that was neither a critical nor a financial success. After the enormous success of *Crimes of the Heart*, how did you cope with such failure?

BH: I had dual feelings about it. I was brokenhearted in that I really loved the director and the cast. On the other hand, it was sort of a relief 'cause I had felt so strange getting all that success from *Crimes*. I mean, I was getting *praise* heaped on me. And people were getting sort of strange. You know—"She's won the Pulitzer Prize. She's not going to be my friend anymore." So I had to go around pretending I was just the same and being extra nice to everybody. It was such a bore.

Being from the South, you're used to women being sort of downtrodden. But my mother was always raising her fists and saying, "You can't keep me down! I can do this!" So after *The Wake*, I had a chance not to be so humble anymore and to stop being so careful not to be conceited when everybody was telling me how wonderful *Crimes* was. When people tell you you're a shit, then you can be brazen. That was the nice part of the failure. It taught me strength.

KS: Into what sort of work did the experience propel you?

BH: I immediately went back to Los Angeles. I mean, even today, just looking at the print of the *New York Times* makes me nauseous. I started working on *The Debutante Ball* with a vengeance. And out of a kind of anger.

KS: Although your film *Nobody's Fool* was somewhat wistful, it *too* was full of anger.

BH: I first wrote the screenplay in 1977. The first version was even more angry and victimized. But I think as I grew up, I didn't like that victimized part so much.

KS: One of the things you were quoted as saying about *Nobody's Fool* was that "[t]here's no time for self-indulgence or bitterness in this story. Oh no, it is designed to get Cassie out of her despair. Maybe she should paint her nails. Or even try to kill herself. Either one is a positive act to catapult her out of that pain." Do you really consider suicide a positive act? It plays a big part in *Crimes of the Heart*, also.

BH: Yeah. Sure. I'm always thinking about killing myself. Aren't you? Sometimes I just sit with a knife and wonder if this is the time I'm going to stab myself—you know, when I'm in the kitchen or something. I just can't imagine that people don't think about killing themselves or dying. I think it really saves you a lot of times. The fact that you have the choice to live or die is a triumph, in a way. When my characters try to kill themselves, it's always like, "Okay, I know how to solve this problem—I'll kill myself! That's what I'll do! I'm in control!" And it's an exhilarating feeling.

KS: Well, you're lucky you have your writing. . . . Maybe that's what prevents you from stabbing yourself. It's a way of "painting your nails."

BH: In a sense, I write to survive. When I first sat down to write, I did it out of desperation. It is a lifeline to me. It keeps me from being bored. I'm heartsick when I don't have a play that I'm working on, 'cause I don't know what to think about when I'm in the shower or in the grocery line. Or even how to survive the night without being able to dream about my characters. It makes life so much more exciting for me.

KS: Do you consider yourself an intuitive playwright, or do you set out with an intellectual road map?

BH: I never know what the "message" of a play is going to be, but I do a lot of planning regarding the characters in the story. Generally, I'll have an image that will run throughout. For example, in *Crimes of the Heart* I knew that there was going to be a birthday cake at the end. At the end of *The Wake* I knew somebody was going to be playing the spoons. I also rewrite a whole lot, but generally the first draft has the basic structure and characters.

KS: Why have you chosen to live in L.A. rather than New York?

BH: I'd been to New York when I was young and poor, and it was horrifying. I got lost in so many subways. I slept on floors and in kitchen bathtubs. It just seemed so intimidating. I'd never been to California, but I had friends there, so I said, "Why not?" It takes some time getting used to. But compared to New York it is rather quiet and slow—like Mississippi.

Beth Henley

Cynthia Wimmer-Moul / 1991

From *The Playwright's Art: Conversations with Contemporary American Dramatists*, edited by Jackson R. Bryer (New Brunswick, NJ: Rutgers University Press, 1995), 102–22. Reprinted by permission of Cynthia Wimmer. Cynthia Wimmer is coeditor of *Teaching Performance Studies* (2002).

Beth Henley was born in Jackson, Mississippi, in 1952. She received her undergraduate education at Southern Methodist University and did graduate work at the University of Illinois. Her first professionally produced play, *Crimes of the Heart* (1979), won the New York Drama Critics' Circle Award and the Pulitzer Prize. Her other plays are *Am I Blue* (1972), *The Wake of Jamey Foster* (1982), *The Miss Firecracker Contest* (1984), *The Lucky Spot* (1984), *The Debutante Ball* (1988), *Abundance* (1990), *Signature* (1991), and *Control Freaks* (1992). This interview took place on October 23, 1991.

Interviewer: Why did you become a playwright?

Beth Henley: My mother was an actress (she still is an actress); so I started going to the theater when I was very young, and I always loved reading dialogue. She picked plays for the season at the theater in Mississippi, and I would read the plays. I read plays early, and I loved the kind of magic of the theater. I don't know; I just grew up with it.

Interviewer: Did you go to the rehearsals and get involved in the actual production of the plays by watching what was going on?

Henley: Yes. Seeing them tear down the sets afterwards, going back to the dressing rooms, and helping her learn her lines; it was a sanctuary for me, and it still is really.

Interviewer: Now that you're writing plays, are you still a large part of the play in the rehearsal process, or is the rehearsal process where you're letting go? Do you enjoy the rehearsal process?

Henley: Yes, I do. I love the rehearsal process because that's what theater is about. It's this collaborative art, and you get to see other people enhance your work. Sometimes they "de-hance" your work, but it's just thrilling when someone throws an insight into something that you didn't know was there or when the melody of the lines goes together exactly right. Everybody is so passionate about it; it's always exhilarating to be around people that are filled with passion about what they're doing.

Interviewer: How old were you when you first started writing, and were plays the first thing you wrote?

Henley: I remember being really small, and I had a book where you're supposed to draw pictures and write a story, and I remember being so frustrated—I must have been very small—because I had so much to tell and I couldn't figure out how to tell it. I wrote a play in sixth grade, a musical called "Swing High, Swing Low," that I tried to produce with some friends. We included boys, and that was just hopeless because then it got way out of hand. Nobody would rehearse, and I was not very good at being a dictator. Then I took a creative writing class in which I wrote a story and had to read it in front of the class. It wasn't completed, and I hated it so much that I scrunched it up and threw it down and ran out of the class, but I didn't get in trouble. I was always shocked that I didn't get in trouble for behaving so hysterically.

Interviewer: How do you usually start when you write a play?

Henley: I always start with a blank page and a lot of exasperation and self-loathing because I haven't written anything in so long. I've got inner turmoil; it's like a dam which is about to break.

Interviewer: What gets you started?

Henley: I wish I could figure out how not to get started this way, but really it seems like it's some sort of explosion or pain or desire to understand something.

Interviewer: Do you get an idea for a character first, or do you begin with a plot, something you want to see happen on the stage so you want to write a play around it?

Henley: It varies. Most of the plays I wrote early were based on a situation. *Crimes of the Heart* is based on the situation of a sister shooting her husband, and everyone has to come back in this traumatic event and deal with old wounds. *The Miss Firecracker Contest* is obviously based on a beauty contest and the events around that; *The Wake of Jamey Foster* is about a wake; *The Debutante Ball* is about a debutante ball; *The Lucky Spot*, my next play, was about the opening of a taxi-dance hall in the sticks of

Louisiana in the Depression. Oftentimes it has been around an event. I fig-ure out who would be there and what they would want, why they would want to be there or not want to be there, what their dreams would be in this situation, and what this event could mean to them. My later plays, like *Sig-nature* and *Control Freaks*, aren't so centered in an event, I guess. *Control Freaks* is about these people who try and open up Furniture World and end up murdering each other.

Interviewer: Do you write from an outline?

Henley: I have basically a lot of the theme, images, or dialogue, and I'll have "sister's dialogue" (things I think this one particular character may say) or things I think another character may say. Then I have miscellaneous dia-logue, things that I don't know who says, or I don't know if anybody says them.

Interviewer: How do you do rewriting?

Henley: I'm good at rewriting because it's so much easier than writing the original thing. I like to do rewrites after hearing the play read or see-ing it in previews. Previews are great because you can do the play at night and then you have five hours the next day to rehearse it and make changes. Oftentimes if you leave a piece alone for a couple of months and come back to it, cuts are obvious, or ways to fix things become really clear that you were stuck on in production.

Interviewer: Did that happen with *The Debutante Ball*? You worked on that over a period of time, didn't you?

Henley: Yes. That's the most torn-apart-and-put-back-together play I've written, because I wrote it over a long period of time. I didn't sit down and write it all in four months or whatever. I had a production of it done in Cali-fornia, and then I had a whole other production done in New York—and my rewrite between the production in New York and the one in California was really bad. It wasn't either this or that, and then I had to go to really chang-ing it to make it more like that.

Interviewer: Do you start with a title?

Henley: Not necessarily, although my titles, as you can see, are sort of bland: *The Debutante Ball, The Miss Firecracker Contest, The Wake of Jamey Foster, The Lucky Spot*. I kind of got on a roll—and then *Abundance*. I saw a boat called *Abundance* and I thought, "Isn't that the most beautiful word?" Who ever has an abundance? Of course, it's meant ironically, I guess, in the play. With *Signature* I did, too. That's a good question. I never knew it, but I do usually have a title when I start, sort of.

Interviewer: What format do you use if you don't really have an outline, and how do you maintain the discipline to keep working?

Henley: Writing the first line is always so scary, because I think in the first page you've got to have tone, you've got to have character. There are just immeasurable amounts that you need before you can write one line and let the characters start talking. Although I don't have an outline, I have done much preparation, and I may well have an outline for the first scene. I will say, "Okay, there is going to be a scene between Lenny and Chick. We're going to get that there is a problem with Babe. A gift's going to be given, and here is a couple of lines that might go in that scene." Then I'll say, "Doc comes, a horse is dead, and then so-and-so comes in." That's all I know: so-and-so is going to come in. It gets less and less specific until I really don't know anything until I've written that first scene.

How do I have the discipline? Sometimes it's very hard. You have to allow yourself to be idiosyncratic, and if you want to walk around and pick up lint off the carpet, just understand it's part of your process. I can understand why a lot of people don't write, because it's hard to have the discipline. If you do it for a long time, sometimes you get to where you like to be alone. It's sort of frightening, too, but I've always liked to be alone. Sometimes you have to sit there in a chair for two hours and not know what to do. You just think about the play. Because a play is so small, it's like a little chess puzzle, and you can't really go too far askew or you're going to be off the beam. It takes a lot of discipline just going in there every day even if you don't write. I've spent times when I couldn't write and I would just make myself sit there for five minutes with a blank sheet of paper, and then the next day ten minutes with a blank sheet of paper, and then the next day it would be fifteen minutes and I would draw some zigzags. You have to be willful.

Interviewer: Can you talk more about your preparations before you write the first page?

Henley: It's different for each play. With *Abundance*, I had to do so much research because it takes place in the nineteenth century and it deals with Indians and all sorts of things I was completely ignorant about. With *The Lucky Spot*, I had to do all this research on taxi-dance halls and the Depression; but with *Control Freaks* I just really had to enter my own psyche. With *Control Freaks* I would write pages and pages without even thinking about what I was writing, pages and pages where nothing has to make sense, and then go back and say, "Well, this character may say this" or "This might be said in the kitchen" or "This would be said in the yard" or "This would be seen." I went back and categorized it like that, still without putting any pressure on myself to have answers—like an actual plot or a story or interconnections.

Interviewer: So you don't necessarily know exactly what the message is prior to writing the first page?

Henley: Not even prior to the last page. I don't believe in a message. I think it would be disastrous if you could say what the message of *Hamlet* was. Even with a minor play, everyone is going to come away with something different depending on if they've just left their lovers or if they've just had a child or if they've just been fired. You're going to connect with the work in your own way. If you're too cold or if you're hungry, you'll get a different message. I think that's inevitable and sort of wonderful.

Interviewer: You've lived in California for quite a while now. Has that changed the kinds of plays you write? The early plays were very much about the South. Do you see yourself moving away from the South dramatically at all, or do you still feel that because your roots are there you will always write about the South?

Henley: Well, my last three plays have not taken place in the South, so I feel like I am probably moving away from that a bit as a locale for my work.

Interviewer: Do you miss the South?

Henley: In a personal sense, desperately yes.

Interviewer: How do you think your life in the South affected your writing?

Henley: I'm from Jackson, Mississippi, which is the capital of Mississippi and is in the center of the state, and I think it had a very profound effect. My first play takes place in Hazlehurst, which is where my father's family is from; the second one takes place in Brookhaven, where my mother's family is from; the third one takes place in Canton, where I went to camp; the next one takes place in Hattiesburg, where my aunt and uncle and cousins live. It was a mysterious world, and it was the first world I was familiar with.

Interviewer: You once said that writing helps you not to feel angry. Do you think that's still accurate, that that's one reason you write—so you don't feel angry about something?

Henley: Sometimes when I'm writing about something I get in a rage. The last time I was writing I was screaming at my typewriter and I was getting very angry, but I think it's a good kind of anger because it's focused and alive; it's not in on yourself or destructive to other people.

Interviewer: Why do you write?

Henley: Why do I write? I write because it makes me feel like I'm alive.

Interviewer: How did you get into playwriting?

Henley: I started at a university in a theater program in which I was majoring in acting. That was invaluable because I took a lot of theater history classes where I read plays from all times, and also style classes where you would do Restoration plays and you would have to study art from the period and dances from the period. You would have to memorize lines if you were in a play. If you were in *A Midsummer Night's Dream*, even if you had a tiny part, you would hear that poetry over and over again, the structure of it. If you had one little speech, you'd have to memorize each word of that speech. I think I only took one playwriting class. The only good thing about that is that it gives you this time set aside to write a play. Also you were onstage and you realized that it's easier if I have props, or it's not easier if I have props, or I don't have time to change from this costume to the next—just very practically about getting people on and off. You learned how to think about a character very specifically, like what do I want in this scene and why am I here?

Interviewer: Was the play you wrote in playwriting class *Am I Blue*? If so, where did you get the idea for *Am I Blue*?

Henley: Yes, it was *Am I Blue*. I remember I was taking summer school and staying in a dormitory and I was studying Shakespeare. I remember getting some idea about a play I wanted to write. I really can't tell you exactly what the genesis of the idea was. I just thought something about a girl who was sort of wacky and not invited to her senior prom and a young boy who has been given a pass to a prostitute. I just remember thinking, "I have this idea," and I couldn't stop thinking about it and putting images together. I remember thinking, "I've almost got this written in my head; I should take this course because that would be an easy job. That will be one less thing I'll have to do." I'm sorry, but I can't exactly quite recall. I know I'd been to New Orleans and I was enchanted and mystified by the city.

Interviewer: What terrifies you?

Henley: Doing interviews.

Interviewer: Creatively, what terrifies you?

Henley: It has terrified me a couple of times when I haven't been able to work. I generally say it's part of the process, but it's very debilitating not to be able to write.

Interviewer: Would you rather be heard through the plays than through interviews?

Henley: Definitely, absolutely.

Interviewer: Do you feel that the plays have in them certain things you have repressed in your own dealing with other people? Has being a playwright enabled you to write about certain things that you've repressed in your own life?

Henley: I don't know. I write about things I'm concerned with, that are troubling me; and I suppose some of what you write is unconscious and subliminal. That's sort of where the magic comes from; it's not plotted logically like "This is something I want to explore." But it does come from inside you.

Interviewer: Is it still hard for you to get your plays done, now that you've had a Pulitzer Prize and some commercial success?

Henley: It's pretty hard. I had to go to Poughkeepsie and live in a dorm for my last play. It's difficult if you write a play that's not something that immediately makes sense to people as commercial. I certainly send out many plays that get rejected from theaters as well, but at least they will generally read them.

Interviewer: Your last play to be produced was *Signature*, wasn't it?

Henley: Yes, that was the one done in Poughkeepsie.

Interviewer: It's about the future, isn't it?

Henley: Yes. It takes place in the year 2052 in Los Angeles. It's about Boswell, who is an art philosopher who finds out he is going to die and goes to a graphologist who tells him he can change his life by changing his handwriting. It's really about what is your signature, what do you leave in life, what's important that you've done or haven't done—or is anything important? It's sort of uncommercial; that's why it was done in Poughkeepsie.

Interviewer: Do you think it's easier for women playwrights to be produced now than it was ten or twelve years ago?

Henley: It seems to be, actually. There seem to be more women playwrights, and I have no idea why. I may be completely mistaken.

Interviewer: Do you think that the non-profit theater network—like Poughkeepsie—is a good place to try out your plays? Do they give you a chance to develop them?

Henley: Yes, because a lot of times you can get very good people to come out of town, and that's the most important thing—having an excellent cast and a good director. I think with *Abundance* I probably pushed it to New York too soon before I had gotten to see enough various productions to find exactly what tone I wanted and everything. *The Debutante Ball* has never been produced in New York, and it has had more productions than some plays that have gotten to New York right away and have been slaughtered. Sometimes if you keep something out of New York, it enhances its life.

Interviewer: Can you speak about *Abundance*?

Henley: I spent a lot of time working on *Abundance* because it takes place in the nineteenth century. It's about two mail-order brides who come out West for adventure, and it takes place over a twenty-five-year period. It really is about how insidiously people's dreams are taken away from them. You come out here with all this hope and energy and desire, and suddenly you sell yourself out for a warm cup of coffee without really realizing you've done it. I loved working on that piece because I loved doing research on that period.

Interviewer: It's set in Wyoming?

Henley: It takes place in the Wyoming Territories. Most of my plays have been very classically structured and all take place over a twenty-four-hour period. This is the first one which is much more fragmented. That was really exciting, to see if I could put the essence of ten years into one scene. It was a challenge.

Interviewer: I found the relationship between the two women fascinating, especially how it changed over the twenty-five-year period.

Henley: Yes. It's about how somebody starts out with somebody else looking up to them and how that power can corrupt a relationship. When the second banana suddenly becomes even more powerful, one sees all the resentment that goes with that. Suddenly the person that used to be your lackey is now in a position of power; so it was also about shifts in power and how important it is, if you are going to maintain long-term relationships with people, that you be able to change. People shouldn't shrivel; people should let each other grow and face the consequence that maybe they won't need you if they grow.

Interviewer: Do you think that Broadway is some kind of final testing ground for a play? When you write a play, do you always want it to go to Broadway?

Henley: Yes, I want it to go to Broadway and be made into a major motion picture and win Academy Awards and Tonys and Pulitzer Prizes! That's really what I do want, but usually that doesn't happen.

Interviewer: It did once!

Henley: I love Broadway theaters. It's so great if it plays in a Broadway theater; there's just nothing cooler, except for seeing your play done well.

Interviewer: How do you feel about critics? What kind of job or function do they perform, and have you learned from them when you've read things that they've said?

Henley: I don't want to get started on critics. H. L. Mencken said that asking a playwright what he thinks of critics is like asking a lamppost what he thinks of a dog.

Interviewer: When you're writing, do you have a particular audience in mind?

Henley: I know this may sound pretentious, but I do try and write for myself, because anyone else is too hard. If you're writing to please someone else, it's too hard to be alone that much. I must write about something that really really concerns me, that I'm desperately passionate about or interested in or upset about; but I do always fantasize that it will be well received.

Interviewer: What's your writing process?

Henley: Do you mean when do I write?

Interviewer: Yes.

Henley: This is so boring. I write on spiral notebook paper. I don't have a computer, so then I'll type it up on a typewriter and Xerox it and make changes and turn it over to a typist. I usually write from about eleven in the morning till four or five in the afternoon, unless I write in the evenings. I usually don't know where my piece is going. I never know where it's going, but I do a lot of preparation before I write the first line. It's very important to me to do a whole lot of work on the characters and the situation and the ambiance, the atmosphere.

Interviewer: One of the biggest movements in theater now is toward multicultural and color-blind casting. Have you had to take that into account in writing your more recent work?

Henley: *Signature* takes place in the future, and the stage directions read that this is best done with a multiracial cast because I want to get the feel of a cosmopolitan future. The only stipulation is that the two brothers should be of the same race, but their race isn't important; they could be Asian or African-American. I feel that way with *Control Freaks* as well, but I haven't consciously decided to do that. It depends on the type of play you're writing. If you're doing something like *Waiting for Godot*, where we don't know where those people are coming from or where they are going, it's all right; but if you're writing about a specific time or place, as in *Crimes of the Heart*, then obviously race is important because there is a segregated bigoted thing going on. I just think it depends on how specific you're being about the character's background as to whether that's an issue.

Interviewer: When you're writing a character, how much of their history do you know? Do you feel that you really know where they come from and their surroundings and how they were educated?

Henley: Very much, because I write each character as though I were playing them, as if I had to perform them, and I really want to know. Every character has a secret, every character has a reaction to the other characters, every character has a greatest fear, and every character has a greatest dream; and I want to know what their sense of humor is and what their sexuality is and how they dress and how they talk. It's great because you can play all these parts you'd never be cast in.

Interviewer: Do you merge with your characters when you're writing them?

Henley: Yes. You have to look at things from their point of view. They do not judge themselves in the same way the people reading the play may or may not judge them. They have objectives that are so strong, like these people that murder people. It's so scary to write about evil people. *Control Freaks* is the first play I've written about evil people. I really wanted to understand the banality of evil, and you have to find it in yourself, I think, to portray it.

Interviewer: Isn't it hard to merge with that kind of mind-set when you're writing it?

Henley: Yes, it's challenging and it's hard, but I like things that are hard.

Interviewer: What do you think will keep the American theater active and healthy?

Henley: I don't know. I feel so bad because this theater I love in Los Angeles just closed. It was the Los Angeles Theatre Center and it closed last week. A friend of mine was in a play running down there at the time, and they had the most brilliant production by Rosa Abdul, who's really a theater genius. It just broke my heart to see this theater close, and I feel so helpless.

Interviewer: Is it finances?

Henley: Yes, finances. That's something that's so troublesome to me, but I don't worry about it because I figure the most I can do is to keep working. I don't know how to fix that problem, that the arts are just dying.

Interviewer: There are easier and more lucrative ways that you can make a living, even as a writer. Why do you write plays rather than novels or movies or TV scripts?

Henley: I've also written screenplays. I don't believe I can write novels; they seem so big. If you write a play, then there are at least some times when you're not alone. The reason I love the theater, as I said earlier, is because it always felt like such a sanctuary to me from the real world. It was such a magical world where everyone was passionate about something; they felt so alive when they were there, and they really cared that their water be set exactly here and not here. It made you not think about dying.

As a playwright, you maintain your copyright; you have so much more control than you have in the movies. Screenwriters sell their copyrights. They can fire you, they can have somebody rewrite you; it's really a director's medium. It's not your vision, whereas I think a play is so much more the author's vision. It's more of an actor's medium as well, because they can't cut things that you did. I love to go to the theater so much more than movies because generally you see much more of a personal vision in plays because you only need a hundred people out there. In movies, you have to open wide, you have to sell the video; so a bunch of people at a table sit down to figure out what will sell the most. Theater is just more interesting to me.

Interviewer: You have just finished doing a screenplay of *The Lucky Spot*, but you were asked to do that, weren't you?

Henley: Yes, and I certainly didn't turn it down. My last play was not a big financial boon. *The Lucky Spot* was slammed in New York, and it kind of disappeared and then was done in this tiny little theater in London. A director [Lewis Gilbert] came to see it, really loved it, and he wants to make it into a movie; so I've just finished the screenplay. Who knows if it'll get made into a movie, but they pay you ridiculous amounts of money. I was literally sitting there with scissors and tape—here's some good lines; paste them in there. It's so easy, and now that will give me some money to go work on another play. I'm going to take *Signature* to Chicago in March, and I won't have to worry about how to pay the rent for my expensive hobby.

Interviewer: Besides doing screenplays, are there other things that you write?

Henley: No. I've done a couple of screenplay adaptations. I did a Reynolds Price book called *A Long and Happy Life* and a John Kennedy Toole book called *A Confederacy of Dunces*. I think doing that has helped me a little better with prose. You see how beautifully they can stretch it, and you study it so you can understand their mind-set and their tone and the way they do dialogue. I feel like they taught me that and paid me, but they never made the movies.

Interviewer: Do you think Hollywood respects playwrights?

Henley: No. Hollywood has an unmitigated disregard for writers in general, but that's why I live in Hollywood. The good thing about being in the theater world in Los Angeles is that there really is none, so you don't feel disturbed that you're not a success and that you're not "with it." You just go and do your work. It's been really good for me to be able to go to New York and have a play that's a hit or a play that's a flop and just go back and say, "Okay, that's done, that's good; now I'll go start again." That's what really ends up making you find life bearable anyway.

Interviewer: Do you think that your plays have suffered in their transfer from the stage to the big screen?

Henley: No, I think I've been extremely lucky. I don't feel like there has been a definitive version of any of my plays that I've seen. I think I've seen what I feel to be definitive performances by actors, but it's never all come together in this one wholly perfect experience. I think that's okay because it's still alive, and maybe it'll be perfect somewhere somehow years from now or maybe not, but that's why I don't expect the film to be perfect either. In the movie versions of *Crimes of the Heart* and *Miss Firecracker* there are really great lines and really creative moments. It's exciting for me to see how those two directors saw the works, and I felt like they were both sincere to the spirits of the pieces on different levels.

Interviewer: You were satisfied with the film version of *Crimes of the Heart*?

Henley: Yes, I was happy with it. I can't watch it because it hurts me to watch my own things, but I really was when I saw it. I was very moved and very pleased; I have it on video, and someday I'm going to watch it again.

Interviewer: How do you go about structuring your work when it's intended for the stage as opposed to for the screen?

Henley: A screenplay, I think, is much easier to write, because you can virtually have as many characters as you like and go so many places compared to the stage. In *Control Freaks*, she's standing on the balcony and she's talking to her dress; then she drops her dress down, it floats downstage, and he picks it up and starts dancing with it. Somehow that's very theatrical, but it's not something you would do in a movie. People actually get to see the dress fall, and they know it might hit the ground, and there's something about that that's alive and fun. Sam Shepard is great at that. He'll have toasters all over the stage, and then the toast starts coming up. Then you smell the toast and see the toast and it's a surprise. The audience is delirious. If you did that in a film, it just wouldn't be the same.

Interviewer: Cutting a lemon onstage you would smell the lemon.

Henley: You'd smell the lemon, you'd see the juice come out, you'd see the knife, you'd see him wipe off the knife, you'd see that there was a knife between them that was real. It's interesting.

Interviewer: Is there one play you've written that you think you've learned the most from?

Henley: *Control Freaks*.

Interviewer: That's your most recent one.

Henley: I'd probably say that about any of my most recent ones, but I do feel that now at least.

Interviewer: What kinds of things did you learn?

Henley: It's very succinct; it's about an hour and a half, and it's all in one shot. It starts and doesn't stop. It starts very controlled, and it unravels until everything is just insanity. It was very challenging because you had to be extremely succinct and everything had to build exactly structurally right. I was so afraid of the chaos coming because how can I write chaos? I really had to let go; it was extremely exciting and scary. Also, writing about these evil people was challenging because they weren't people I loved. In all my other plays, even though people behave very badly, I love them. I didn't love these people, but they were real; so that was interesting.

Interviewer: Do you have any favorites among your characters that are special to you?

Henley: Boswell in *Signature* and Popeye in *Miss Firecracker.*

Interviewer: I always wondered why Popeye was given the gift in the first scene.

Henley: Those earrings?

Interviewer: Yes.

Henley: I don't know if it's just in the South—this happened to me in Hawaii as well—but people give you things because they have such a desperate need to be liked. Later in the play, the character reveals that she hated those earrings; they pinched her ears, and she was glad to get rid of them. Something that appears to be a generous act—I'm trying to make myself look good by giving you something that I really don't like—the duplicity of that act, I think, reveals something later about Elaine. It's also the magic that a gift like that would hold for a character like Popeye. How extraordinary that would be, to have something hanging off your ears! For somebody who's never had something hanging off their ears and who hears voices through their eyes, it seems completely unbelievable.

Interviewer: Is there anything you would like to do besides write plays and screenplays?

Henley: Ski.

Interviewer: What appeals to you about skiing?

Henley: You asked what I wanted to do and I said I wanted to ski; I've never skied in my life.

Interviewer: What do you expect?

Henley: I just love the existential idea of nothing but white and going down at breakneck speed. I think you would feel so alive. I think it would make me laugh and laugh if I did that.

Interviewer: Is there anything in theater that you'd like to do? Do you want to direct?

Henley: I'd like to direct. To direct you have to have a sense of self, and I so often want to hide what I'm thinking that to be able to talk to people and tell them what you want would be a challenge. I always want to make people feel good; I always tell actors, "You did great," and then I go to the director and say, "Would you fire them!" I always think it would be a challenge to learn to interact more forthrightly with people, so I'm thinking of maybe directing *Control Freaks*.

Interviewer: Is *Control Freaks* the one you wrote the part for Holly Hunter in?

Henley: Yes.

Interviewer: Can you tell us a little bit about that part and why it was for her?

Henley: Holly Hunter was in *Crimes of the Heart* on Broadway; she was in *The Wake* on Broadway; she was in *Miss Firecracker* Off-Broadway; and she did the first production of *The Lucky Spot* at Williamstown. She's just an actress that I feel an extreme affinity for. I'm working at this small Equity theater in Los Angeles that Holly is a part of; so I thought, "I want to write a play for her." I don't generally do that—write a play with an actress in mind—but I wrote this part for her. This part is basically a woman who is not integrated, so instead of playing one part she is sort of several people. Basically she's two people: one person that's violently enraged all the time, and the other person that's real sweet. Holly has this real range; I know Holly has the technical facility and the emotional guts.

Interviewer: Have you always been interested in those split images, the two sides that you were just talking about?

Henley: Have I always been interested in that? It's hard to think of what you've always been, but I know I've always had a fascination with darker images because they frighten me so much. I think I'm always confronting myself with them. I remember I made this glass hand with a knife, and I would drip red candle wax over it all the time; I don't know what that comes from. I think it's sort of the complexities of life that I find most real. If you get things that are just Disneyland, it doesn't seem real to me. The six o'clock news is real, and that's got a lot more grotesque things in it than my plays.

Interviewer: Your favorite holiday is Halloween, isn't it?

Henley: I love Halloween. The autumn is my favorite season, and Halloween is my favorite holiday.

Interviewer: Are you going to dress up for Halloween?

Henley: I think so.

Interviewer: How do you put the humor in your plays?

Henley: I don't know. It's not deliberate exactly.

Interviewer: Do you think they're funny?

Henley: When I saw *Crimes of the Heart*, I was really amazed at how funny it was to people. I just think it's the way your mind works. Coming from the South, people didn't have much patience with you embracing your own pain, groveling in it. It was always, "So big deal, the house is burned. There goes Atlanta, sorry." I think it's a part of the country that has been destroyed and has had to have this sort of grit. They face it much more front-on. People are just almost ostentatious about their pain.

Interviewer: In so much of your work you have the dark side and the comic side together like two halves of a split image. You've said that you first saw that in Chekhov. Is that so?

Henley: Yes. A moment in theater that changed my life happened when I was in New York—I must have been nineteen or so. *Three Sisters* was going to be produced at the university I was going to, and I said, "*Three Sisters*, great! Parts for women; I'll read this." I kept reading it, and I didn't get it. What is this? Who are these people? Then I went to see an all-Black production of *The Cherry Orchard* starring James Earl Jones and Gloria Foster, and I started to get it. It was like a satori when James Earl Jones as Lopakhin came back in after buying the cherry orchard and said, "I bought it." It was the greatest day of his life because he was no longer a serf, but also it was the worst day in his life because he had betrayed his dearest friend. All through that speech he was zing, zing, zing, back and forth between despair and joy, madness and sanity, and regret and not caring. I was screaming in the theater; I thought I was going to be evicted. I started crying and laughing and I couldn't stop. Then, after he leaves, Gloria Foster falls out of her chair and has to be carried off. It was just absolutely a revelation about how alive life can be and how complicated—and beautiful and horrible; to deny either of those is such a loss.

Interviewer: Do you think that *The Debutante Ball* is your most daring play?

Henley: No, *Control Freaks* is.

Interviewer: I haven't had a chance to see that one yet; but in *The Debutante Ball* there are some really daring moves that you make. Tell us a little bit about the play's production history and about why it's daring.

Henley: It's very Jacobean. It has everything thrown in it. There's a beautiful ballroom with a balcony but also a bathroom onstage. The essence of it all is these people trying to look beautiful for this ball, but they're like animals and they're going in and having to pluck out hairs and shave their legs. Their facades cracking is really what it's about. The debutante slices her face with a razor; then, later, her mother beats her up and she has a miscarriage onstage in her debutante gown. There is the deaf cousin who has a lesbian affair with the sister. The last scene is just the mother getting into the bathtub with psoriasis on her skin and the daughter bathing her. These people have so many scars and are trying to be so beautiful and have so many secrets. It's about secrets as well.

Interviewer: Would you say that's the focus of The *Debutante Ball*?

Henley: Secrets? One of them, I think.

Interviewer: Any others that come to mind?

Henley: Secrets and lies.

Interviewer: Can we talk about *Crimes of the Heart* a little bit?

Henley: Sure.

Interviewer: What are the crimes?

Henley: I guess Babe's crime is shooting her husband because he hurt someone who was innocent. I guess her mother's crime was killing herself and leaving her children because she could no longer bear the pain of being left by her husband. Meg's crime was being so afraid of Doc she left him with his broken leg saying she would marry him and went off to Hollywood. Lenny's crime is more of a crime to herself in that she won't tell the truth to the man she is in love with because she is afraid if he knows the truth he won't love her so she just chucks the whole thing. I guess a lot of it is them coming to terms with their crimes and trying to unshackle themselves from the past.

Interviewer: Do you think there is a way in which each of the sisters experiences a freeing from the expectations of the society that they were in, and of their family, during the play?

Henley: Yes, I think so. Lenny calls up her boyfriend and she tells him the truth, that she can't have children, which is her secret. She was afraid he would leave her; in fact, it turns out that he hates kids! Meg, I think, feels reconciled with Doc, even if they're not together; and Babe gets so desperate that she tries to commit suicide. But one of the things that plagued her was why their mother killed herself and hanged the cat; then she realized she hanged the cat with her so she wouldn't be alone; and Babe realizes she is not alone. All three of the sisters have really kept their most precious pains a secret from the other sisters; they've been ashamed or afraid to share them; and by the end of the play, I think, they—like it or not—have had to share these secrets. Babe never told anybody her husband beat her, Meg never told how bad she felt not being a success and how bad she felt about leaving Doc, and Lenny hasn't revealed to them her great wish not to be alone. She has made it seem like it was okay that she took care of Old Granddaddy.

Interviewer: You've talked elsewhere about when you were going to write the ending of *Crimes of the Heart* and you thought Babe was going to die.

Henley: I had gotten to Act III, and I just had images. I knew there was going to be a birthday cake, and I knew there was going to be a rope or a suicide. Then I discovered it was Babe and I said, "Oh no, Babe's going to die? Oh well, you have to keep writing! This is really going to be a tragedy. I thought this was kind of being comedic, but no, it's a big tragedy, and they're going to have to have the birthday cake without her!" You just have to trust. I wanted this scene between Lenny and Babe. I really saw it vividly—Lenny in the ecstasy of joy and Babe in the ecstasy of despair and then colliding with each other in the scene right before Lenny calls up Charlie and right before Babe goes to hang herself. I knew somehow that that was exactly right, but then I said, "Oops, now Babe is going to hang herself?" Luckily, I heard a thud from upstairs: it didn't work!

Interviewer: How did you decide to have Babe hit her head on the oven?

Henley: That was developed in performance because I realized a fallacy in the logic. Once Babe realizes that her mother killed herself because she was afraid of being alone, that would give her a reason to live because she understood something that she had been so afraid of. But then I couldn't have her get her head out of the oven because that wasn't as dramatic as Meg coming in and finding her with her head in the oven. So I had to have her say, "Oh, I see!" like she had the idea and she would have gotten out but she got knocked out. Patricia Wettig, who was in *thirtysomething* dying of cancer last year, played Babe in that production, and she was so diligent, because we were going over the logic of it and she said, "Yes, but now I have to get out of the oven!" I'm saying, "No you don't. You've got to stay in the oven." I said, "Okay, so you hit your head." It's great to have really good actors because they challenge you and they're thinking things so specifically that it makes it good for you.

Interviewer: Do you give very specific stage directions to the actors in your plays, and has that changed from your earlier work to your later work?

Henley: I don't think I overdo stage directions too much. I have had productions in which the actors played it so dead wrong that then I tried to write heavy stage directions, but that really doesn't work, I've realized. I just try to have the stage directions give an essence of the whole feel. If this is funny, I try to make them a bit humorous; if this is dead serious, I try to tell the tone through stage directions.

Interviewer: There seem to be some links between *Crimes of the Heart* and *The Wake of Jamey Foster.* Could you talk about those a little bit?

Henley: There is a balance of characters that is similar, and they are getting back there for a tragic event. Katty in *The Wake of Jamey Foster* is somehow another version of Chick in *Crimes of the Heart*. I felt like Chick was very one-dimensional, and I wanted to try and get more into a woman who was so controlling, so needing to be liked, and so needing to be perfect. Who was she really? That's what I tried to explore with Katty.

Interviewer: Most of your plays focus on women and their relationships with each other and with society. Would you say that your plays are feminist or women-centered?

Henley: Do I have to pick one or the other?

Interviewer: No, you can pick something else entirely!

Henley: I just think they are about people. I don't necessarily think I'm going to write a women's play or a feminist play. I just think of a story I would like to tell, and whoever ends up being in the story, I'm grateful.

Interviewer: But you have said you are a feminist, haven't you?

Henley: Of course. People say, "Are you a feminist?" like I'm saying I'm a liberal or something; so I looked it up in a dictionary and it says that you believe women should have equal rights with men. No, I believe they should have less rights than men? Absolutely I'm a feminist, absolutely vehemently so.

Interviewer: Do you think there is a way that, because you're a woman playwright, you're sometimes asked to speak for all women?

Henley: Yes.

Interviewer: How does that make you feel?

Henley: I feel inept. I feel incapable. I sometimes feel I can hardly speak for myself. I think people have such a fear of not having things categorized, and a way to grab hold of things that they want is to say this is a woman writer, this is a southern writer, this is a Black writer, this is a Black woman southern writer. The more categories they can get you into, the more secure they feel so they won't have to feel what you wrote. I just feel sorry for them.

Interviewer: Some women playwrights have talked about how they feel that women's lives are changed through conversation and dialogue. Have you thought much about that? It seems that in *Crimes of the Heart* the sisters' lives are changed through their conversations with each other.

Henley: I don't know why it would be limited to women. I certainly think I've had some conversations with men that have spiritually enlightened my life, and I *know* I have enlightened theirs!

Interviewer: How would you characterize the bonds between the women in your plays? Have you drawn on the fact that you have three sisters in those relationships?

Henley: I think in *Crimes of the Heart* very much; growing up around women, I mean. Just having a family, I think, is different from not having a family. It is so strange how you can feel that the connection with these people is so primal and basic, although sometimes you would not be with them if they weren't your family. You are inextricably bound to them, concerned for them, and enraged by them or enraptured by them. Families are a peculiar sort of situation.

Interviewer: Could you tell us a little about your early days with the Actors Theatre of Louisville?

Henley: That was my very first professional production, which was exciting for me in an almost unbearable way because I was so frightened. It was January and it was cold, and I remember standing in the parking lot watching people park their cars and walk into the theater to see my play at a first preview and just crying because I couldn't believe they had gone out in the cold and gotten babysitters and were going to drive there and see my play. I just remember I've never felt like such a charlatan. I couldn't believe they were coming to see it, and it had been very rocky; the director had been fired and replaced by the producer of the theater, who was also directing three other plays at the time, so we had to start rehearsal at 8 a.m. I was quite prepared for it to be a horrible debacle, but actually I was blessed by really having two of the greatest actresses I've ever ever worked with, Susan Kingsley and Kathy Bates, and they worked miracles, so I was very lucky.

Interviewer: Are any of your characters autobiographical?

Henley: Autobiographical? That implies that they are about me?

Interviewer: Yes.

Henley: I would say all of them, absolutely all of them.

Interviewer: Have any of your plays been performed in other countries, or have they been translated into other languages?

Henley: Yes, *Crimes of the Heart* being the most done, but even *The Debutante Ball* has been done in London and Germany quite a bit. My most exciting trip was when I went to see *Crimes of the Heart* done in China. That was just spectacular. It didn't go over; but it was the year before Tiananmen Square, and everyone was so alive. There was just this wildness about it.

Interviewer: When you go to write a play, do you think stylistically? Do you try to put it in a category—that it's comedy or satire or a particular kind of play—or do you think more eclectically about the play?

Henley: I think more specifically, in that it's almost like a smell I get or a feeling I get about a play, rather than in a generalized category. It's just much more intricate than that. Getting the tone of *Control Freaks* was quite difficult.

Interviewer: What writers, dramatic and nondramatic, are you influenced by?

Henley: I love T. S. Eliot, but I wouldn't defame him by claiming to be influenced by him. I quite love reading Flannery O'Connor; I think it's been a revelation to me. Willa Cather, William Styron, Dostoyevsky (not to be pretentious, but I do love those Russians). Gorky was in my childhood. I like to read. I'm reading now this wonderful man named Denis Johnson that I just found out about, and Richard Ford is a big favorite of mine from Mississippi as well. I have to say I was particularly influenced by Reynolds Price and John Kennedy Toole from getting to work so closely trying to adapt their books into screenplays. I feel a special kinship to them.

Interviewer: What dramatic writers do you like?

Henley: Chekhov and Shakespeare and O'Neill, Tennessee Williams and Beckett and David Mamet. Ibsen has become a new favorite of mine. I just saw this amazing production of *Hedda Gabler* in London and this amazing production of *Wild Duck*, and I was just enthralled by how absolutely stunning he is.

Interviewer: Do you have any favorite women dramatists?

Henley: Weren't there any women on that list? I guess Lillian Hellman would be my favorite, and Carson McCullers. *The Member of the Wedding* is a beautiful play, but it's a beautiful book as well. I love *A Taste of Honey*; that's a beautiful play. So I suppose there are some.

Interviewer: Is there a drama critic whose opinion you respect?

Henley: Well, I guess it would have to be someone like an Edmund Wilson or George Bernard Shaw.

Beth Henley Takes the Director's Chair for *Control Freaks*

Hedy Weiss / 1992

From the *Chicago Sun-Times*, September 20, 1992, *Arts & Show*, pp. 1, 4. © 1992 Sun-Times Media. All rights reserved. Used under license. Hedy Weiss was the theater critic at the *Chicago Sun-Times* from 1985 to 2018.

When Pulitzer Prize-winning playwright Beth Henley began thinking about her new play, *Control Freaks*, the dominant image she had in mind was one of flying.

"All the people I write about have desperate needs," said Henley, explaining the relevance of the flight metaphor. "And I believe that a play is only really watchable if it has characters who have something powerful to hope for."

Control Freaks, which receives its world premiere at Center Theater on Sunday, also marks the playwright's directorial debut.

To some observers, it might seem surprising that Center Theater, a seventy-five-seat space in the Rogers Park neighborhood, would be able to snag Henley for such double duty.

But the small Equity company has had remarkable success with two of her earlier plays—*The Lucky Spot*, a story about an eccentric love triangle that was staged there in 1990, and *Abundance*, the luminous, tragicomic tale of two mail-order brides in the Wild West. Center gave *Abundance* a remarkable production last season, with masterful performances by Robin Witt and Kathy Scambiatterra.

Control Freaks is the story of a Los Angeles family—a brother, sister, and sister-in-law—who try to open a business called Furniture World. As in many family business situations, the blood-linked entrepreneurial push can end with a rude shove and an unquenchable desire to murder one another.

Those familiar with Henley's work, including *Crimes of the Heart* and *The Miss Firecracker Contest*, will quickly sense that such a cataclysmic clash of personalities is bound to bring out the wildest and wackiest aspects of the secret souls of each of her play's four characters. And Henley is most intrigued by the unpredictable souls of her characters.

"The crux of this play has to do with secrets," Henley said. "It's about the things you hide from yourself and from other people. And it's about the realization of how dangerous these secrets can be, and how powerful. Mostly, it's about a character coming into a consciousness about herself."

Henley has been friends with Center Theater directors Dan La Morte and Dale Calandra since they all went to graduate school together at the University of Illinois at Champaign-Urbana in the mid-seventies. Earlier this year, La Morte, Center's artistic director, made the playwright an offer she couldn't refuse.

"He allowed me to do a ten-day workshop of the play last January that came with no strings attached," Henley said. "There was no pressure in the form of a final reading or studio performance. I could have just worked on a single sentence if I wanted. I also had a great group of actors." (The cast now includes Robin Witt, Marc Vann, Marlene DuBois, and Clark Champ.)

Dressed like a fashionable flower child in pindot shift, jeans jacket, and western boots, the shy, soft-spoken forty-year-old writer, whose Mississippi roots are betrayed by the gentlest of southern accents, seems nothing like the zany, outspoken characters of her plays. But the writer's imagination is a wonderful thing, and looks can be deceiving: Her characters often fly off the handle with a tragicomic logic that all but defies gravity.

During the workshop, Henley ended up tracking her characters through the action. "*Control Freaks* is very poetic and was written emotionally rather than logically," she said. "It's part fairy tale, part ultra-real, and part fake-real. It's not naturalistic or literal at all. So I just needed time for my rational mind to take in everything my subliminal mind had done."

In writing the play, Henley said, she used clichés in an almost poetic way. "The characters are so controlled that they *depend* on clichés because any language that was more individualistic would be too dangerous. There is a deep human need in these characters—a lack of centeredness—and that's what creates their need to be control freaks."

Henley wrote this play very quickly—three months of thinking about it, followed by another three months of writing. "And then, of course, a year of *rewriting*," she said, laughing. "But the speed of writing was a quest for a sense of unity in the action as things move from control to chaos. Everything happens in ninety minutes with no blackouts."

Reared in Jackson, Mississippi ("during a very ugly time in the South"), Henley is the daughter of an attorney father and a mother who acted in community theater.

"My mother used to take me to watch rehearsals, and from the very beginning, I thought of the theater as a kind of sanctuary. In fact, one of the places she performed in was a tiny little converted church. But I always thought it was *better* than church because people laughed and clapped and cried there."

Henley was a theater major at Southern Methodist University, where she focused on acting. But she also took a playwriting class, and out of that came her first work, *Am I Blue*, which was produced in Texas.

The study of acting has helped her tremendously as a playwright. "It helped me know what actors need onstage, which very often is more action rather than dialogue."

As for the seemingly genetic disposition for writing associated with growing up in the South, Henley said she was wary of making such generalizations, but admitted, "We probably tend to be more eloquent.

"But I think more than that, we have a profound understanding of irony that I don't see elsewhere," she said. "I know that in the house I was raised in, nothing was ever seen as completely tragic or completely comic. At any funeral, you could turn the pancake over and see the humor in it all.

"Maybe this sense of irony developed because we were beaten in the Civil War. There's something dreadfully unsentimental and enduring that grew out of that fact."

Certainly that quality of bemused unsentimentality surfaces in Henley herself, when she's asked if winning the Pulitzer Prize for her first major play—at the tender age of twenty-nine—had opened doors, destroyed her life, or altered her future irrevocably.

"A, B, and C," Henley answered, with a rueful smile. The one thing the Pulitzer did *not* do was cramp her creativity. She went on to write the Academy Award-nominated screenplay for her own *Crimes of the Heart* (1986), Bruce Beresford's film version that featured the all-star cast of Diane Keaton, Sissy Spacek, and Jessica Lange. She did the same for *Miss Firecracker* (1989), which starred Holly Hunter. And she recently completed a screenplay based on *The Lucky Spot*.

A longtime California resident, Henley transformed her newfound infatuation with the West into *Abundance*. The play explored "the feeling of being a pioneer and sensing the limitlessness of life, as opposed to the inevitable way our dreams tend to become shrunken as we sell them out for a pittance, in an almost insidious way, year after year."

Shortly before *Control Freaks*, Henley wrote another play, *Signature*, which will be given a reading at Lincoln Center in October. Set in Los Angeles in the twenty-first century, it's the tale of two brothers—one who believes he can change his imminent death by altering his handwriting, and the other who becomes a guru of love and the most poetic figure of the century.

While admitting she would love to direct again, Henley said that staging her own work has nothing to do with being an artistic control freak.

"Actually, it involves letting go a lot," Henley said. "I have no secrets from the cast, and there's been a huge amount of group participation. And while I may have started off knowing more about the characters than the actors did, at this point, they know more than I do. My job is just to keep an overview of the rhythm of the play.

"Unlike movies, the great thing about theater is that it's so alive and changeable. Every production incorporates the qualities of a whole new set of actors, so the play never becomes stagnant. I love writing screenplays and thinking cinematically, where the pictures are the poetry, rather than the words. And it's easier than writing a play.

"But I'm hooked on the sheer challenge of theater. And when I get back home, I'm going to start work on a new play. It's about people who have dreams, and those who don't."

Henley said she definitely falls into the dreamer's corner.

Beth Henley

Mary Dellasega / 1993

From *Speaking on Stage: Interviews with Contemporary American Playwrights*, edited
by Philip C. Kolin and Colby H. Kullman (Tuscaloosa: University of Alabama Press, 1996),
250–59. Reprinted by permission of Mary Dellasega. Mary Dellasega was the director
of theater at Augustana College in Rock Island, Illinois, and at Capital University in
Columbus, Ohio.

Beth Henley is a native of Jackson, Mississippi; born on May 8, 1952, she
is the daughter of a lawyer and an actress and is the second oldest of four
sisters. She attended Southern Methodist University, where she graduated
with a bachelor of fine arts degree in theater in 1974; for one year she worked
toward a master's degree in acting at the University of Illinois. When she
moved to Los Angeles, she intended to be an actress, not a playwright.

Henley's previous efforts had been one-act plays written as class assign-
ments. One of these, *Am I Blue*, was produced at SMU, but the playwright
was too shy to allow her name to be used on the program. In Los Angeles,
frustrated with the lack of acting opportunities, she began writing her first
full-length play, *Crimes of the Heart*. The play was written for one indoor
set and six characters to make it more attractive to little theaters. When a
friend in Louisville submitted the play to the Actors Theatre's third annual
Festival of New American Plays, it was an immediate success. *Crimes* was
produced at three other regional theaters before the Manhattan Theatre
Club staged it in New York. Before moving to Broadway the play had won
both the New York Drama Critics' Circle Award and the 1981 Pulitzer Prize,
making Henley the first woman to receive the award in twenty-three years.

Crimes demonstrated a sense of comedy also seen in her subsequent
plays: it is based not on one-liners, but on empathetic understanding of her
characters' desperation. Frank Rich has observed that she "gets her laughs
not because she tells sick jokes, but because she refuses to tell jokes at all.
Her characters always stick to the unvarnished truth, at any price, never

holding back a single gory detail. And the truth—when captured like light-ning in a bottle—is far funnier than any invented wisecracks" (*New York Times*, November 5, 1981). Henley herself has noted in an interview, "I've always been attracted to split images. . . . the grotesque combined with the innocent, a child walking with a cane; a kitten with a swollen head; a hunch-back drinking a cup of fruit punch. Somehow these images are a metaphor for my view of life; they're colorful. . . . Southerners always bring out the grisly details in any event" (*Washington Post*, December 12, 1986).

Henley has often been compared with other southern writers, such as Flannery O'Connor and Eudora Welty, largely because of her penchant for writing about eccentric, colorful characters in southern settings. Most of her plays have been set in the South: *Crimes of the Heart* (1979), the story of the Magrath sisters, takes place in Hazlehurst, Mississippi; *The Wake of Jamey Foster* (1982) centers on a family reunion in Canton, Mississippi, for the purpose of burying the title character, who has been kicked in the head by a cow; Carnelle Scott, who dreams of changing her image by winning *The Miss Firecracker Contest* (1984), lives in Brookhaven, Mississippi; the char-acters who dream of striking it rich with a dance hall called *The Lucky Spot* reside in Pigeon, Louisiana; and *The Debutante Ball*, which Henley calls, in the preface to a 1991 printed edition, "one of my stranger plays," in which the characters are "fighting to pluck and spray and shave away their true natures—adorning themselves with lies," is set in Hattiesburg, Mississippi.

Beth Henley has adapted two of her plays into screenplays. The film *Crimes of the Heart*, starring Jessica Lange, Diane Keaton, and Sissy Spacek, received an Academy Award nomination for best screenplay in 1986. Holly Hunter reprised her role as Carnelle Scott in the film version of *Miss Firecracker*, one of several projects on which she and Beth Henley have collaborated (Hunter has appeared in *The Debutante Ball*, *The Wake of Jamey Foster*, and *Control Freaks*). Henley also cowrote the screenplay for *True Stories* with musician David Byrne and actor-director Stephen Tobolowsky, with whom Henley lived for several years. (Tobolowsky, who was in the cast of *Wake*, directed *The Debutante Ball*, *The Miss Firecracker Contest*, and *The Lucky Spot*.)

In spite of their southernness Henley's plays have also been well received abroad, particularly in Britain, which has seen multiple productions of *Crimes of the Heart* and *The Miss Firecracker Contest*, as well as *The Lucky Spot* and *The Debutante Ball*. However, her latest plays move away from her familiar southern territory: *Abundance* (1989) is set in the late 1860s in Wyoming Territory; *Control Freaks*, which opened in August of 1993 as her directorial debut, is set in Los Angeles, Henley's adopted home.

This interview took place December 15, 1993, when Henley was working on her new play, *Revelers*.

Mary Dellasega: I know your mother, Lydy Caldwell, is an actress. Did she inspire you or influence you to work in the theater? I believe you both acted at the New Stage Theatre in Jackson.

Beth Henley: Yes. We worked at Jackson Little Theatre, and then later they had the New Stage Theatre, and she worked at both. So I really grew up around the theater, and it absolutely did inspire me. My mother was often on the play selection committee and she had Samuel French versions of plays around, so I got into the habit of picking them up. I really enjoyed reading dialogue. I also loved going to see her act in plays and going backstage.

Dellasega: Is there anything in particular you remember that she did?

Henley: *The Glass Menagerie.* She played Laura, and she was so beautiful with all those little glass animals. She used to limp around when she went to the grocery store, trying to pick up cans that Laura would pick up. I coached her on her lines a lot. I know practically all the lines to *A Streetcar Named Desire* because she played Blanche.

Dellasega: And your mother still acts, I believe.

Henley: Yes, she was just in a play this last year, *Lend Me a Tenor.*

Dellasega: You originally moved from Mississippi to Los Angeles for an acting career. What changed your goal to playwriting and screenwriting?

Henley: I think, the fact that I could. [*Laughs*] You just have a pencil and paper and you can write, but you have to get an agent and get cast in something to act. I loved acting in college because I was always doing wonderful plays. But in the real world there are so few opportunities to do great pieces, and I found that very discouraging. Plus kind of horrifying, when I had to have pictures made of myself and send them out to strangers. I hated that.

Dellasega: I know people have told you that *Crimes of the Heart* reminded them of their relationships with their sisters. Did you see yourself or your sisters in the characters?

Henley: I think the relationships and the way sisters interact are definitely based on my family: people remembering little things for years on end, you know, and bringing them up at just the right moment to drive you crazy. [*Laughs*] I didn't think about it at the time, but I do also think they are all kind of different split visions of myself, the characters—different things I myself was grappling with.

Dellasega: I've heard that *Crimes* was submitted to the Actors Theatre without your knowing about it.

Henley: Well, that's sort of the glamorized version. My friend Fred Bailey, who had won the contest the year before, sent the script in and told me about it, so I knew it had gone there. When Jon Jory called me, he thought I didn't know about it, but that's just because I'm so shy. I was so nervous when I talked to him, I could hardly speak.

Dellasega: How did it feel to have the play performed in Louisville by professional actors?

Henley: It was so frightening. I had had a play done in college, *Am I Blue*, in 1973, but this was the first time people were paying to see it. It was January and it was freezing and it was snowing. I remember standing in the parking lot, and these people in fur coats were getting out of their cars. And I thought, "Oh, my God, they paid money, they hired babysitters, and they came out to see this," and I started crying. I was terrified that I was going to be arrested for fraud. [*Laughs*] It was really scary.

Dellasega: And you were pleased with the production?

Henley: Yes. Actually, it had two of the greatest actresses that have ever been around, Susan Kingsley and Kathy Bates, so I was very lucky.

Dellasega: I wanted to ask what inspired some of the changes made in translating *Crimes* and *Miss Firecracker* to the screen, for instance, the very interesting change in the character of Popeye, the seamstress who makes Carnelle's dress in *Miss Firecracker*.

Henley: You mean to make her Black? Well, that was actually Tommy Schlamme's, the director's, idea, because we were looking for locations, and he said, "Gosh, there's such a discrepancy between where the Black populations live in these towns; it literally is the other side of the tracks." And also what inspired me was his mention of Alfre Woodard, who is one of my favorite actresses. I wasn't as interested in changing it to a Black actress as changing it to Alfre Woodard; I like her work so much. And also to bring in that world, which is so present—the Black world, which is still fairly segregated from the white world—and to incorporate that world. However, this is something we did more in the original screenplay we talked about than in the eventual screenplay we did. There was a blues scene that we never got around to, for instance, because the budget couldn't incorporate it.

Dellasega: I was thinking, too, about the confrontation between the two women toward the end of the film, when Carnelle discovers Elain *did* bring the red dress but didn't give it to her to wear in the contest.

Henley: Yes, that's new. Actually that was inspired very much by Tommy, who thought they should have a confrontation, which they actually don't have in the play. But it was a tangible thing that could be discovered, that could symbolize their whole relationship, which was, I thought, very smart of him.

Dellasega: It was a very effective scene. And after that we see Carnelle alone, watching the fireworks, rather than with Popeye and Delmount.

Henley: Yes. That play really opened up. I think it was required. The play all takes place backstage, and it's very Greek, with people running on- and offstage saying what tragedies just happened, and that works in the theater. But in a movie you want to see the contest. I got very excited at the idea of actually seeing all the scenes that had been in my mind, to actually get to see them. It just made more sense, sort of spiritually, for Carnelle to be wholly alone—wholly in the spiritual sense of the word—and for the lovers to be together, and for Elain to be in her own trap. So I liked how we were able to do that.

Dellasega: Many critics have commented on the eccentricity of your characters and the frequency of grotesque images and bizarre events. What is the connection between the southern locales and the vivid characters and situations? Do you yourself see the characters as strange?

Henley: I looked up that word—let's see, I have it here: [*drawing the word out*] "strange!" What does it mean? "Unusual or queer" or "new." Only in the sense that all human beings appear unusual to me. No stranger than anyone I know, certainly no stranger than people you see on the news. Or how about those police shows, now that they have those "reality" shows? Basically when I write I try to discover what I can strongly relate to about the characters. To write them I find what's the same about me that's the same about them. Things that I'm afraid of or things that I need or I can see people need or I've seen people dream of. I don't think I take them out of any sort of life I've observed or experienced.

Dellasega: Do you still go back to the South for inspiration?

Henley: It's always inspiring to go home, simply because people are such good storytellers. I don't know if it's my family particularly, but they always inspire me because they've always got so much life going on around them. I live a fairly secluded life, you know, being a writer, and they seem to be so much more out in the world and know what's going on. It's pretty exciting.

Dellasega: Is *The Debutante Ball* the first time you portrayed a lesbian relationship onstage?

Henley: Yes. I think one of the things that the play is really about is love and self-love and also seeing through facades. I wanted it to express that these women really connect on some essential level that doesn't have to do with the fact that one's from the country and one's from the city. It's just a need they both have, a desperate need to be loved and to be seen, and this need and acceptance of each other overcome other elements, such as that they're both women, or that one speaks French and one doesn't, or that one has probably never had a lover at all and the other one has had many. I wanted to illustrate something that many people would say wouldn't be right—and then turn it around because love is right.

Dellasega: I have a very beautiful edition of *The Debutante Ball* that was illustrated by Lynn Green Root. The two of you seemed to share a wonderful tragicomic vision. How did this collaboration come about, and are you going to do it again?

Henley: I would very much love to work with Lynn again. I think this idea was from JoAnne Prichard, the woman who is an editor of the University Press of Mississippi. I've known Lynn since we were children. Actually I was ahead of her in school, but I knew *of* her. And I just loved her sketches when she sent them to me in her portfolio and got very excited. We had hoped to do a version of *Abundance*. We applied for a grant, but we didn't get it. So we would love to work together again, but it just hasn't worked out yet.

Dellasega: I would love to see that. That brings me to *Abundance*. Most of your plays have been set in the South and in fairly contemporary times. With *Abundance* you moved to the Wyoming Territory and the mid-nineteenth century.

Henley: I think I have a sense that the first plays that I wrote, *Crimes of the Heart, The Miss Firecracker Contest, The Wake, The Debutante Ball*, were all set in Mississippi and vaguely in the past, more like in my childhood than in the eighties when I was writing. And then I went to *The Lucky Spot*, which took place in the thirties, and then I just kept going farther back. *The Lucky Spot* was set in Louisiana, and then I went farther west, to the Wyoming Territory. But one thing that inspired *Abundance* was this book, *Wisconsin Death Trip*. I saw this book, and I was just stunned because of the harsh reality of the West it showed, which was not portrayed in the cowboy movies or the Westerns of the time. I was fascinated with the specifics of everyday life and how brutal they were. They triggered my imagination, who these people actually were and their madness. People were eating the heads off matchsticks, and then they would print it up in the paper so matter-of-factly. And something about that book made me get interested also. After living in California for so many years, I like the idea of having the West symbolize hope and new things and danger—you know, you can move west and change things.

Dellasega: Often the women in your plays find support from other women more than they do from men. Does *Abundance* show a darker side of female relationships? The mail-order brides, Bess and Macon, swear eternal friendship and then seem to betray each other.

Henley: Yes, they do. Of course I don't see women being that great to each other throughout my plays. Elain's not that great to Carnelle. And Chick is just a horror. But I think I was dealing with what happens with people's dreams in *Abundance*—how people come out to California so full of hope to be an actress or to be in movies and slowly they find themselves working at Chicken Bob's, or they want to be great novelists and they're trying to write bad TV scripts. How do your dreams get chipped away? And these two women—one has a dream to find true love and the other has a dream to find her adventurous spirit and daring. And they each betray their own dreams, and that's betraying themselves, really. And I'm fascinated by the insidiousness of how this happens in life, how this is a process in which you're hardly to blame because it's so invisible how it seduces you. Suddenly Macon really wants that copper kettle instead of just taking off. So I think it was more an exploration of that, and at the end it wasn't an easy fix. But I think by looking at the deeper aspects truthfully, there is something much deeper about the shaft of hope that *is* there at the end.

Dellasega: Bess wins a certain amount of autonomy by selling the story of her abduction, and yet to do so she gives her approval to the idea of the extermination of the Indians.

Henley: Yes. That to me shows how far she has gone away from her dream of true love because I feel that she did love Ottawa and her children. But she feels *he* betrayed *her*, and so that's her revenge. She agrees to that, and it's really kind of blood-curdling. It's amazing what people will do when they've been hurt, how they will strike out viciously. And it costs them so much, eventually, as far as their hearts go.

Dellasega: Would you discuss the recurrence and significance of women in your plays who are in or have been in relationships with men who are emotionally or physically abusive? Is it a comment on marriage that the married female characters so rarely seem happy? I was thinking of Katty in *Wake*, Jen in *The Debutante Ball*, Bess in *Abundance*, and Babe in *Crimes of the Heart*.

Henley: Yes. That's one side of the coin. You're leaving out the other side of the coin, though: Barnette and Babe and Pixrose and Leon have positive relationships, and Sue Jack and Hooker have a volatile romance, but at least they come together at the end. I think there are all aspects of human connections that I try to show in my plays. But I do very much believe that men and women have a hard row to hoe, connecting with each other, as do women and women and men and men. But I think because of the sexual thing, there's something a lot more volatile.

Dellasega: I know you've identified yourself as a feminist in previous interviews. How do you think your feminism is reflected in your plays and in your female characters?

Henley: I don't know. I cringe at that word, *feminist*. I always look that up. Okay, you're for female rights—well, of course! But I don't favor women over men characters when I write them. I try to understand each. I certainly like Delmount more than Chick, if you want to know the truth. I just try to look at people more than at just the sexes and hope that it'll be more a human point of view rather than having some sort of agenda to show that women are better, because I don't actually think they are. I think some women are better than some men. I know that sounds equivocating, but it's just true. And some men are better than some women. But to me it's not a question of better. My favorite characters are the ones that screw up most.

Dellasega: Which ones are you thinking of?

Henley: Well, I do love Meg, and she's insane, you know. And Sue Jack is a very destructive person. Boswell in *Signature* is awful, he's really conceited. I love and I understand Bess when she seeks revenge on Macon, but I understand Macon when she chains Bess up. I am so excited by people who are driven to extremes because of their passions.

Dellasega: That leads to my next question. You have often been compared with Chekhov, I think partly because you show your characters' flaws and foolishness without judging them, simply revealing them.

Henley: Well, I'm very complimented by that. I do try to track the characters' throughline, from their point of view, and try to understand, even if it makes no rational sense whatsoever, what is compelling them to behave the way they do.

Dellasega: Do you see your sense of comedy as being at all similar to Chekhov's or as an inspiration to you?

Henley: Definitely an inspiration. Very much. I always look at *Crimes of the Heart* as a real steal from *Three Sisters*. *Crimes* is a much less brilliant and inspired version. But I always think they could be played in repertoire with Irina as Babe, Masha as Meg, Olga as Lenny, Natasha as Chick, and Vershinen as Doc.

Dellasega: That's a wonderful idea. I wanted to ask you about Holly Hunter, who's worked with you on six plays now.

Henley: Five, I think.

Dellasega: Do you see qualities in her that are particularly appropriate for your characters? Or by this time are you sometimes writing with her in mind, and how does this affect your writing?

Henley: Actually I wrote *Control Freaks* with her in mind, because I wrote it with four characters and on one set to do at our theater here in L.A. But I just think anyone would want Holly in anything. She's extremely versatile and extremely brilliant.

Dellasega: Would you discuss your recent play, *Control Freaks*?

Henley: The plot of it? It's about this family that tries to open up Furniture World together, and they end up killing each other. It's got four characters: Carl and his sister, who's called Sister, and his new wife, Betty, and then Paul, who was kind of a guest whom they're buying the space from for Furniture World.

Dellasega: Would you call this play something of a departure for you?

Henley: Yes, because it takes place in L.A., and it's extremely expressionistic and theatrical rather than a more naturalistic story like *Crimes of the Heart*. I mean, the props are extreme—they have bubbles for breakfast in the frying pan, and there's flying onstage. It's a bit odd and more theatrical.

Dellasega: The language and the sexual situations are also something of a departure?

Henley: It's a play about incest, basically. That's one of the themes that is the darker side of the human spirit and passions. In that sense I think it's kind of the path I was on.

Dellasega: Do you think your vision has turned darker with your later plays?

Henley: I think they have a darker vision, but it's only because my vision is broader. I suppose I mean by that that I feel more able to embrace the endlessness of our mysteries and risk the darker waters without that paralyzing fear of drowning. Why I feel more able to do this, I don't know. Practice?

Dellasega: Will you be turning more to California or L.A. for inspiration now?

Henley: I don't know. I've got some notebooks, and I'm not sure where my next play is going to take place. The one I wrote after *Control Freaks* actually takes place around Lake Michigan and is entitled *Revelers*. *Revelers* is actually about going to sprinkle the ashes of a friend around Lake Michigan. And these characters all started working together at a theater in Chicago when they were young and have taken divergent paths and are coming back for this ritual. It has a light touch to it. They do this performance for the deceased, and it's a bit *Midsummer Night's Dream*-y.

Dellasega: Your first time directing was for *Control Freaks*. What was the experience like?

Henley: Very challenging. And really sort of monumental for me because I had to take responsibility to communicate and to really go with a vision without leaning on a director and being able to leave when things got boring or heated. It was a big leap—but hard.

Dellasega: I read somewhere that you were working on a screenplay for *A Confederacy of Dunces.*

Henley: I've done a version of that, but as far as I know, that version is shelved.

Dellasega: What a shame.

Henley: Yes.

Dellasega: What was it like adapting another writer's work?

Henley: I just fell in love with John Kennedy Toole. It's a very sort of spiritual connection you have. I wanted so much to meet him.

Beth Henley: Signature of a Nonstop Playwright

V. Cullum Rogers / 1995

From *Backstage* 36 (March 24, 1995): 23, 44. Reprinted by permission of *Backstage* and V. Cullum Rogers. V. Cullum Rogers has been a political cartoonist, caricaturist, theater critic, and freelance writer-illustrator since the late 1970s. For several years in the 1990s, he was the southeastern correspondent for *Backstage* in New York.

There may be no such thing as an overnight success in the theater, but Beth Henley will do till one comes along.

"I wrote one one-act play at SMU [Southern Methodist University] in Dallas," the Mississippi-born author said from her home in Los Angeles last week. "It was done [as a major production] with another one-act called *The Bridgehead*, written by a friend of mine named Frederick Bailey. They were doing his play and needed another to go with it, and I won. . . . After I graduated, I came out to Los Angeles, and I wrote *Crimes of the Heart* right after that."

The rest, as they say, is history. Henley submitted *Crimes* to the 1979 Great American Play Contest, sponsored by the Actors Theatre of Louisville, where it shared top honors before going to Broadway and winning the 1981 Pulitzer Prize. Her second full-length play, *The Miss Firecracker Contest*, was produced by the Manhattan Theatre Club in 1984 and starred Holly Hunter. Her third, *The Wake of Jamey Foster*, was directed on Broadway by Ulu Grosbard—and closed twelve days later.

Does Henley, now forty-two, have any advice for young writers whose plays close after twelve performances? "Find a good bar." More seriously, she went on, "I've always made it a policy to keep working. As great as it is to win a Pulitzer—to win anything—the thing that really keeps you going is the writing."

That writing has since included several screenplays, plus the plays *The Debutante Ball* (1985), *The Lucky Spot* (1986), *Abundance* (1990), *Control*

Freaks (1992), and *Signature*, which was written in 1990 but will have its world premiere next week at the Charlotte Repertory Theatre. It runs March 29-April 9 at the Blumenthal Performing Arts Center in downtown Charlotte, N.C. CRT Artistic Director Steve Umberger will direct.

"It's about two brothers and their travails about love and life in the twenty-first century," Henley said. Why the twenty-first century? "I could make up language and not have to adhere to what we know. . . . Most of my plays are kind of in the past. *The Lucky Spot* is in the 1930s, *Abundance* is in the nineteenth century. I pushed this one into the twenty-first century because I wanted to get into the present."

It must have worked. *Control Freaks*, which was written right after *Signature*, is set in Los Angeles—now. There are four characters who open a business together, and end up trying to kill each other.

"The darker side of life has always appealed to me. I like to have a big perspective on things: The reason things can be so funny is that they can be so sad; the reason they can be so beautiful is that they can be so ugly. If all there was to life was anguish, it wouldn't be so bad." That characteristic mixture of light and dark—call it Gothic whimsy—shows up in the play's [*Signature*'s] main character, Boswell, who comes to believe he can save his life by changing the way he signs his name.

"I was in a depressed state and there was this graphologist on Melrose Avenue, and he read my handwriting, and it was such a dark portrait of a human being," Henley said of the event that sparked the central image of *Signature*. "All my plays are psychically autobiographical. I'm always dealing with things I'm tormented with or wrestling with. . . . Once I'm working on a play, everything [that happens in my life] starts to construct itself around it. . . . There's an uncensored outpouring of feelings and obsessions. I don't start with clear-cut characters. . . . I never know how I'm going to end the play at the beginning. I try to get a very strong sense of the first scene. . . . I do a lot of pre-writing work [in notebooks]: smells and images and bits of dialogue."

When not writing, Henley said, "I try to have a life—shopping, doing the laundry." She writes by hand in a spiral notebook, "so I can do it all over the house. . . . I usually like to write from 11 [a.m.] to 4 [p.m.]." After finishing a first draft, she'll type it up on an IBM Selectric and show the results to selected friends. "I really trust their opinions, and I know they'll overpraise it," she said. "Later, I'll show it to people who are more critical. The last thing you want after working on something for five months is to have someone tell you it's no good."

The public got its first view of *Signature* in the summer of 1990, at a work-shop mounted by the New York Stage and Film Company in Poughkeepsie. "They sort of ran out of money for costumes and some of the actors had to wear their regular clothes," Henley recalled, "but they knew their lines and there was an audience, so I consider it a production." The script being pre-sented by the CRT, she said, is "a pretty final version," and she expects to do little in Charlotte beyond "rewriting moments or noticing changes to make in other productions."

Her latest work for the stage is *L-Play* ("that's letter-L-dash-Play"), which she describes as "eight different mini-plays in different theatrical styles with different characters." All eight plays have titles starting with L. "Loneliness, Loss, Lunatic, Loser. . . . One is southern, one is western, one is prehistoric." She's also working on "a screenplay based on a non-fiction book by a Cana-dian journalist called *The Stopwatch Gang*. It's about a group of gold robbers who came down and robbed a bank in San Diego."

What would Henley do if she weren't a writer? "I shudder to think," she laughed, adding that just before *Crimes of the Heart* was produced, "I nearly took a job sorting spare parts at TRW," the computer manufacturer.

When not writing, she serves on the board of the Met Theatre in Los Angeles, and she directed the first two productions of *Control Freaks*—at the Center Theater in Chicago in 1992 and at the Met Theatre in 1993. "It was extremely challenging," she said. "They ended up being two entirely different productions of the same script. . . . I learned [from the Chicago production] that it should really be away from any sort of naturalism or whatever. . . . [In L.A.], it was like this grotesque ballet of a poem that never stops."

But Henley largely limits her theater work to writing, even though she majored in acting at SMU and believes playwrights can learn some of their most valuable lessons onstage.

"If you have to be in a play, you hear it over and over and learn it by heart," she said. "If you're doing Shakespeare, you learn how he put a play together, and what better class can you have in form and structure?

"Another practical thing is that you learn what's fun to do onstage. It's fun to throw glitter. It's fun to walk out in a hat with a big plume. So you write those things."

Playing Dollhouse on a Huge Scale: An Interview with Beth Henley

Bonnie Lyons / 1997

From *The Muse Upon My Shoulder: Discussions of the Creative Process*, edited by Sylvia Skaggs McTague (Madison, NJ: Fairleigh Dickinson University Press, 2004), 145–59. Reprinted by permission of Bonnie Lyons. Bonnie Lyons is professor emeritus of English at the University of Texas at San Antonio. She is the author of *Henry Roth: The Man and His Work* (1976) and of four poetry collections, and is coeditor of *Passion and Craft: Conversations with Notable Writers* (1998).

Beth Henley is best known for the astonishingly successful *Crimes of the Heart*, which was awarded the Pulitzer Prize in Drama, the New York Drama Critics' Circle Award, and a Tony nomination in 1981. Since then she has written widely for both the stage and films. In addition to the one-act *Am I Blue*, which she wrote while a student at Southern Methodist University, her other plays include *The Wake of Jamey Foster, The Miss Firecracker Contest, The Debutante Ball, The Lucky Spot, Abundance, Signature, Control Freaks, Revelers,* and *L-Play.* Her newest play, *Impossible Marriage,* is scheduled for production at the Roundabout Theatre in spring 1998. She was nominated for an Academy Award for her screenplay for the acclaimed film version of *Crimes of the Heart.* Her other screenplays include *Miss Firecracker, Nobody's Fool,* and *True Stories,* which she cowrote. Acclaimed for her rich characterization and complex combination of comic and serious elements, she has written in a variety of styles and set plays in various locations and time periods.

The following interview took place on a brilliantly sunny afternoon in November 1997 in her office in Los Angeles. Although her office has the usual office equipment, it has the homey feel of a comfortable living room. Casually dressed in a skirt and sweater, Beth Henley revealed the humor, warmth, and unassertive, clear intelligence so evident in her work as she discussed her overlooked interest in images, her dramatic debt to Chekhov and Beckett, the differences in writing plays and screenplays, her artistic intentions, and writing practices.

Bonnie Lyons: Has being one of four sisters had any effect on you as a writer?

Beth Henley: I'm sure it did, especially with *Crimes of the Heart*, which is all about sisters and the interaction among sisters. I think men are still something of a mystery to me in a way they wouldn't be if I'd grown up with a brother. I have a little boy now, and it's such an odd thing seeing growing up mean trucks and cars and boy books. I even know what a backhoe is now. The differences are right here from the beginning.

BL: Did your own sisters think they were the sources of the sisters in *Crimes of the Heart*?

BH: I think they did a little bit here and there. None of the Magrath sisters were drawn from my sisters directly though. I think more than seeing themselves in the characters, my own sisters felt that I got something right about us growing up together.

BL: Did you identify with one of the characters?

BH: I really identified with all of them at different points of my life. As a writer you don't always fully understand what you're writing. You sense things and know things in different ways and at different times.

BL: In some of your plays various characters complain about being labeled by their families or compared unfavorably with their siblings. Do you think that comes from your own experience?

BH: As a writer I certainly can understand a deep sense of jealousy. I understand the dynamic of wanting to be special, of wanting to be visible and also the dynamic of wanting to be invisible. In my own family I was the shy one; I was shyer than my sisters.

BL: How does that relate to your early interest in becoming an actress?

BH: Everyone talks about that, but my interest in acting was really brief. It was just a foray in college. I think acting is a very appealing profession for shy people, because you get to express things but you don't have to be yourself. That's true of writing too, of course. When you write, you get to do all the characters, you get to try out all the roles including men. Writing gives me extraordinary freedom.

BL: Going back to your college days, what made you choose SMU?

BH: My whole college application process was helter-skelter. I had not a clue. I did know that I didn't want to go to college in Mississippi. My mother wanted us to have more perspective of the world. She told me this was my big chance to get out of Mississippi. She said, "You've grown up here all your life. You should experience something different." I didn't have great grades or test scores either. I remember one college in Memphis turned me down. When I did get accepted by SMU I was very happy. I knew that they had a very good theater department, and I wanted to major in theater.

BL: How has the extraordinary success of *Crimes of the Heart* affected you?

BH: It was very exciting and overwhelming. And I'm very grateful to have had that success in my life. It's something many people never have. Winning a Pulitzer Prize has given me a kind of credibility. The success of *Crimes of the Heart* has given me the freedom to be a writer from a very early age. And my dream of what to do with my life was always to be an artist. Because of that success I didn't have to go back and work horrible jobs. It has given me the freedom to write things I cared about all these years.

BL: Has that early great success had any downside?

BH: The only downside was at the time I felt unworthy and overwhelmed. Suddenly I was at the top of my profession and talented people who were my comrades were still struggling.

BL: Elsewhere you've mentioned that you fell in love with the theater when you first saw a Chekhov play. Could you talk about that a little?

BH: I fell in love with Chekhov when I saw a production of *The Cherry Orchard* with James Earl Jones. When I was auditioning for the part of Irina in *Three Sisters* I was reading the text and I kept thinking, "Why is this so great? I don't get it." Then I went to see a production [of *The Cherry Orchard*] and I started weeping and laughing. I remember Lopakhin saying buying the cherry orchard was the greatest moment of his life and the most despairing moment. And I thought that the way Chekhov caught that was genius, real genius. I remember thinking, that's it, that's the real thing.

BL: Did you get the part of Irina?

BH: No, but years later I wrote *Crimes of the Heart*, which is really a total rip-off of *Three Sisters*. The two plays could easily be played in rep by the same actors. Lenny is Olga and so on.

BL: Do you see any other connections between your work and Chekhov's?

BH: I'd like to say yes, but his work is just beyond anything I could even aspire to. I'm in love with him—and it's so great to be in love with somebody that's not here but you feel like he is. When I saw pictures of him in a theater program I started weeping because I thought, "I should have married *him*! He's so sweet, so adorable." I thought he was right for me; I don't know if I was right for him, but he was right for me.

BL: I associate your interest in combining the comic and tragic with Chekhov.

BH: What I am able to accomplish is a much cruder version compared to his orchestration and the way he unravels things mysteriously. He is such a genius that I think you can't really learn from him. He seems to create out of thin air, so you can't really copy him.

BL: Elsewhere you've been quoted as saying the way to write a play is "You just take two characters and get them into an argument." And that made me wonder whether you see conflict as the heart of drama and whether that conflict was primarily between individuals or within an individual.

BH: First I think you have to have the sense of every character wanting something, or needing something, or fearing something. I do think conflict is crucial but that conflict can certainly be internal. In *Control Freaks* I have a character who has three different voices that speak to that character, so that play has my most obviously internally conflicted character. In *The Debutante Ball* the mother is in conflict with society because of her great desire to make a place for herself but there is also internal conflict there as well because there is a part of her that is really vulnerable and the harshness of her actions is in conflict with that part of her.

BL: I was surprised to see you quoted elsewhere as saying, "I cringe at the word feminist," because I think your work is feminist. What about that word makes you cringe?

BH: I can't remember ever saying that. Perhaps I was just responding at someone's clichéd use of the term. I consider my plays adamantly feminist according to my understanding of the word. To me feminist implies women are equal to men and also that women for many, many years have had their arms tied and their mouths bound. I think there is rage about that and some repercussions from that lack of freedom. Many of my women characters are in a rage about it or have some sort of self-loathing because of it. I think feminism is a very strong factor in much of my work.

BL: Has your own career as a writer been affected by your gender?

BH: That's a hard question to answer, because I feel I've had a really easy lot, easier than many men and women who have also had gifts. So I don't have any complaints about my personal career. In fact I think my work came at a moment when women playwrights were being lauded and accepted, and the work of women playwrights was something to write about for about ten minutes.

BL: Why do you think that women playwrights have come into their own so much later than women poets and fiction writers?

BH: Well, in Shakespeare's time there weren't any women connected with the theater, period. And as recently as the nineteenth century actresses were perceived as harlots. At least Jane Austen and Emily Dickinson could sit at home and write. It was more ladylike and they could keep their faces away from the crowd. But drama is so public, and as a playwright you're down at a nasty, dirty theater with these horrible, scummy people called actors who enter through the back door. Until very recently you basically had to proclaim yourself a prostitute to be a playwright. Writing a play at home is not the same as seeing it done at a theater and working on it in production. Whereas if you write a poem or a novel it's complete on the page. You can even be like George Sand and send it in under a pseudonym. But a play is a public, collaborative art.

BL: As you say, playwrights, unlike fiction writers and poets, have a dual life—one very private and solitary, the other quite public. Do you like both sides equally?

BH: I really do. I wouldn't want to be a novelist and have to be constantly, constantly alone when I worked. I love the production part when I get to go out and be around people. It's such an extreme high to hear actors say your words and make them even better than you thought they might be and to see costumes that someone has created. It's like playing dollhouse on a huge scale.

BL: Your dollhouse analogy suggests women should be drawn to playwriting more than men since very few girls didn't love playing dollhouse.

BH: Yes that's true, and there were more women than men in my class at Columbia.

BL: How do you teach writing plays? Do you rely on techniques you learned as a student?

BH: The students at Columbia were advanced graduate students so I had them bring in something they were working on and then I would listen to it and give them an exercise that I thought might help fill out some things that seemed to be lacking.

BL: For each student you had a unique exercise?

BH: Yes, based on the characters in their play. It was a lot of work, but it was also engaging and fun for me, and I think more useful than giving a general exercise because not everyone has the same concerns. Some of the students lucked out more than others because their exercises proved more helpful, but they all were happy that I had actually engaged with them as playwrights.

BL: Can you remember any of the exercises?

BH: It really varied, but I might say, have a character dream that every-thing will turn out right or have a character write a letter telling another character everything he loves about her. Or have a character's dead mother write him a letter from heaven and tell him what her hopes for him were.

BL: From your examples it sounds like the students were creating char-acters without enough depth, that you were trying to get them to have a deeper feel for their characters' psychology.

BH: A lot of it was character work, but some worked on things like set-ting. I asked some of them to sum up their plays in two pages. They were close to finishing their plays and they had worked through intuition, so now it was time for clear thinking. They needed to see that they had made cer-tain choices and to understand why they had made those choices and to see if their play worked through those choices.

BL: Are these techniques you use in your own writing?

BH: Subliminally, but sometimes when I was teaching I'd think to myself, "I should try this." Actually I do a lot of preparation before I write. I write notebooks and notebooks of images and possible scenes and possible dia-logue. If a student hadn't finished a play I might say, give me three images that you know will be in the next scene. Something like someone lights a match and it goes out, or someone puts on a slipper and it falls off. Or some particular color or taste or smell. Things like that.

BL: Are you interested in teaching plays as well as teaching playwriting?

BH: I would like to teach drama sometime. Actually I'm taking a Shake-speare course myself right now. The teacher, who teaches at Loyola, comes to our house and we're a small group, mostly novelists and screenwriters and one architect. Every three weeks we study a different Shakespeare play. We've gone through the tragedies and we're studying the comedies now. I love Shakespeare but I'm sure that if it weren't for this course I'd never get around to reading *Titus Andronicus*.

BL: Do you have any favorite playwrights among your contemporaries?

BH: Mamet and Sam Shepard and I also like Nicky Silver, who is really new on the scene. His plays are very verbal and full of mad dialogue.

BL: How do your plays begin? Do different plays begin differently?

BH: I always have notebooks and notebooks of intuitions or images before I start writing, and I never know where a play is going. I never work from an outline of a whole play.

BL: Do you usually start with a character?

BH: Some begin with characters, but a lot of times situations or events like a debutante ball or a wake or a contest are the beginning. Actually

The Debutante Ball was based in part on a true story. There was a female socialite who supposedly shot her abusive husband in Mississippi; everyone thought the daughter did it, but the woman got off because her husband was abusive.

BL: Do you often rely on news events as sources?

BH: Sometimes something I read or hear creeps in. Before writing *Crimes of the Heart* I read a story about Walter Cronkite visiting in the South and how when an African-American boy came to the door to deliver ice cream, some man yelled at him to use the back door. That image of unmitigated cruelty, of a stronger person abusing a weaker one, was behind Willie Jay and Zackery in *Crimes of the Heart*.

BL: Do you see yourself as a southerner or yourself as a southern writer?

BH: I don't like the responsibility of being tied down to the South, but I do feel sort of grateful to be a southerner, because I feel that I'm from someplace. And Mississippi is a wonderful place to visit and about as opposite California as possible. I love the trendiness and triviality of Los Angeles, where people have these dreams, no matter how pathetic and vague and woeful they may be. Whereas in Mississippi people know where they are going and what china is going to be used for which holiday. That has its charms, but it is also restricting.

BL: Do you know other southern writers and their work?

BH: I like Richard Ford's work. He went to the same high school in Jackson I did a few years earlier. I see him down there occasionally, and Willie Morris and Barry Hannah. I've met Eudora Welty too; she's a goddess.

BL: How about Tennessee Williams's work? His plays seem to ask the audience to sympathize with the outsiders and misfits rather than the so-called normal and successful people. Isn't that true of your work too? Doesn't the audience sympathize with the Magrath sisters—not with Chick, for example?

BH: I think I do have an affinity for outsiders. But to tell you the truth the fact that Chick is so unsympathetic is not a great thing about the play. In *The Wake* and other plays I've tried to make characters who are somewhat like Chick more multidimensional.

BL: As far back as your first play, *Am I Blue*, isn't there a criticism of the hardness and cruelty of many successful people? Doesn't that young girl criticize the fraternity boy for having a "management mind" and for being a sheep?

BH: It's really hard for me to remember that play, but yes, he's more straight and she's more idiosyncratic and they both have their problems because of their families and their choices. When the fraternity boy and waif girl finally dance at the end I think the audience is supposed to feel that they are both simply people with human needs.

BL: People often talk about the South having a strong oral tradition. Do you think that's true?

BH: Very much. People there are more loquacious and just brimming with stories. And they enjoy just sitting around talking. When I go home my mother and I just sit around and drink coffee and talk. Then we go to the grocery store which takes forever because when we get there we have to talk to everybody. Then we come back and talk some more. It's the opposite of life here, where everybody runs around and also has everything delivered.

BL: Is anyone in your family a particularly good storyteller?

BH: My mom is a great storyteller. Another thing she is particularly good at is perceiving things in the moment, knowing what's really going on here and now. She's got a keen eye and sense of when something is phony. Actually all my family are witty and fun.

BL: Was it hard for you to leave the South?

BH: Actually I left Mississippi at eighteen and never moved back. The big move was coming to L.A. I was terrified and I should have been. Actually I was not nearly terrified enough. I felt really foolish for many years about trying to do something that was just impossible.

BL: When people like me ask you questions about being a woman writer or a southern writer, do you resent being categorized? Would you rather be seen simply as a playwright?

BH: These kinds of categories help people organize their thoughts, but at the same time, sometimes people use categories to pigeonhole you as a barrier to a direct connection to your work. I would say, read the play and see if anything comes alive for you, rather than looking at it as a feminist play or a play by a southern woman writer. Too much context can kill you and prevent you from looking. Instead you just leap to say, "I've got this figured out."

BL: Your first play takes place in New Orleans and you've written a number that take place in Mississippi, but you've also gone far afield in both time and place recently. Do you think you've said all you want to about the South?

BH: Actually my newest play, *Impossible Marriage*, which will open at the Roundabout next season, takes place in Savannah, Georgia. It's about a wedding. The lead is a pregnant woman named Floral, who is the sister of the bride. Floral's younger sister is marrying a much older man, a writer who has left his wife of twenty-three years and all his children for her. His son arrives with a message from the ex-wife threatening to jump to her death if the wedding takes place. Then it comes out that the pregnant sister is not pregnant by her perfect husband but by the reverend who is supposed to conduct the ceremony. It's quite farcical. It's Aubrey Beardsley on the outside and Chagall on the inside, or Oscar Wilde and Chekhov. I am delighted that Holly Hunter will star in it and Stephen Wadsworth will direct it.

BL: Holly Hunter and you have a long history together. Did you have her in mind when you wrote the play?

BH: Not really, but when we had a reading of the play last year I asked her to read a part. I thought she would be perfect for it. Holly doesn't do many plays and being in a play eight times a week is very different from making a film. Acting in the theater is more challenging and fulfilling because the actress gets to orchestrate her whole performance from the first moment to the last. Theater is much more of a writer's and actor's medium than film.

BL: Do you think Holly Hunter has a special sense of who you are as a playwright, or do you think she is simply a wonderful actress?

BH: I think she has a great sense of me as a writer, of my tongue and style, and she knows how to make my work as rich and powerful and fun and sad as anyone on this planet. There are many great actors who don't have that affinity for my work for whatever reason. It's not that they are not talented, it's just something you can feel.

BL: When she started playing in your work she wasn't as well known as she is now, was she?

BH: No, she was very young and just starting out as an actress. She was working as a secretary and living in the Bronx, I think. I first saw her when she auditioned for *The Wake of Jamey Foster*. Our careers have intertwined over the years and we've remained personal friends as well.

BL: You've set plays in Wyoming in the 1860s and Louisiana in the 1930s and so on. Do you do a lot of research for those plays?

BH: I love to do research of all kinds. I read history books and diaries, and for plays or films set in the present I sometimes do interviews. I wrote a film about Canadian bank robbers [an adaptation of *The Stopwatch Gang*], and for a film based on an actual murder case in Florida I did a ton of research including reading court transcripts and local newspaper articles.

BL: Tell me about the advantages of writing plays or screenplays.

BH: With a play you get to approve the choice of director and actors. With a screenplay you have much less power. But I say if you're going to take the money, don't whine about it. I can't stand it when screenwriters whine that their dialogue has been changed. They sold their copyright, they sold out, face it. That's the truth and I'm grateful that I've got somewhere that pays me money for my work.

BL: Does lack of control over the end product keep you from taking your screenplays as seriously as your plays?

BH: I don't think that's possible when you're working on something. I've always worked with a director, not a studio, because that way I feel that I'm in a collaboration with a creative person. I've never had a bad experience working that way. But not every screenwriter has the option of working directly with a director. You have to take what you can get.

BL: What are some of the advantages of writing screenplays?

BH: You make money writing plays, but not at the ridiculous level you can make money writing screenplays, and screenplays are easier to write.

BL: Why easier?

BH: A film is not ruled by time and space, so you don't have to worry about a stage or a set. And you don't have to worry about the number of actors your script calls for. With a play if you have over six actors, producers start to get financially worried. In a screenplay you can have a person say one line and never appear again. And one scene can take place on the moon and the next in a zoo. It doesn't take the same amount of imagination and skill to write a screenplay that it does to write a play.

BL: Is it hard for you to go from writing a play to a film or vice versa?

BH: It's harder to go from a screenplay to a play because of the things I just mentioned, but I like the difficulty, the challenge, of it. And in a play your personal voice, your personal point of view, has a much better opportunity of being demonstrated. For one thing, films have to please a much broader audience; plays can be more specific and personal and idiosyncratic and verbal. Language is so much more an intricate part of a play. I think in a play an audience wants to hear a unique voice, while in a movie the unique voice is usually the director's, if anyone's.

BL: Do you think characterization is your major strength as a playwright?

BH: Characters more than plot, that's for sure. Plots are tough. I love people's complexities; and the endless, endless spectrum of nuance and variations on a theme within people fascinate me. How they try to connect and try not to connect. I like losing myself in other souls. But I also like experimenting with different styles and exploring the power of style. Recently I'm leaning away from naturalism. The magic onstage is different from the magic on film. When you blow bubbles on a stage it has a different magic than it would on film, because it's alive and you know it's going to pop and there it is and then there it's not. I'm interested in theatrical images, images that work primarily on a stage, the kind of thing Sam Shepard is so great at.

BL: When you write screenplays do you get involved in thinking through the camera, or do you mostly write dialogue?

BH: I do a tiny bit of indicating shots, and I have become much more visual as I've written screenplays, and much less reliant on dialogue alone. I love the idea that in a film you can tell a story through images. You can just show a little haiku of a scene and that's it and cut to something else. That's much more difficult to do on the stage. I love the poetry of film.

BL: Could you talk a little about creating characters? Has your process changed over the years?

BH: It's hard to keep track of, but I do know that I often rely on old acting exercises like asking questions about the characters. What is their greatest dream or fear? What do they want from another character? What is their education, their background? Some of this doesn't always apply. Sometimes you make the characters deliberately flatter depending on the style. That's a decision too.

BL: In a stylized play do you use flat characters more?

BH: I don't think you ever want them to be emotionally flat, but historically flat. They don't have major histories the way characters usually do in a naturalistic play. They can be very deep, complicated people, but we don't necessarily know that they had a mother who beat them or how much education they got. These aren't relevant; what is relevant is what is happening now, that the boot has a hole in it, you know.

BL: You're talking about *Waiting for Godot*?

BH: Yes, I read Beckett in high school and it really was an eye-opener for me. That his insane cruelty could be humorous was a revelation to me. I remember I got obsessed with Pozzo and Lucky. Beckett was not an optimist; he was not a happy boy and his vision is not necessarily a kind view of the world but it is very alive. And his plays are rhythmically perfect, that's where the life of it is.

BL: Do you remember anything else you read as a young person that influenced you?

BH: Of course I read Shakespeare but it was so belabored in high school that it wasn't until I read it in college that I really got a grasp of Shakespeare. But I'm still fascinated by some of the images that fascinated me in high school like Claudius pouring poison in Hamlet's father's ear while he was sleeping in the garden. The poison and the garden really grabbed me. I remember reading a lot of Carson McCullers and Sartre's *Nausea* and existential ideas and Abbie Hoffman's *Steal This Book*. And I remember being fascinated by the brutality of *Who's Afraid of Virginia Woolf?* I don't know that I read Tennessee Williams but my mother was an actress and I remember when she was learning Blanche's part that I went over and over those lines with her. When I saw Jessica Lange play that part a few years ago all that gorgeous language just came flooding back to me. My mother was also in *The Glass Menagerie* and I worked with her on those lines too. I think that when we're young our brains are literally still growing, and I think that what helped me be a writer more than anything else was night after night hearing those lines. When you hear lines again and again, something has got to sink into your brain about structure and movement and characters.

BL: Speaking of characters, I'd like to know if it's harder for you to create male characters than female characters.

BH: I think it's fun for me. I love the freedom of getting to be a man and exploring the power of it and the mystery. But I think I do lean more toward women characters. I'm probably more innately at home with them.

BL: Are your male characters ever as central as your female characters?

BH: Only in *Signature*, where both of the main characters are male. It takes place in the twenty-first century so I was inventing a whole new language and so forth. That play was totally an act of imagination, and I think that kind of lent itself to the freedom to do those characters.

BL: Elsewhere you've said that your favorite characters are the ones that screw up most. Is that because they are the most interesting to work with dramatically or do you have a special sympathy for them?

BH: Something about people being driven to extraordinary acts, even criminal acts, is fascinating to me. I'm interested in what pushed them to that point; it wasn't necessarily evil circumstances. It could be very human circumstances.

BL: You've said that the book *Wisconsin Death Trip* was an important inspiration for *Abundance*. Have other books been important for other plays?

BH: Reading Willa Cather was also important for *Abundance*, but with other plays the inspiration was different. My obsession with the music of the era was important for *The Lucky Spot*.

BL: *Abundance* seems to me to be an extraordinarily ambitious play covering twenty-five years of your characters' lives. Was it very hard to write a play covering that many years?

BH: As I recall, at the time I was really sick of doing plays in the classical form and was excited at the idea of having to write so many short scenes, the necessity of getting them exactly right. And I was interested in the theme of growth and change and how you can suddenly realize that you sold out, that you've lost everything that was important to you but not in any noticeable fashion or in one big moment.

BL: What about adapting your own plays for film? How has that been?

BH: That's been easy and fun and profitable.

BL: What about the changes from one form to the other?

BH: With *Crimes of the Heart* the director really wanted to keep the characters in the house, to keep the feeling of these characters trapped together back home for a while. So that wasn't changed much. But with *The Miss Firecracker Contest* something that works on the stage—messengers from the big tragedy coming and telling what's going on—would not work in a film; the audience would get irked. So that play lent itself to being more opened up. I consider the film an interpretation of the play in a different form, and since the script for the play exists, the original form is available too.

BL: Was one of your plays more difficult to write than the others?

BH: *Control Freaks* was the most emotionally difficult. But they have all had a stage of seeming impossible. They all have a terrifying stage.

BL: When does that usually occur?

BH: I think it's mainly before I start writing, when I've gathered a lot of data and information and have to begin the actual writing. I think, if I make one wrong step, it will be all wrong.

BL: Do you write a play from beginning to end, or do you say you have a feeling for a scene and write that when it comes to you?

BH: Generally I write pretty linearly and let the play evolve.

BL: Have there ever been major changes from what you first envisioned?

BH: In all of them. I never really know where they are going. I remember when I was working on *Impossible Marriage* that I was supposed to bring the completed play to Chapel Hill where I was teaching. But I hadn't finished the last act, and I really had no idea what was going to happen. I just had a couple of images that I saw.

BL: It sounds like images are absolutely central to you, that you think in images.

BH: Yes. An example of that is when I was writing the third act of *Crimes of the Heart*. I knew there was going to be a suicide attempt and I was assuming the character would die. I had this horrible feeling that the play was going to be a tragedy. That there was going to be this uneaten birthday cake. When I got there I was delighted to see Babe was going to live!

BL: All of a sudden that scene when she puts her head in the oven but doesn't die, which is such a great scene combining the grotesque and comic and terrible, reminded me of that part in *Waiting for Godot* where Gogo attempts to hang himself with his belt and his pants fall down.

BH: Oh yeah, Part IV, read it. It's just so ludicrous but the most tragic.

BL: It sounds like for you writing a play is a really exploratory process.

BH: It's much like going into the ocean in a little boat. You don't know what you might run into. It's very scary and it takes a lot of faith.

BL: Does the faith come from your previous success?

BH: No, I don't think that helps unfortunately. I think the faith has to come from somewhere inside. I think it comes from having a deep respect for the characters and letting them speak and trusting where they go.

BL: Do you write lots and lots of dialogue that you end up throwing away?

BH: Some, but not as much as some playwrights who write draft after draft after draft. Once I start writing, a ton of work is done including subliminal work. I don't begin to write until I feel ready. Then the writing itself usually takes about four or five months and that's the fun part.

BL: How do you feel when you finish a play?

BH: There's a feeling of great relief and I'm ecstatic for about ten minutes. And then I say, "What am I going to think about when I'm driving my car or at the grocery store or in the shower?" Writing a play makes my internal life so interesting, trying to figure out a scene or thinking about a character. When that's over I'm suddenly forced to look at the price of fish.

BL: Are you ever afraid another play won't come?

BH: I just sort of consider writer's block part of the whole process. If I'm not writing I tell myself that's because I'm clearing my brain for another play. I don't get in a huge panic. Just a small one.

The Mellowing of Miss Firecracker

Pamela Renner / 1998

From *American Theatre*, November 1998, pp. 18–19, 61. Used with permission from Theatre Communications Group and Pamela Renner. Pamela Renner is a theater journalist, poet, and teacher.

Could it be that Beth Henley, our premier American playwright of girl-powered lunacy, has grown up? That's the news hinted at between the lines of *Impossible Marriage*, her new play currently running at New York's Roundabout Theatre. It's clear that the precocious, Pulitzer-winning writer of eccentric works like *Crimes of the Heart, Abundance, The Lucky Spot*, and *The Debutante Ball*, who carved out a niche for herself in the eighties as a chronicler of high-octane dizziness, has undergone something of a shift in perspective in the nineties. Call it a maturation, if you will, but the wild gal has turned Wildean satirist.

"In this play I wasn't thinking in terms of naturalism or realism," Henley confides. "I just wanted to create a world where people are incredibly rich—the timeless aristocracy. They have endless time on their hands to contemplate love. To look at their souls becomes even more difficult."

At forty-six, Henley has had plenty of practice peeking into cloudy souls. Whether writing about a dancing floozy with six toes in old Louisiana, or the way abduction by Indian tribes can reinvigorate a lackluster family life, Henley has been a wry observer of youthful infatuation and emotional disarray. No matter how outlandish the situations she's chosen, her plays invite a total absorption in her illusory worlds.

Now her palette seems to be changing from florid goth scarlets to softer tones. The desperate enthusiasm of her protagonists has mellowed, too. There's a tinge of amusement in the way that Henley speaks about coming to accept the passage of time. In *Impossible Marriage*, a captivating young bride named Pandora is nervous about losing her moment. Her author, however, knows such moments come and go throughout one's life. Seize the day, or seize the morrow; it doesn't necessarily stop there. "It's a youthful perspective, that terrible fear that *this is it*—'This is as beautiful as I'm going to be. This is as adorable as I'm going to be.' Later you realize you were just kind of confused and miserable, even though you looked good." It's important not to stagnate, but there's no magic way around accepting life's flux: "You keep growing, evolving, changing. If you're graceful in life you embrace that. You're able to let go."

In her personal life, Henley has likewise embraced a radical change. Three years ago, while working on the current play, she became pregnant and gave birth to her first child [Patrick Henley]. Motherhood has meant tremendous joy—and that she's had her hands full. In recent months, nevertheless, Henley finished a movie script about Canadian bank robbers, recovered from a strength-sapping illness, and collaborated intensively with her Roundabout director, Stephen Wadsworth, on the casting of *Impossible Marriage*. It's no wonder that she expresses a yearning for a little quiet time to relax with her family in the "really sweet yard" of her California home.

Meanwhile, her characters are also going through an evolution. It's not that the wild southern gamines of her best-loved early plays have disappeared from view—it's just that they've undergone a ripening process. Holly Hunter's new role is emblematic of the change in viewpoint. A veteran of six previous Henley productions, Hunter memorably played Pixrose, an incendiary teenage orphan in *The Wake of Jamey Foster*; Carnelle, the overzealous beauty contestant in *The Miss Firecracker Contest*; and Sister, a triple-layer cake of split personalities in *Control Freaks*. In *Impossible Marriage*, Hunter's newest part is Floral, elder sister to the bride, trapped herself in a loveless charade of domestic life. A wellspring of the play's mischievous vision on the pitfalls of conformity to social rules, Floral is also a casualty of sorts, leaking tears and bitter regrets, and pining for something she can't articulate.

"Holly has a strange ability to be passionate and vulnerable, but extremely tough and rageful," Henley says of her longtime collaborator. "Also, she knows how to walk the edge between truth and humor. Holly hears the music of what I write." Although Hunter is identified in the popular press as the star of films from *Raising Arizona* to *The Piano*, a big part of her acting life has been tied up with Henley's idiosyncratic heroines, to whom she brings a peculiar poignancy. Ever since she appeared on Broadway as a replacement for Mary Beth Hurt in *Crimes of the Heart*, the union between playwright and actress, both southerners, has been one of the happiest constants in both their careers. They know each other's work inside out.

As the sardonic Floral, unhappily married and enormously fertile, Hunter projects a character long past innocence but not yet ready to resign herself to corruption. She rebels against boredom, shunning her handsome and insufferably adoring husband. We watch the actions of the play through her eyes, and its epigrammatic manner might very well be Floral's inner voice speaking. Disappointment hasn't stilled her spirit, but it has given her a less-than-sanguine view on the imminent wedding of Pandora (played by Gretchen Cleevely), her lyrically beautiful younger sister.

As for Pandora herself, she's a cauldron of conflicting emotions. Alone for a moment onstage, the young woman spins around in a private dance, going faster and faster until she nearly topples over with dizziness. As she twirls, she feels her world is exploding with possibility—if she pauses for even a minute, it may disappear. "Everything's in bloom and I'm dancing in the night. I'm spinning under all these stars and I can't stop. Never. Never."

Henley's women often appear this way in her plays—breathless and impetuous, daring their fates. Orphaned by reason and good sense, they live by feeling alone. The playwright comments, "All these women are cursed with the ability to see the truth, if not to live the truth. They're sort of exposed to themselves in a way a lot of people aren't." Their exposure brings them very little safety. "To see and really love somebody is one of the most dangerous things you can do. It can kill you." Still, even an inappropriate passion is better than the spiritual torpor of a conventional and loveless union, like the relationship Floral and Pandora's mother (Lois Smith) endured silently for many years. Henley muses, "There are so many things that can work in this world if you follow your instincts and your heart instead of some predestined structure."

It's clear that Henley's own heart lies firm in the theater. The daughter of a dedicated community theater actress in Jackson, Mississippi, Henley grew up an intimate acquaintance of the seductive world of adult make-believe. Her mother's playscripts lay in perpetual abundance about the house, just waiting to be picked up and browsed through by her four daughters. As a child, Henley recalls going backstage and learning about the craft of mounting and staging a show. She studied how the illusions worked. "I just loved seeing how they built the set. It was like your own little dollhouse." She recalls the sense of exultation within this miniature world. The actors were plastic, malleable, awaiting their lines and cues. Becoming a playwright was a natural role for Henley to take up, and her contributions to the theater over the years have been prolific.

To date, Henley's mother remains the single most formative influence upon her writing. When *Impossible Marriage* was in the works, Henley says,

"My mother told me, 'Write a happy play because you're pregnant. You don't want to write anything dark.'" The result was her larkiest play in years. Its setting is a bosky, dream-haunted wood in Savannah, Ga., but in wit and style it is indebted to an Edwardian age of drawing-room repartee.

After twenty years as a professional playwright, Henley retains her sense of delight. "I'm not in the least bit jaded," she says. "I haven't had a play in New York for many years, so this is very exciting for me. I'm thrilled." Henley has written for film, but avows that there's just no replacing the sensation of a live performance: "It's like walking a tightrope and you could fall. You don't know what's coming next. A sigh in the audience affects a performance."

Stage-Struck in Screen City

Don Shirley / 1999

From the *Los Angeles Times*, January 5, 1999, pp. F1, F10. Reprinted by permission of the *Los Angeles Times*. Don Shirley wrote about theater for many years for the *Los Angeles Times*.

Playwright Beth Henley struck gold with her first professionally produced play: *Crimes of the Heart*, which was introduced at Actors Theatre of Louisville in 1979, played 535 performances on Broadway in 1981–83, and won a Pulitzer Prize and the New York Drama Critics' Circle Award as Best American Play.

Her most recent play, *Impossible Marriage*, closed Sunday Off-Broadway at the Roundabout Theatre in New York. Starring Holly Hunter, it marked the first time one of Henley's plays received its first full production in New York.

The Mississippi-reared Henley also has been active in Southern California theater. The premiere of her *The Miss Firecracker Contest* opened the Victory Theatre in Burbank in 1980, before becoming a movie starring Hunter and Tim Robbins. Two of her plays during the eighties, *The Debutante Ball* and *Abundance*, premiered at South Coast Repertory. In 1993, Henley's *Control Freaks* received its second production at the Met Theatre in Hollywood, again featuring longtime collaborator and friend Hunter.

Henley, Hunter, and Ed Harris were among the group who revived the Met Theatre in 1991, and they were among the group who bolted from the Met in 1996 to establish the still-fledgling Loretta Theatre. The Loretta plans to move into a space on Main Street in Santa Monica, recently vacated by the Santa Monica Museum of Art, but the board is still raising money.

The playwright is also a screenwriter, not only converting her own plays into movies, but also working on original material. She's currently writing a script for director Jonathan Demme, as well as a new play.

Henley, forty-six, lives in West L.A. with her husband and a three-year-old son. She maintains a homey-looking office in an apartment within walking distance of her home. That's where she answered questions on a recent chilly day.

Question: Is being a playwright in America getting any easier?

Answer: It was a joy getting *Impossible Marriage* produced because it was commissioned by the theater, they did a reading, and then they produced it. That's much smoother than what I'm used to.

Q: What are you used to?

A: Trying to get a production somewhere, possibly in Poughkeepsie with two weeks' rehearsal, then trying to get people in to see it and get them interested in taking it to New York. My career seems to come and go in waves. Suddenly you have a piece of luck, as with this play. With *Control Freaks*, it was more arduous, doing a workshop and production in Chicago, calling friends for money to do a production here. But just today, I heard that a company wants to do *Control Freaks* in London. A playwright friend of mine in London says they're interested in more tough-minded pieces.

Q: Does Broadway matter to you?

A: Getting your play done on Broadway absolutely enhances its life. More regional and international theaters will know about it and want to do it. It will make more money when you sell the rights. It helps you be able to afford more plays that don't do well. I'd love for every play I write to go to Broadway. You get a bigger audience.

Q: But is the Broadway market for nonmusical plays shrinking?

A: For me, it's shrinking. [*Laughs*] It feels really hard. But there are quite a few plays on Broadway. Ionesco's *Chairs* at the Golden Theatre [on Broadway]—that's amazing.

Q: How did this recent Off-Broadway experience compare to Broadway?

A: *Impossible Marriage* was part of a season. It didn't have an open-ended run, but it wasn't going to close overnight. That's a safety net.

Q: How often do you go to the theater?

A: Here in L.A., I go less frequently because I'm involved in my life. I have a little baby. When I travel, I'm more free. And when I go to New York, none of my friends there have been to see anything there. You have to make time for yourself to see theater, and I'm not an expert at that.

Q: What have you seen lately?

A: I really loved *Side Man*, by Warren Leight. But when you're rehearsing all day like I was in New York last fall, the last thing you want to do is go sit in a theater and watch people act. I was doing tons of rewriting. It was intense.

We changed the ending three times during previews. So I didn't see anything this fall.

Q: Seen anything here recently?

A: I loved *Peter Pan* at the Pantages. My son kept saying, "I just want to talk to that Peter Pan."

Q: You've said you find yourself turning away from naturalism. Why?

A: I got sick of always having pots and pans and props. My play *Abundance* just had too many props. It needs to be spare. It needs to be about the relationships and the words and even the movements of people. It got cluttered. I wanted to think more expressionistically.

Q: *Abundance* was first produced at South Coast Repertory, as was *Debutante Ball*. Is there some reason why you haven't gone back there?

A: I definitely let them see my plays. [*Calling out*] Guys! Guys! I'd love to work there. I love the people there. For whatever reason, my plays haven't got into their seasons.

Q: Though you're one of the best-known playwrights living in L.A., your recent work isn't produced at the major L.A. theaters—Center Theatre Group, the Geffen, Pasadena Playhouse. Is there a story behind that?

A: I submit plays just like everybody else, and most of the time people say no. I would so much like to work here for so many reasons.

Q: Is the Loretta an attempt to provide . . .

A: A home for me, but also I know of so many artists I'd love to work with. I'd like to have some sort of world-class theater here that has collaborations with artists who want to do something amazing. Not just L.A. artists, though those are the ones primarily involved.

Q: Can a world-class theater work under Actors' Equity's 99-Seat Plan, as the Loretta will?

A: I never think of it as too small. I just get so happy: "We're full!" A full house is a full house. For me, it's just like church—it's more about the quality of what's happening than the amount of people who see it. That has to be, or why do theater? There are always going to be a million more people who see any bad movie.

Q: But isn't it harder to get great people to work for the token salaries they get under the 99-Seat Plan?

A: That's true. But you can get people to give extra money for a particular artist who needs it. I guess these are highfalutin expectations from ninety-nine seats. But in a way, there is such freedom in a smaller theater. You don't have a huge budget.

Q: Would you like your plays to have their first full productions at the Loretta from now on?

A: Absolutely. I'm writing a new play for the Loretta. Of course [*laughing*], it could easily be turned down by the board. As a playwright, you never know. It's so easy not to get your play done.

Q: Why do you live in L.A.?

A: I love it. It's a great place to write plays. If I lived in New York, I'd be of the petty nature of looking at the *New York Times* every day and trying to figure out: "What is the trend? Look who's doing well and I'm not." It's good to dissociate myself from that and just write what concerns me. L.A. gives me that opportunity. And I love that people here have dreams. There's such a lack of tradition, which is the opposite of where I grew up in Mississippi. Even though they're foolish and fanciful dreams and probably doomed to failure, at least people have them, and I love the energy of that.

Q: You write movies here, too.

A: I love to write movies. It's so much easier than writing a play. You get so much more money, and I work with really creative people who teach me a lot.

Q: All of these are reasons why many playwrights who move here stop writing plays. Why do you continue?

A: Because I'm obsessed with theater. I love it when a roomful of people respond to something that's really alive. Also, you sell your copyright when you sign on to be a screenwriter. That is demeaning for a creative person. You don't do that when you write a play.

Q: Have you received more money in total from your movies than from your plays?

A: So, so, so, so much more. A play is like an expensive hobby.

Q: Has the recent drama in Washington, D.C., inspired you at all as a playwright?

A: It makes me want to write about people as they truly are, not about this black-and-white "You did bad and we did good." All the ugliness and piety and hypocrisy of impeaching the president is scary. I want to go into this new year with hope and diligence.

Q: With President Clinton and Paula Jones coming from the South, does it inspire you at all to write about characters like them?

A: It certainly reminds writers that there is a lot to write about. Never let it be said that it's not a fertile world. Plots, characters, situations—it's amazing.

Beth Henley

Alexis Greene / 1999

From *Women Who Write Plays: Interviews with American Dramatists*, edited by Alexis Greene (Hanover, NH: Smith and Kraus, 2001), 200–224. Reprinted by permission of Alexis Greene. Alexis Greene is the author of *Lucille Lortel: The Queen of Off Broadway* (2004) and *Emily Mann: Rebel Artist of the American Theater* (2021), coauthor of *The Lion King: Pride Rock on Broadway* (1998), and coeditor of *Frontlines: Political Plays by American Women* (2009).

Beth Henley was born in Jackson, Mississippi, where she also grew up. Although Henley has lived in Los Angeles since 1976, and has written her plays there, she has spent a good part of her career introducing theatergoers to the people of Mississippi, whom she dramatizes with an acute eye and ear for their eccentricities, furies, and vulnerabilities.

In 1979, Henley wrote *Crimes of the Heart*, a poignant comedy about the lives and loves of the three Magrath sisters in the small Mississippi town of Hazlehurst, and in 1981 she was awarded the Pulitzer Prize for Drama. Subsequent plays include *The Miss Firecracker Contest* (1980), *The Wake of Jamey Foster* (1982), *The Debutante Ball* (1985), *The Lucky Spot* (1987), *Abundance* (1990), *Signature* (1990), *Control Freaks* (1992), *Revelers* (1994), and *Impossible Marriage* (1998), a comic fantasy about unpredictable love. In addition to writing plays, Henley has written filmscripts, including *Crimes of the Heart* (1986), *Nobody's Fool* (1986), and *Miss Firecracker* (1989).

Henley lives in Los Angeles with her son. This interview took place in Los Angeles on July 15, 1999.

Alexis Greene: In 1995 you gave birth to a first baby. Congratulations.
Beth Henley: Thank you.
AG: Why did you want to have a child at this point in your life?
BH: I pictured five or six lives. In one, I pictured myself with eight kids, and cooking spaghetti with an apron on. Well, no. Just lots of dogs and a husband who works and loves me. That was one version of a life that I didn't

have. I'd probably kill myself immediately after ten minutes of it, but one fleeting image of it sounds good. To love my son is so great. To be in love with somebody like I'm in love with him. My heart soars. Just to be with somebody like that is so rare. And that's how much I love him.

AG: Are you writing about this yet?

BH: No. No. That sounds too saccharine, to write that. But I probably will write about him someday in some coded version.

AG: Are you raising him by yourself?

BH: I have a nanny, but my nanny doesn't live with me. She picks him up from school or wherever.

AG: You once told an interviewer that you wished you were the sort of woman who wanted children, but you were not.

BH: I didn't want children, that's true. I was totally terrified of children. I didn't want the responsibility. I didn't want the distraction. I didn't want the domesticity. I really, really wanted to do my work. And to be free, in the sense of guilt-free about being able to travel. If you are in the theater, you really have to be a gypsy, unless you have a home in New York and your plays are always done there. But there are about three people in the world that applies to.

AG: In *Impossible Marriage*, your heroine, Floral, is enormously pregnant. Which came first, your pregnancy or your play?

BH: The pregnancy. I got the play commission, and my mother said, "Would you please write a happy play," because I had been writing these dark plays. "You're pregnant and you don't want to upset this baby." So I wrote part of the play before the baby was born and finished it afterwards.

I had been at a wedding while I was pregnant. Actually, I had been the bridesmaid. It was such an odd notion, being a bridesmaid while pregnant, and there was the beauty of the wedding. The idea of impossible marriage— me having a child was the impossible marriage as far as I was concerned. I was dealing with how to live with polar opposites and not diminish either of them. I was also reading Oscar Wilde, and then I was looking at Aubrey Beardsley drawings and Chagall drawings, and I said, "Those Chagall people ought to be inside these Beardsley people." That's really what I tried to do.

AG: Are impossible marriages the best kind?

BH: I think they're the only kind.

AG: Do you think of Floral as in tune with her pregnancy?

BH: When she connects to it, she totally connects, as much as she might be denying it. The actress has to find where the connection between Floral and her baby is, at different moments in the play.

AG: I was thinking about images of pregnant women on the stage, and few come to mind. The duchess in *The Duchess of Malfi*. In *Auntie Mame*, unmarried, lumbering Agnes Gooch is supposed to be funny. There's a pregnant woman in your play *The Lucky Spot*. Floral is somewhat awkward, as Holly Hunter played her. But she's also sensuous.

BH: Yes. It was interesting—at the Roundabout, the costume designer was doing Floral's dress for Act Two, when everybody is dressed up, and I said, "Show some shoulders. She has to be alluring. She is sexy. She's very sensual and appealing. Maybe particularly so, because she's so robustly pregnant."

AG: She responds to nature. The characters who respond to nature in *Marriage* seem to handle life better than the others. Floral's husband, Jonsey, doesn't seem to know what life is about.

BH: I don't know which characters in that play know anything about life. I felt very bad for Jonsey at the end. The others I felt all right about, even good about some of them.

AG: Do you mean they are going to be okay?

BH: Well, no. They aren't. But, you know, I thought they would have a good day.

AG: When did you first meet Holly Hunter?

BH: We were doing *The Wake of Jamey Foster* on Broadway, and she came to audition.

AG: She has been in more than seven productions of your plays. That's an unusual collaboration these days in the American theater.

BH: That's a shame really, because it's so great to work with actors that understand your voice.

AG: Have the two of you ever discussed this affinity?

BH: Not deliberately.

AG: Undeliberately?

BH: We just talk about the work. I think she's a great actress. I feel confident she can get a tone of truthfulness and oddness. She always has hope and energy. She'll see the humor, but she won't play the humor, and that's crucial to my plays. I've had very good actors come in to do readings, and they don't get the tone. Don't get the irony or the heart, and how they connect, and the frightfulness of it all. Holly does. But I do think that when you know people, and they see you in real life, it helps. If the actors in a production get to know me, they seem to be able to look into the material with a keener eye.

AG: Before writing *Impossible Marriage*, you had written *Signature* and *Control Freaks*, both of which are set in Los Angeles. Why did you return to the southern landscape for *Marriage*?

BH: I wanted an environment where there were more boundaries, where marriage was an institution that was valued and would put Floral more on a pedestal than, say, Los Angeles. I wanted an environment where there's an organized society for the characters to bounce off of. A pregnancy from an out-of-wedlock affair would have more mileage in that environment.

AG: Could we talk about the mother in *Impossible Marriage*? She initially appears shocked and disturbed by her daughters' goings-on. But ultimately she supports their love affairs.

BH: I think she takes a bit of a journey in the play. And she's keeping a secret. They're all keeping secrets from each other that they think the others can't deal with. She's keeping the secret that she's ill.

AG: And that she had an unhappy marriage.

BH: And that she had an unhappy marriage. But when she sees that Floral has been keeping a secret from her—because Floral was afraid of losing her love—there is movement to the mother's character. There has to be movement to where, at the end, the mother is going to be eating raspberries and letting the juice drip, because, well, thank goodness there's a boundary so I can go outside it. Basically she's intuitive and intelligent. When Floral says, "People can change. . . . I've seen it happen," she means her mother. Her mother has changed from caring about public opinion to saying essentially, "Oh, who gives a damn? We lived and touched real life and inevitably we had some scandal."

AG: A number of the mothers in your plays are not so supportive or balanced, or even present.

BH: *The Debutante Ball*—now there's a mother.

AG: Yes, there's a mother. Was she modeled on someone in particular?

BH: Well, it's based on a true story, a murder that I heard about when I was growing up in Jackson. A woman murdered her husband—shot him—and the daughter was there, and there was the rumor that the daughter did it and the mother took the rap. And we knew it was the truth, since her daughter was friends with one of my sisters. The mother ended up getting out of jail on self-defense or something, but this society-woman-in-jail situation stuck in my mind. A mother taking the rap for the daughter and actually making things worse.

AG: Jen, the mother, is obsessed with externals, with how her daughter, Teddy, looks and behaves. Every time Teddy goes into the bathroom, she puts more makeup on. I have the idea that her face is a grotesque mask by the time she goes to the ball. Cinderella in reverse.

BH: The more secrets you have the more facade you need. They think that nobody will have to know Teddy killed her father, and the family will be accepted again. If they have the right boy and the right dress and the right presentation, then they will be seen as the mask they put on. They can't be seen as they are, because it's too horrifying.

AG: Since you set this story in the context of a debutante ball, which is *the* white-glove female experience in the United States, the ball feels like a metaphor for what women do to themselves in order to appeal to men.

BH: The notion behind the debutante ball is historically frightening, if you think about these virgins being brought out on display at the time of their blossoming, in the white dresses, presented by their fathers to the young men of a certain financial or social status, to hopefully mate with one of them. It's a mating call. And it's done quite seriously.

AG: Were you a debutante?

BH: No. My older sister and my younger sisters were debutantes.

AG: How did you escape?

BH: I just said I didn't want to do it. I can be really . . . stubborn. I become very unengaged.

AG: Jen, too, is trapped inside her body.

BH: Yes. Her literal body is decaying as much as her secrets have decayed her insides, because her insides are becoming harder to mask. Everything that has been internalized and hidden is now coming through.

AG: But at the end, mother and daughter come to an understanding.

BH: Yes. They share an honest moment. They have a cigarette together. They've both been lying about smoking, too.

AG: A number of people lie about smoking in the play.

BH: Teddy admits she killed the father. That she's pregnant. I wanted the image to be a peeling off, a renewal, a washing off, an applying of ointment to the wounds. "I'm going and I'm telling you I'm going, instead of sneaking away."

AG: Frances, the niece of Teddy's stepfather, is deaf. Was there a particular reason you wanted that character to be deaf?

BH: Actually, I wanted to work with the actress Phyllis Frelich. I had loved her in *Children of a Lesser God.* So she played Frances at South Coast Repertory. I also wanted to write a part for a deaf person that didn't have to be sweet and perfect. I wanted to write a real person. And there are so many images in that play of isolation, of people having the need for love and not being able to express it. Frances's mother is dying, she's out of place, she doesn't fit in, and she's fallen in love with a woman and didn't even know she was interested in women. Having Frances in the play sort of embodies people trying to communicate. How do we connect? How do we love? The struggle when somebody is deaf, or for you, if you're deaf. Something in you is cut off or not open. All of that is in there. My agent got a letter from some theater saying the character was an insult to deaf people. It's not my most politically correct play, but I didn't care.

AG: The love relationship between Frances and Bliss seems to be the only one that works.

BH: Well, it probably won't work out eventually, but it will be good for a while. They both need each other so desperately and they've both been cruel to other people. But I don't know how it will end.

AG: In *The Debutante Ball* and other plays of yours, it sometimes seems that the daughters have to separate from the mothers in order to find themselves.

BH: That's definitely the theme of *The Debutante Ball*. Teddy is guilty over her mother going to jail for what she did. They're enmeshed psychically. All of that has to get bashed rather quickly for Teddy to go on. And for the mother to go on, so she can let go of that obsession of keeping Teddy perfect, keeping her safe.

AG: Even the three sisters in *Crimes of the Heart* have to separate themselves from their mother's suicide, or at least learn to accept what happened.

BH: I think that same thing about the suicide, but it's when Babe tries to kill herself that the sisters start to think, "We can't do this anymore, it's getting to be a thing in our family, we have to let that option go." Probably once your mother commits suicide, that is always an option. The door's always ajar in that way. I suppose I was trying to shut it. "We have each other."

AG: You often mention in interviews that your mother had a formative impact on your writing. In what way?

BH: Well, in that she was an actress and took me to the theater. She worked in theater, and I got to be backstage. Also, she would pick plays, and since this was the community theater in Jackson, they used a lot of Samuel French and Dramatists Play Service scripts, and I loved the dialogue. For a long time I didn't write descriptions; they would bore me. I didn't care about the trees and the smells. I preferred the people. It's really taken me quite a time to develop an appreciation for narrative. Plays are about people.

AG: Would you call your mother a feminist?

BH: Oh, sure. Oh, definitely. There's no question she's a feminist. I don't know if she would call herself that. To say she's a feminist is to box her in, because she's much more than that. Sometimes she can be the opposite of feminist and be, you know, real and practical.

AG: I get the feeling you don't have a high regard for being a feminist.

BH: I do have a high regard for feminists. But you could never box my mother into any label she wouldn't shoot out of.

AG: Did you want to be like your mother when you were growing up?

BH: She was such a goddess to me, it wasn't even a question. I just wanted to worship her, watch her put on her makeup. Talk to her. Adore her. And I still do.

AG: What was your father like?

BH: My father was very emotional, in an odd way for a man. He could get very angry or very moved, and be very demanding. He was not the type that would let you win at chess or tennis. "Why do you let the kid win?" Which was sort of a relief when I was a child, because once I did beat him at chess and I felt great, because I knew I'd really won.

He was a lawyer and a politician—he was in the state legislature. He loved history more than the law practice. He was a good lawyer, but he had dreams. I really regret not getting to know him longer as an adult. Part of him was terrified of children, and he had these four daughters. He had older brothers and not a clue as to how to deal with daughters. So he was always sort of shy and sad.

AG: You've said on occasion that he did not smile on your writing.

BH: Well, he died before I wrote *Crimes of the Heart*, so you can understand it.

AG: *Am I Blue*, which you wrote in 1973, is a good play by a young playwright.

BH: I guess he went to see that. There was another play on the bill—*The Bridgehead*—written by my friend Frederick Bailey, a wonderful writer. It was an incredibly violent Vietnam play set in Cambodia, where they shoot a Cambodian spy in the head at the end, and it was followed by my little play set in the French Quarter, where two virgins get together and dance at the end. And my father of course loved the guy play. He'd been in World War II; he was fascinated by the dialogue. It was real quick, quick male dialogue. So I got the distinct impression he preferred that play. But why wouldn't he? And then I wrote the book for a musical about World War II, about a 4F guy who has to stay home . . .

AG: *Parade*?

BH: *Parade*. And he didn't get it. His brother was killed in World War II, and I think he found it upsetting that the musical was fanciful. And not researched enough. Not serious enough. Had he been alive when I won the Pulitzer Prize . . . he would have liked *Crimes of the Heart*.

AG: From the moment *Crimes of the Heart* appeared, critics began to place your work in the tradition of Southern Gothic writers. Do you agree with them about that?

BH: I don't know what it means to agree with them or not agree with them. If they meant it kindly, I was grateful; if they mean it unkindly, I'm not. I don't particularly like to think in those big terms. I like to read something and glean from it what's personal and specific to me, and get a communion going between whoever is writing it and myself. To say, "Oh, it's Southern Gothic," it's like, "We've got that settled. We don't really have to feel what she's feeling or think about what she's thinking about, because it's in that tradition." I suppose that's useful to a degree, but I don't think, when I read Shakespeare, "He's Shakespearean." I think, "That's beautiful. That just blew my head off." You nab from different things that will help you tell a particular story. I don't say, "Okay, I'm going to follow this style exactly," unless that's going to help the story.

AG: When you were growing up, did you read the southern writers, like Faulkner or Flannery O'Connor?

BH: I didn't read them as much as you would think. I read Tennessee Williams, Eudora Welty. I guess they had more influence. Flannery O'Connor—I love her, but I didn't start reading her until after I wrote *Crimes of the Heart* and the reviews said, "You write like Flannery O'Connor." For some reason I totally missed O'Connor. But it would have been impossible to steal from her, because she writes too intuitively. She wouldn't be possible to copy.

AG: In terms of style, *Signature* and *Control Freaks* feel different from anything you wrote previously.

BH: All my plays seemed to be set in the past. Even *Crimes of the Heart. The Lucky Spot* does go back in time. *Abundance* goes to another century. So I decided to catapult myself into this century by going to the future. *Signature* and *Control Freaks* take place in L.A. I was trying to write more about now than about my nostalgic past. That's kind of how that happened.

AG: Was there a particular inspiration for *Signature*?

BH: Yes. I was walking down Melrose Avenue with a friend, and I was having a bad time, just depressed, and there was a graphologist on the street. He read my friend's handwriting, and it was "great, creative, spontaneous, genius," and mine was like, "Oh, yours is a measly life. Wretched and tormented." It hit me in a profound way. I knew it was not real, but in my reduced state I felt overwhelmed by this total stranger's version of me and my life. I started pondering the notion of signature. What is our signature, what do we leave that's important to us? Is it our work, our family, our life, our love? Is it the evil things we do? I pondered that notion. And L.A. seemed the perfect town where people are looking to leave a signature.

AG: You invented a new language for *Signature*.

BH: I'd been doing a lot of research, particularly for *The Lucky Spot* and *Abundance*. I researched *Abundance* for five years—I became obsessed with the late nineteenth century and the American West. And I loved the idea of not having to do research because—it hasn't happened. The notion of inventing language and new concepts was fun.

AG: You invent a world in great detail. There is a euthanasia hotline, video divorce, up-and-coming obits.

BH: Yes, but sometimes it makes no sense whatsoever. But I feel that'll do. That's the way that world is: the outfits they wear, the things they eat, their philosophies and art.

AG: Speaking of which, the "art philosopher," Boswell T-Thorp, is a futuristic critic who promotes his "Box Theory." What does "Boxdom" mean to you?

BH: "Boxdom" means a reduced way of thinking, in which you can put a box around anything. If you make a box big enough, it will fit around anything. If you make this truism big enough, it's a fear of the unknown, a fear of the mysterious and the spontaneous—it is what Boswell has. That's what this philosophy connotes.

But despite the futuristic world, I thought of the characters as very human in their fear of not being loved, fear of professional failure. Boswell and his terror of dying. Not getting along with your family. The wife of Boswell's brother, Max, leaves him, and Max goes crazy. She gets successful and dumps him. That seems quite the standard.

AG: Could you talk about the character of the Reader, the graphologist to whom Boswell goes for advice?

BH: The Reader is a mysterious character. She's hard to pin down, because she is a lunatic and a poet. And a criminal. All of those things that make people creative, that they struggle with. She's definitely a scam artist, but she's also intuitive and brilliant; she's using fortune-telling as an art rather than a science. And she does have a gift for it. But also, she's literally crazy and ends up in the insane asylum. Who do you listen to? Boswell chooses to listen to her and at a price.

AG: The play is wonderfully crazy, satiric, dark. In this universe you invent, people can't look at the sky directly; they see it on video. Outside this enclosed world is a desolate, threatening downtown, rolling in garbage. What have productions looked like?

BH: The first production, in Poughkeepsie, was very spare, because it was a workshop. But it was wonderful in its sort of coarseness. There was just a little box onstage, and some of the interns would walk on and play the people on the TV screens. There weren't actual videos. It was very simple and low-key, and I liked that a lot. The costumes were spectacular. Until they ran out of money, and then a couple of people didn't get costumes.

It was much more elaborate when it was later produced in Charlotte, North Carolina. And it was done [at Passage Theatre] in Trenton, New Jersey, and there was a nod to the futuristic 1930s. The way people envisioned the future in the thirties? That was a great concept.

AG: Why did that work so well?

BH: I don't know. I think that's the era I was meant to be in—the twenties or thirties. The production used odd funnel machines that looked like something people might have imagined in the thirties for the future. People came in and out of stalls that reminded you of bath houses in the 1920s.

AG: How did you come to write *Control Freaks*?

BH: I was working with a theater company in Los Angeles, Met Theatre, and I was thinking of writing it for actors there. Two men and two women. Also, I was getting to a point where I was tired of literal props and things. I just wanted everything to be more stylized and simpler. So I wanted to play around with the style of it. It was written for a simple space. Not a huge production necessary.

AG: Did Met Theatre produce it?

BH: Yes. First I directed it at Center Theater Ensemble in Chicago, then I directed it at Met.

AG: What performance style were you looking for?

BH: It was interesting, because I spent a lot of time paring things down when I was doing it in Chicago, but it still had a bend toward naturalism. When I directed it out here, there was this atmosphere of chaos that we created, and we really invented a style. The actors invented a way of walking. The sister and brother had a way of walking together that was almost like a two-headed dragon. The style was very organic, in the sense that it was from the characters and their inner worlds, but it was not at all naturalistic. I loved it.

AG: What kind of tone resulted from that approach?

BH: There was a starkness to it that unraveled. It went from a totally controlled, severe beginning to a totally chaotic, colorful end, littered with blood, stabbing, and screaming.

AG: Did you feel as though you had explored a new stylistic realm with *Signature* and *Control Freaks*?

BH: It's certainly not a conscious progression. But I do think things get stale for me, so I try something different. A new play I've written—*L-Play*—is twelve different scenes in twelve different styles. It's totally out there. A non-linear piece. I was exploring style. I get interested in something and start obsessing about it. *Family Week*, my newest play, takes place in the desert and is very stark. It's sort of lacking in poetry, as opposed to *Impossible Marriage*, which is more poetic and more of a return to a former style. I'm writing shorter plays. Which I like.

AG: In *Control Freaks*, one of the characters defecates in his backyard. This is something I never expected in a Beth Henley play. There has always been grotesquerie, but this is drawing the curtain back.

BH: Yeah, I know. It was great fun to write, but it was terrifying. Then sitting with my agent was horrifying, because he was befuddled. Actually, some of the grotesqueries in that play are more theatrical than literal. The idea of defecating behind a bush onstage can be much worse than seeing it. And then someone steps in it. It's just playing with the audience's senses.

AG: Comical.

BH: Well, there's a nod to whimsy.

AG: There's certainly whimsy at the end, when Sister flies off after taking her revenge on Carl. It would probably be clear if I saw a production, but how many people does this character split into?

BH: She's a split personality into three different people: Sister, Spaghetti, and Pinkie. Pinkie knows about Spaghetti, and Spaghetti knows about Pinkie and Sister, but Sister doesn't know about any of them. Holly Hunter did the part here, and she's so brilliant she came up with three totally different characters. Completely and utterly transformed herself within moments. It was staggering to be present.

AG: What personality did she project as Sister?

BH: Well, when Sister was talking about jury duty, she was proud, sort of plain, and a good girl. Wanted to please. Everything was held in but steaming underneath.

AG: And Spaghetti?

BH: Spaghetti was very sexual and wry and Mae West. Precise and cutting and cynical, and terrified of things.

AG: And Pinkie?

BH: Pinkie was the person who was the most whimsical. Innocent and flighty and always believing in the spirit.

AG: The split personalities feel like a woman's attempt to be nice on the outside, while inside, savagery reigns.

BH: The play definitely says something about women's and men's roles in the world. About constantly trying to fill them and not being able to. Carl trying to be the man who comes in with the tie and has his breakfast and goes off with the briefcase. Betty, Carl's wife, trying to be the little woman with the apron running around making breakfast and going shopping and having pretty underwear. The grotesquerie of trying to fill those roles.

AG: What is it like to live in Los Angeles and be in theater?

BH: It works well for me, because I like the notion of doing a play in New York and then coming back and either licking my wounds or just going on. Living here makes me think more about the work than about trying to be in the scene. I love New York; it remains the most romantic city for me on the planet. But I can't work there. It's too much fun. I don't know how people get anything done in New York City. In L.A. you're more isolated. I need a break from that energy.

AG: What amount of energy do you draw on to write plays and films?

BH: It takes more energy to write a play, because you start from scratch. Unless you're writing an original screenplay, which I've only done once. It's much harder to create all the characters and the story. I've mostly done adaptations of my own scripts or other people's for movies.

AG: Is your process at all the same when you're writing a play and a filmscript?

BH: In many ways, yes. But screenplays are in a lot of ways easier, because you're not dealing with time and space in the same way you are in the theater. You can go anywhere. You can have a thousand characters, you can show things visually. I used to have an aversion to descriptions, but now I love to tell things through images in a movie. It's easier than a play. There's something more restricting about a play, which makes writing a play harder but more interesting.

AG: When you adapted *Crimes* and *The Miss Firecracker Contest* for film, were there things you felt you gained or lost?

BH: The main thing to keep in mind is that the movie is not going to be the perfect production. It's going to be a version. Hopefully it will be a good version done as a movie. There is no ideal play version. A play is always transforming, and maybe the greatest production ever will be in a hundred years. Or it's already been in Japan, and I missed it.

It was fun filming *Miss Firecracker* because you could see the beauty contest. In the theater, it's theatrical to have that action offstage and have people come on to give accounts of it. But you wouldn't sit for that for a minute in a movie.

AG: In *The Miss Firecracker Contest*, as in *The Debutante Ball*, a character is concerned with beauty, although she gives up that dream.

BH: She gives up her dream to win the contest. When she comes in fifth or whatever. She gets to that point of, "What can we hope for? Not much, not too damn much, but there's always eternal grace." A letting go of the answers to what's going to make her life better and make people love her, and make her respectable and not Miss Hot Tamale. It's sort of the theme that people think they know the answers and try to fulfill that vision. "If I get to be Miss Firecracker, win the contest, I'll be loved." Which isn't true. But that makes her need to do it so extreme. Because she's not really doing it to win; she's doing it to be loved and accepted.

AG: But as with *The Debutante Ball*, it happens in the context of an American beauty ritual: the beauty pageant. Every American girl's dream.

BH: Well, I think everybody wants to be beautiful. I think we envy beauty. People get better seats in restaurants if they're beautiful. I'd love to be beautiful. I know it has its problems, but beauty is an asset. Just as intelligence is an asset. I've become more in awe of beauty the older I've gotten. I just love to look at somebody who's beautiful.

AG: Did you feel this way before you moved to Los Angeles?

BH: Well, no. I just think human beauty is great. It's sad that people go to extremes, but frankly, your looks mean something. That's a hard thing for me to admit because I hate to think I believe that, but I think it's a primal thing. Looks and presence and smell and the way you hold your body—all that counts.

AG: A version of that attitude exists in *Abundance*. Macon Hill prefers sexy, abusive Jack Flan to her husband. Jack is one of the most disgusting characters you have ever created.

BH: I know. I really love him.

AG: Why?

BH: Well, he's just so selfish. He represents that affliction women have with the wrong guy. Both women fall in love with him. You see it in life all the time. There's this wonderful guy who only has one eye whom nobody wants. And then there's this horrible guy. He's totally lazy, totally deranged, totally sexy, and everybody wants him. I've seen it over and over. "You should go for the guy without the eye." "I know. But I want that other one."

AG: The women start out as friends, but they betray each other.

BH: It is a cautionary tale. How not to live your life. But I was entranced by the idea of California during the Gold Rush, and going West, and seeking new life and new fortune, a new self even. In many ways, I guess we're always dealing with two parts of ourselves. A part that wants to be this great writer and totally independent, and a part that wants somebody to love and have them love us. For different reasons, each of the women in *Abundance* gives up her primary desire. Macon relinquishes her search for adventure, to get more land. Bess allows herself to be abused, as she struggles to be loved. It's almost insidious how we let our dreams go when we lose that energy to go on. It's frightening to me how we turn away from ourselves.

And another frightening element is how tangents just take some people. These people end up with things they didn't even want. They destroy their lives for things they don't want. I do feel sorry for human beings, because they start off wanting things simply and innocently and truthfully, and getting through life can be so treacherous.

AG: The characters in *Abundance* try to control each other in various ways. Could you talk a bit about people who have power in your plays and people who don't?

BH: I think nobody in my plays basically feels they're empowered. I think they're all struggling with that issue and doing cruel things to empower themselves, or get what they feel would be empowerment. Macon just can't stop flirting with Bess's husband and making herself into the powerful woman of the house. Not sharing the power or even relenting, but "You're under me and I'm over you, and that's how I'm willing to keep it in every small thing I do and say." The oh-so-small ways that Bess can't really notice. Until she does. And then she uses her power to destroy Macon by taking everything away from her.

AG: What does empowerment mean? Are there different kinds?

BH: I guess empowerment is acceptance of your own worth and value and not the fear that you're invisible. The belief that you count. Which is what so many of my characters want to feel. They want to shine, they need to show. The idea of just *being* totally eludes all of them.

AG: All of your characters?

BH: I'm not sure all of them. You do get somebody like William in *Signature* who understands that she is a mother and that she wants her children, and that gives her something very clear to be. Something clear to do with her life that is worthwhile. She likes cleaning the animals. But she can't help but love Boswell, and Boswell manages to make her feel invisible and worthless. Still, I think as a person, she has a clearer sense of self than many of the characters I write.

AG: The women in *Crimes of the Heart* have more of a sense of their worth at the end.

BH: Well, so many of their secrets have been revealed. Meg, that her career failed, and although she doesn't reveal it to her sisters, she admits to

Doc about having a breakdown. Lenny reveals to Charlie about her shrunken ovary, and she also reveals that Granddaddy didn't think she was worthy of him. Babe reveals the truth about having this affair, her husband beating her. Letting themselves be seen for who they are to each other makes them closer, or a little more empowered to just be.

AG: That's sort of what happens at the end of *Debutante* and the end of *The Miss Firecracker Contest*.

BH: The end of *The Wake of Jamey Foster*. Just letting go and sleeping. Just finding some peace in all the turmoil.

AG: And *Control Freaks*?

BH: Well, at the end of *Control Freaks*, Sister is empowered because she can finally be one person. Pinkie finds out about Sister, and then Sister finds out about Pinkie and Spaghetti, and they can all be together again, or at least try to reunite in a certain broad way.

AG: Whom do you write for?

BH: Gosh. Myself. Period. When I write plays. It's not true always for a film studio.

AG: How is that different?

BH: I've only written screenplays with a director involved, but it's more of a collaborative thing than totally on my own. With a play, I own the copyright, so that's for me. That's not to say I won't change things if a director asks, but I don't sit down and say, "I'm going to write this for young people, I'm going to write this for a New York audience"—because I don't really know what that is. Basically I'm writing something that I'm totally concerned with and interested in, and upset by. Generally I'm upset by something or haunted and intrigued by something. So it's, in that sense, a selfish occupation.

I spend a lot of time with characters before I even start writing, but a lot of times I've got a situation. A debutante ball, a wake, the Miss Firecracker Contest. Some event. *Abundance* is kind of a circular play to me. Writing about two mail-order brides who come out West with hopes and dreams, and what happens. So a little bit of both. In *Impossible Marriage* there's a marriage. *Family Week* is about going to a treatment center. A week in a treatment center.

AG: What kind of treatment center?

BH: Well, that's a good question. For people who can't handle the world.

AG: And *L-Play*?

BH: *L-Play* is really about trying to connect, trying to make the box. It's about how we go about finding anything solid in this world, where it can be the Marquis de Sade's world, Disney's world, Woody Allen's world, Degas' world. So many different perspectives on this one world that we live in. A look at "How can anybody have a clue as to what's happening in the world?" All the scenes start with an "L": Lunatic, Loser, Learner, Lost.

AG: Do you make detailed notes about characters?

BH: I spend a lot of time filling whole pages of notebooks. Several, several notebooks. Then I work from the notebooks, and I'll figure out, "Well, this applies to this character," and put it under that character, "and here's an image for that character, and here's a piece of dialogue that character might say." I really work out of total chaos before I even start writing. I have a thing with images. What are the themes? I write those down without questioning anything. I write everything down without thinking about it. Some of it doesn't apply, but I don't censor. And style. I write possible style things, or books to read. But mainly on the characters. The characters' things are really extensive.

AG: Physical as well as internal things about characters?

BH: Yes. And dialogue. Even some scenes will come to me. I'll say, "This thought, or this philosophy, would go to this character. This character I see doing this image." I write in notebooks and then I write on my computer, and then I take it to a computer typist, who types it up neatly.

AG: When do you know that you are ready to sit down and write?

BH: It's a feeling of a certain deep amount of self-loathing that finally I can no longer ignore.

AG: Have you made a living as a playwright?

BH: I've made a living as a writer. I haven't figured out if I would have made a living as a playwright. Early on, I sold *Crimes of the Heart* as a screenplay for a considerable amount of money. So as a playwright, I probably could have made a living, but it would be very tight. This would not be my office, this would be my house. Because it's tough. You're lucky if you can sell a play to the screen and make some cash.

AG: Has being a woman helped your career or hurt it or not figured at all?

BH: I think it has hurt and helped. It hurts in that the stories I write are from a woman's perspective and feature women primarily, although not in *Signature*. And there are just more men in charge of theaters and more men directors, more men actors, and they can't help themselves. Like my father. I see a movie about Vietnam soldiers where I want to see a movie about somebody going out on a date. I want to see a woman. My son likes to see shows about little children. If a play is totally great, by some genius writer,

I don't care if it's about men or women. I saw *Art*, which I loved, which is about men. But if I'm just going to see a play—is there a woman in it? Oh, good, at least there's one woman in it.

On the other hand, being a playwright is such an obscure profession, and being a woman playwright is even more obscure. Nobody would have the guts to do a male playwrights book. They'd have to be more politically correct. Different races and at least two women, so we might have a chance to be one of the two women.

AG: Does it bother you that this book is exclusively women?

BH: No. No, I'm relieved because I'm in it. Did you ever read Tillie Olsen's *Silences*? It's such a beautiful book. I do believe so many women have been silenced. I think it's great to give them a voice. Growing up with all these John Wayne things—not that I don't love John Wayne—but . . .

AG: With your son, you may have a lot of that.

BH: I know. I'm falling in love with trucks for the first time. And machinery. He's transfixed with the beauty of machines. I've never noticed. I don't care what I drive as long as it goes. But he can look at trucks, their design, their beauty.

AG: A number of the women I've talked with have complained about how critics see their work.

BH: I only read the *New York Times* review of *Impossible Marriage*, because it came to my hotel and I couldn't resist. I didn't read any others. I know the play got mixed reviews, and that's all I can stand to know. That seems wimpy, but I've got to go back and write. Even when I get a good review, I'm of such weak character that it can obsess me in the wrong direction. I can start thinking that I'm just too wonderful to work.

AG: Did that happen after *Crimes of the Heart*?

BH: No, but I do recall reading quite a few more reviews for *Crimes of the Heart* than for *The Wake of Jamey Foster*. Actually I have a kind of contract with myself to always have a new play started before I have a play done in New York. Because no matter how bad the reviews are, I don't want the critics to have the power to make that be my last play. I want to be into another play that I'll finish.

AG: Is there life after winning the Pulitzer? Was it hard to come back from that?

BH: It was harder than I thought at the time, because I was really busy. There were repercussions from winning that I denied, and they came back to haunt me. But it's hard to be anything but unspeakably grateful for winning the Pulitzer Prize. It made me think of myself as a writer. It made my family excited. It gave me a life. I get to have a life as a writer. I was working in the TRW parts department, and not to have to waste my life doing day jobs was a total gift. And it was glamorous and ridiculous, and I was young enough not to take it that seriously. I remember thinking, "I could win a Pulitzer Prize. It must not be that much at all." I'm glad I'm forty-seven and not longing to win a Pulitzer Prize.

AG: Do you have advice for women who want to write plays?

BH: I love them. I love them if they're going to write, period. And then if they want to write in the theater, I really love them. It's a great art form. It's very tough, but it's a life. Even if you fail at being a writer, it's worth the failure. Because things will be revealed to you that would not be revealed by doing something safe. I have many friends who are artists and actors, and maybe it's not working out and they need a day job, but I look at their lives compared to those of people who stay in one place and are safe and have insurance and big cars, and I'd take the artist's life. Maybe I'm saying that because I don't have to work a day job. But I think if you have a desire to do something, you're blessed. The worst thing I've experienced is having passion but not knowing what for. But to find something you want to do. . . . And with writing, you're particularly lucky, because you can just do it. It's not like wanting to be an actor or film director, which take some support. You're just so lucky if you want to be a writer.

Expressing "The Misery and Confusion Truthfully": An Interview with Beth Henley

Jackson R. Bryer / 2002

From *American Drama* 14 (Winter 2005): 87–109. Reprinted by permission of Leah Stewart, Department Head, Department of English, University of Cincinnati.

Beth Henley's first professionally produced play, *Crimes of the Heart*, won the Pulitzer Prize and the New York Drama Critics' Circle Award in 1981 after a successful New York production (prior to New York, it had been done in Louisville, Baltimore, and St. Louis in 1979 and 1980). Her first produced play, *Am I Blue* (1974), was written while she was an undergraduate student at Southern Methodist University. Her works for the stage since *Crimes of the Heart* include *The Miss Firecracker Contest* (1980), *The Wake of Jamey Foster* (1981), *The Debutante Ball* (1985), *The Lucky Spot* (1987), *Abundance* (1989), *Signature* (1990), *Control Freaks* (1992), *Revelers* (1994), *L-Play* (1995), *Impossible Marriage* (1998), *Sisters of the Winter Madrigal* (2001), and *Exposed* (2002). This interview was conducted on September 30, 2002, in the Ina & Jack Kay Theatre of the Clarice Smith Performing Arts Center at the University of Maryland; the audience was composed of undergraduate and graduate students and faculty members.

Jackson Bryer: Can you start by telling us about your first exposure to the theater? As I recall, you became interested in theater through your mother, who was an actress. Talk a little bit about your early interest in theater and also about your time as a student of theater.

Beth Henley: I grew up in Jackson, Mississippi, really in suburbia, so my mother was in community theater plays. They were so magical for me, and one of the most exciting experiences was to go in and see little houses that were built for people to act in and then were torn down. I would also help her with her lines. I remember when she got to play Blanche DuBois and I got to hear those words over and over again when she was trying to learn her lines. Also, I liked to help her edit things. If she was doing a reading for a club or something, we'd have to make Blanche's speeches longer and cut out Stanley's—so I got into editing. Then, when I was a senior in high school, I was kind of bereft and she put me in an acting class. What I loved about the acting class was that you got to think all day long about a person that wasn't you, and figure out why they were sad and what they wanted, what they dreamed. I just loved being divorced from my own wretchedness. Then I went off to Southern Methodist University in Dallas. They had a really wonderful theater department. I regret that I was so not grateful at the time to my professors. We're sort of innocently arrogant about just being young. The class I liked the best, that I think helped me the most, was my movement class because when I got out of high school, I was very hunched over. In movement class, you had to lie on the floor and get your alignment in to pass the class. You had to stand on your head for, I think, three minutes. That transformed me in a way that's hard to speak about. I also took Stage Combat, and I took a wonderful class in Theater Styles where you'd do the Greeks and make your own mask. I remember sitting there with a death mask over me with straws coming out of my nose. I had a really good Theater History class that, at the time, was excruciating. It was at nine in the morning, and I would sometimes go in jeans and my bedroom slippers. But actually that's kind of the way I learned about history. The only foothold I have in world history is through theater history.

JB: All this time, you were doing this in order to become an actress?

Henley: Yes. I was sort of in the acting program. How I got in the acting program is a miracle. Oh, I know how I got in. Anyone could get in! You had to do a general audition for the school when you got in, and I chose to do, brilliantly I think, Willie from *This Property Is Condemned*. And then I did Macbeth in *Macbeth*, which was the only Shakespeare I knew. Somehow, I was in the acting department.

JB: But it sounds like when you talk about your experience with your mother that, even if you weren't conscious of it, you were paying pretty close attention to the words.

Henley: Yes.

JB: Had you been interested in writing at all or were you always interested initially in being a performer—probably because your mother was a performer? Were you conscious of any interest in writing?

Henley: I wrote a play in sixth grade called "Swing High, Swing Low." It was about Dolly, a girl who lives in the suburbs and goes to New York to be an artist. Actually, the character was named Dolly because when she came to New York, they said, "Hello, Dolly, hello!" And the parents back in the suburb were, "Kids. What's the matter with kids today?" I tried to direct as well as write this. I wasn't performing, and we got boys involved. It ended in a debacle. It never ever got on anywhere. It was a summer project. The next thing I wrote was in a writing class at my school. It was about a poor woman who worked at a dime store and who was all alone for Christmas in Laurel, Mississippi. I hadn't finished it and the teacher said, "Just read it anyway." I got up to read it and I was so pained by its inadequacies that I crumpled up the paper and threw it on the floor and ran down the hallway and hid in the restroom for the rest of the afternoon. It's really interesting that whenever you do something that is so out of character, like having an emotional outburst, that you don't get in trouble. I guess they were horrified by the hysterics of a junior high schooler. After that I thought, "You know what? You're not smart enough to write." But when I got to SMU and decided to take a playwriting class, I said this isn't a bad idea. If I write characters, they could be as dumb as me, and I don't have to be very smart. It was kind of enlightening to become a playwright. I wrote a play called *Am I Blue*, which is about a young guy who's very straight and his fraternity's sending him to a whorehouse on his eighteenth birthday and he's a virgin. He meets this young sixteen-year-old girl who's all alone on the night of her prom and lives a very chaotic life. That was my first play that was actually done.

JB: After SMU you went to graduate school at the University of Illinois. What was the impetus behind that?

Henley: The impetus behind going to graduate school was a year after graduating from college spent in Dallas working at the dog food factory and Bank America and not having met success in my chosen field, which at that point was being an actress. I think I had a job in a children's theater. I taught badly because I was into nihilism at the time and that's just not where you go with teaching. Then an old professor of mine went to run the art school at the University of Illinois in Champaign. He said he would give me a scholarship to go there if I would teach. I got there and somehow miraculously lived on $200 a month, which was what I got—and I was happy to have it. I did realize after being there for a year—I didn't complete my MFA—that if they had teachers as bad as me it wasn't a good sign. So I had to move on. I was just restless with being in school; so I went out to Los Angeles.

JB: You've spoken in other interviews about a time when several successful directors came to SMU. Can you speak a little bit about what it means to a person who is an undergraduate in theater to have an actual, successful theater professional present? What kind of impression did it make on you?

Henley: A searing impression. Somehow I got to be one of five or six actors that the directors would use as guinea pigs at this directing colloquium, where people pay to listen to and watch the directors direct. It was painful because I was a really bad actress. I remember I had just done an awful rendition of Juliet, and William Gaskill, this British director, said, "Now won't you just sit on that box and don't move!" Joseph Chaikin came and he read some stuff and he was so brilliant; that was glorious! I've never ever seen anything like that in my life. The spirit, the sort of human, animal, god energy of that guy was just unforgettable. Joseph Anthony came and we saw his film *Tomorrow*, which Horton Foote wrote. They were so artistic.

JB: Another story that you've told—and I don't know when this happened chronologically—is when you went to New York to see a production of *The Cherry Orchard*. When was that?

Henley: I was in college. We were having auditions the following year, so this was after my sophomore year. In the fall, I was going to have to audition for Chekhov's *Three Sisters*. I was reading it and it made no sense. I didn't get it. I probably had a bad translation anyway. I was like "How can I get into this character? Who are these people? They're stiff; they're not people you can really like." Then I went to see an all African-American production of *The Cherry Orchard* with Gloria Foster and James Earl Jones as Lopakhin. I finally got it when he says, "They used to tell me I wrote like a pig." When he buys the cherry orchard, it's the happiest and most devastating moment of his life. It's so big how he did it, and I started having this sort of epileptic fit in the audience. I was crying and screaming; I was really euphoric because I understood how things could be simultaneously tragic and comic and so alive and so real. After that I understood Chekhov, but didn't get cast in *Three Sisters*. I did go on to write *Crimes of the Heart*, which is loosely based on *Three Sisters*.

JB: Don't you think also that the quality in Chekhov of simultaneous comedy and seriousness is something that characterizes many of your plays?

Henley: I like that edge. I like when I see it in writing if it's over the edge. Even something like the Marx Brothers is sort of brutal in how funny it is. Some really good things kind of swing both ways and I like to see people that can swing really, really, really sad and horrible and terrible and really, really, really beautiful and funny. I think Chekhov does that like nobody else. Shakespeare's up there, but . . .

JB: Isn't there something inherently southern about that too, about combining the most grotesque and serious kinds of things with the funny, about being able to see the humor in the grotesque? Why is that? What is there about the South that makes that particularly true?

Henley: That's a good question. I think that people have to be able to see two sides of the coin to survive because it is a racist society, and yet you're being raised by racists. So what are you going to do? There are these people who are feeding you, but they're chauvinist and racist. You kind of have to get a little perspective. You can't go with "They're just evil," and you can't go "Oh, I believe them, I love them." You kind of have to go "This is a little more complicated."

JB: You have to see them with two different sets of eyes.

Henley: At least two!

JB: Was *Crimes of the Heart* the second play you wrote after *Am I Blue*? Were there other plays in between?

Henley: I wrote one play that was only recently done. It was buried in a trunk. It's called *Sisters of the Winter Madrigal*. It was interesting for me to see it done after so many years because I wrote it and I didn't realize what a rage I was in. I always think, "Oh, I'm not a feminist. I like men." But in this play there are these two sisters: one's a whore and one's a cow herder. One wants to marry the shoemaker's son, but the king wants her because of her hair and she ends up with her ear bit off, and the other one ends up with her arm chopped off. It's very Bergmanesque; there are all kinds of pieces of them in the end.

JB: Who did it?

Henley: A friend of mine did it, Frederick Bailey. He and I had had a double bill back when my play was at SMU. We did his Vietnam play *The Bridgehead* and my *Blue* play about two virgins. His play was first and ended with somebody getting shot in the head. Then they had to clean up the blood for my play. It wasn't a perfect double bill! But he is one of my favorite writers, and he'd written a play and he wanted to do these two plays on the same bill; his new play is called *Dirty, Ugly People and Their Stupid Meaningless Lives*. I said sign me up! So he directed both of these pieces and so that's how it got done.

JB: What was it like seeing an early play like that? Do you say to yourself, "How could I have done that?"—or were you rather pleased with it?

Henley: I was touched that I was that enraged. I was happy to know I had that rage and happy that I'd written it then. That's what I was saying earlier. I'm always happy to have written anything because it's kind of a mark of who you were at the time if it's even vaguely honest—though you could never redo it. I couldn't recapture that sort of frivolous rage. It had its moments, so I was really pleased.

JB: Talk a little bit about how you came to write *Crimes of the Heart*.

Henley: My friend Frederick Bailey was doing *Gringo Planet*, a play of his, at the La MaMa Hollywood and he produced the whole thing for $500. I thought, "Maybe I could do that." I'd written a screenplay ["The Moonwatcher," which years later became the film *Nobody's Fool*] while I was out there and I said, "This would be perfect for Sissy Spacek. I love her! I'll call up her agent and see about her reading it." So the agent says, "We don't take unsolicited material. When you get a producer to produce it, we'll be happy to look at it." Then I called up producers and they said they didn't take unsolicited material. It was a Catch-22 thing. I didn't really know how to get it to a producer or how to get it to an agent. Nobody's going to look at it unless it's a success. I wrote *Crimes of the Heart* kind of because I thought, "At least I can do this with my friends for my friends for $500 at the La MaMa." That's why in the very first draft I don't have them cut into the cake because I'm thinking of the budget! We can't have a different cake every night, so the lights go down as they cut it. That's also why it was one set, a kitchen, and modern clothes. I was really thinking practically when I wrote that play; I was thinking about producing it on my own.

JB: Was it done at La MaMa in Los Angeles?

Henley: No, it wasn't done at La MaMa. I didn't have $500! Actually, Bailey, who is so instrumental in my life, had won the Actors Theatre of Louisville playwriting contest with his play *The Bridgehead* the year before, and he sent my play in and it won the Actors Theatre of Louisville contest.

JB: And that was the first production?

Henley: That was the first production, and they were very adamant about it not having been produced anywhere. That's one sort of annoying thing to me about this. Plays are so much more special if they've never ever had a production, but I think you can really work on a play and make it better with each production. Anyway, that was the first place it was done.

JB: What was that like?

Henley: It was terrifying, number one. I remember not knowing what a cue light was because I'd never worked in a production that was high-class enough to have a cue light. They kept saying, "Yeah, we'll do it with a cue light." And I was like, "Yeah, yeah, the cue light. What's the cue light?" But I had two glorious actresses in the parts of Lenny and Meg. Kathy Bates played the original Lenny and this wonderful actress, Susan Kingsley, played

Meg and she was a genius at it. I don't know if I want to get into the ugliness of this, but the director's wife played Babe, and she wasn't as good as the others.

JB: What is it like when you go and you're involved in a production about which you have very definite ideas, and it isn't going entirely the way you want it to go?

Henley: It so depends on the production. The most glorious thing about working in the collaborative art is when you have somebody like Susan Kingsley or Kathy Bates who are better than your play. And you're just "Ahh." That is just extraordinary. You have a director that sees things in the play that you didn't envision and knows how to heighten them and move the rhythm of it and to cover up any faults and make all of the assets really glimmer. I'm very into the first production of a show. I love to see the rehearsals, to sit there throughout the entire rehearsal and hear it over and over because with repetition you can get a sense of what the rhythm of the lines is. When I first started, it was much harder because, in the very first production of the play, I'm thinking, "I really don't know what is the director's fault, what's my fault, what's the actor's fault." It was very hard; they'd say, "Cut this" and I would say, "But I'm not certain that needs to be cut." Now I've gotten a lot clearer on how to sort that out, I think.

JB: And how do you sort all that out?

Henley: I have a lot of meetings in my living room and hear it again.

JB: In other words, today you'll go to rehearsal having a lot more ideas of how things should be, and how they should sound? With *Crimes of the Heart,* when you got to Louisville was that really the first time you had heard the play read?

Henley: I think I did have a reading at my house.

JB: But you hadn't worked on it?

Henley: I hadn't thought of the process, of somebody telling me to cut a line. I love to cut. My fault now is making my plays too short.

JB: Has that been a result of writing a lot of plays?

Henley: It's the result of writing plays and feeling the audience get restless. That to me is like "I want it to move. I want it to move!" Pace, you know. I don't want you looking restless. Because it's so excruciating when you're in the theater and you can feel that "Why isn't this over?"

JB: *Crimes of the Heart* was such a success. It must have been difficult to write the next play. You had a lot to live up to at that point, didn't you?

Henley: When I went to Louisville, I had started on a new play, *The Miss Firecracker Contest.* That was always my inclination, to start on a new play before the other one gets done, because at least you'll have something to go back to if that play gets trashed. It took a long time for *Crimes of the Heart* to get on. It was done in Louisville and in Baltimore, and then in St. Louis. It was round and about before it was actually a big success, so I had time to work on other plays.

JB: Is *Crimes of the Heart* the play through which you got involved with Holly Hunter?

Henley: No. Holly auditioned for *The Wake of Jamey Foster*. There was a part of a seventeen-year-old orphan who's a burn victim, who's a romantic interest of one of the boys. It was so bizarre because Holly and I got stuck in an elevator; we were trapped in this elevator together at this very first meeting. So I thought, "Hmmm." I knew who she was because someone had said that this wonderful, wonderful actress was coming in, but I was too shy to talk very much. We got free. I loved her audition so much for *The Wake* that when we were replacing Mary Beth Hurt in the part of Meg on Broadway in *Crimes of the Heart,* I got her to do that, to be that replacement, but with the stipulation that when *The Wake* started she'd get out of *Crimes of the Heart.* So *Crimes* was the first play of mine she was in; then she was in *The Wake.*

JB: Some actors and actresses have a particular affinity to certain playwrights, and it seems to me that there's something about the way Holly Hunter presents herself onstage that makes her particularly good at the roles you write.

Henley: Absolutely. I'm really blessed.

JB: Have you ever written anything with her in mind?

Henley: Yes, I have. A play called *Control Freaks.* We were working at a theater in Los Angeles together, the Met Theatre, and I wrote a play for her and three other actors and she ended up doing it in L.A. She was wonderful. So that play I specifically wrote for her.

JB: Do you tend to do that often—write for specific actors or actresses?

Henley: Not really, no. Not generally.

JB: How would you describe your relationship with Holly Hunter? When she comes to the play, does she discuss the character with you a lot? Or is it more a matter of watching her and saying things to her through the director?

Henley: It kind of varies because we've worked together over so many years. She particularly likes to explore while she's working and not get a lot of feedback until she's reached the limits of her exploration. It's very fearless and sometimes very bad. That's another point about running a play with actors. They'll risk being just terrible. Holly will come in with ideas that are just brilliant and she'll come in with this idea that makes no sense; she likes to really go with her instincts. Once she has those instincts in play, then you can shape more.

JB: Along with Holly Hunter, you've worked with some other tremendous actors over the course of your career, and you write so richly for actors. What do these great actors have in common in terms of making strong choices for your work?

Henley: That's a good question. I don't know. It's a deep, deep commitment and passion for investigating every facet of every moment. With Holly, it's the things that she'll do for the play, like learn to play the harp, learn to tap dance, learn to twirl a gun around, learn to play the piano.

JB: Have you ever dealt with actors where in the end you know they're going to come up with something really, really good, but to get there you're going to have to let them do that kind of fearless exploration?

Henley: When we were doing *Control Freaks*, it was all about being out of control in rehearsals and then doing a play that is so utterly controlled. Every moment is basically choreographed, and then it explodes into this big mess—but it's a very thoughtful mess.

JB: I've heard playwrights and directors say that one of the talents of being a director and not simply a playwright at rehearsals is knowing that different actors work in different ways.

Henley: Yes, you have actors that are all over the board in how they've been trained and what they like and what they are used to or how they perform best.

JB: Do you speak to actors directly, or go through the director most of the time?

Henley: I'll speak to them directly if the director trusts me or if the director says, "What do you think of that?" Sometimes the director is so burned out talking to the actors, they'll say, "Now, Beth, what did you tell me?"

JB: Would you know in that situation if you had been given permission to talk to the actors or not?

Henley: Yes. I feel very much it's all sort of diplomatic and a sense of trust and deep respect. You can't just go in there and open your mouth until the cast and director feel comfortable with you.

JB: It took you a while to get away from the South, dramatically. But you have with the most recent plays not written as much about the South. What was the source of that change?

Henley: I guess, not living in the South. My first few plays took place in the South and even *The Lucky Spot* was in the thirties but in Louisiana. Then

I moved further into the past into the Wyoming Territory for *Abundance* and then I just decided to thrust myself into the future and wrote *Signature*, which takes place in Los Angeles in 2052. Then I wrote *Control Freaks*, which is very much a Los Angeles play.

JB: You have said that one of the reasons you live in Los Angeles is because no one will bother you; everybody there is involved in film and so you can do your own thing and not feel you're competing with all the people in New York, where there are playwrights on every street corner.

Henley: Part of that is that New York has proved to be too much fun for me to live and work; I love New York so much. It's my favorite city, but it's kind of nice to go back to Los Angeles and just not be inundated with what is the scene and what is hot or what is not. You're just left on your own in Los Angeles, and you can have a nicer place with a yard there.

JB: You have also said that it's a little frustrating in L.A. because everything is film.

Henley: It's not a theater town. It's film and television and that's—entertainment-wise—the heart of the city. Often people will be in plays to get into film and television; whereas, in Chicago or Seattle or New York, they're just in the plays because that's what their passion is.

JB: Do you feel that the people in L.A. support theater? Are there audiences or do you find them so involved with film that theater is a kind of secondary medium to them?

Henley: I tried to start a theater in L.A. and failed miserably, but I was probably not meant to raise money.

JB: Are the theaters in L.A. supported pretty well? Do they get audiences?

Henley: The big places like the Taper do, but some of the smaller theaters, no.

JB: Is it frustrating? When you get your plays done, you don't usually get them done in L.A., do you?

Henley: Not usually, although occasionally.

JB: Isn't it more likely to have a reading of a new play of yours in Washington or New York than in L.A.?

Henley: Absolutely.

JB: Are playwrights treated badly in Hollywood when they write for films or are they being treated with more respect by producers and directors than they have been in the past?

Henley: Here's the thing you have to know about being a screenwriter. I love writing for the screen. I love that they pay you a lot of money. You get to meet fancy people and eat really good food. But here's the thing: What you do as a screenwriter is you sell your copyright. As a novelist, as a poet, as a playwright, you maintain your copyright. If you write a fabulous screenplay, they pay you this chunk of money; it's theirs, they own it. I've always emotionally tried to detach myself from my screenwriting and just love doing it, enjoy doing it, and I try to do adaptations. I did write a couple of original screenplays, but I'd rather write plays. If you are a screenwriter, they can fire you at any moment, and the actors can change your dialogue. It's really a director's medium, where theater is much more a writer's medium; in theater, you have actor approval, you have director approval, you have not necessarily design approval, but at a point you do. They can't change anything, even stage directions, without your approval. Of course they have, I suspect, but at least not when you're on the premises!

JB: What was it like adapting *Crimes of the Heart* as a screenplay? Didn't you have to detach yourself a little from that, almost have to not be the playwright who wrote the original play?

Henley: That's a long story. I was working on *Crimes of the Heart* with Jonathan Demme, and they made us fly in from New York, to have a meeting where the producer told me I was the worst person to write this because I had written the play. So I tried to open it up, and I wrote a version of it and they said it was too much like the play. Jonathan Demme quit on principle because he didn't want to be the person to ruin this beautiful play. Then a couple of years later, I was in London and Bruce Beresford was hired to do *Crimes of the Heart* and I said, "They don't want me." He said, "Well, I want you and I told them I wanted you. And I read Demme's script and it veered too far from the play." I said, "Bruce, I got fired from it!" He said, "Oh, they don't know what they want." So I got rehired with Bruce Beresford, who has brought a lot of plays to film. And he was lovely to work with and it was great; but it was on the verge of being catastrophic.

JB: It sounds like he had great respect for you as the writer of the play.

Henley: He's just a fun, smart guy who respects people; he wasn't afraid of any idea you had because he knows he's really smart. He's really experienced in what he's doing and he knows what he wants.

JB: And how much of that screenplay actually survived to be the screenplay of *Crimes*? Was the screenplay that survived pretty much the screenplay you wrote?

Henley: Very much, because he was very good as well. He wanted it short. He said, "Let's keep it short."

JB: But that's not always the case, is it?

Henley: No.

JB: Don't you have the kind of horror stories about Hollywood that other playwrights tell?

Henley: My horror stories are the screenplays that didn't get made; you get frustrated with that, but you still get paid this enormous amount for them. I figure that helps me with my theater work.

JB: Talk a little bit about your play *L-Play*.

Henley: I couldn't think what to write for a play. I was really fragmented in my life and so I kept scribbling. It's really painful when you're trying to come up with an idea for a play. I decided I would write a play called *L-Play*, which would have twelve different scenes, twelve totally different characters, and twelve different theatrical styles because I was into exploring different styles. The only unifying factor is that the names of the scenes start with an "L." This was completely stupid! But I proceeded in the face of this stupidness and it was really fun because it was a bit like an exercise for me. It was struggling with the fragmented nature of reality, like who is real, Donald Duck or Bergman, or just the different realities that come together in the fragmented world. The Learner and the Lunatic are the only reoccurring characters.

JB: You have said that frequently you write plays about characters who express some part of yourself you wouldn't express any other way. Often, it's part of yourself you're afraid of or that you wouldn't go out in public with on your own.

Henley: The girl, Ashby, in *Am I Blue* didn't get invited to the prom and she is all alone and feels isolated. I did have friends at that age, but what you fear is not having friends. You fear that part of you is not acceptable to be exposed and I think that's a lot of what I look for in my characters. I wonder what their greatest fear is and what their greatest dream is and what the teaching is between the two. Usually their fear is holding them back from their dream, and their dream is giving them hope to fight against their fear. A lot of what I like to write about are things I'm confused about. When I was younger I kept thinking that I needed to write an important play, that I needed to help people understand something and improve the world and enlighten people—except I didn't know anything. This was the big problem. And then I read where Ionesco said: "Oh, I just like to write about my own confusion." I said, "Well, I can do that; I'm certainly confused." It was like this weight was lifted. I don't have to solve anything because there is nothing to solve. It's all a big mystery and if you can express the misery and the confusion truthfully, that might be something worth looking at.

JB: Too often we're looking for answers in plays when plays are really asking you to think. They're not actually looking to solve problems for you.

Henley: People say, "How do you want the audience to respond to your play?" And I say, "As individuals!" I would feel horrible if everyone felt the same thing by the end of the play, and didn't have particular thoughts, particular notions, if some people weren't upset about something and some people enthralled by something.

JB: How do you start a play?

Henley: I think if you're any good you're aware of the notion that you can't start where you want to. I use a ton of notebooks. I write what is the theme and then I write all sorts of different themes; some of them never end up being the theme at all, and then I have images that I see. I see some stage images; like for *Crimes of the Heart*, I see a knife cutting into a lemon. I see there is a birthday cake. I'm not sure whose birthday it is. Or I see somebody roped; somebody's going to hang themselves, but I don't know if they're going to live or not. Images. I do images. I do theme. I do the style, and I've really gotten to be much more cognizant about the style. I have a section in my notebook just called "dialogue," things I've heard that are intriguing to me, or read, that might go in this play. And then there's dialogue for this particular character—what do they do, what is their dream, and what are their feelings? There's preparation before you do it; getting to page one is quite a mess and takes, for me, the most time and is the hardest because they're not talking to you yet. You're kind of planting the seeds so they will talk. When they start talking, don't edit them for a while; let them talk.

JB: Do you know where a play is going when you start?

Henley: No. That's the scariest thing and the most thrilling.

JB: In other words, when you saw that birthday cake, you had no idea that was the end of the play?

Henley: No, I didn't know that was the end of the play. I did know by the time I got to the third act that Babe was going to try and kill herself, but I didn't know that she wasn't going to kill herself up until the moment she didn't. I thought, "No, it's going to be a tragedy. I thought it was a comedy, but I guess it's going to be a tragedy because it's a tragedy when a character kills himself." And then it turned. I always think that although this is very frustrating for the writer, it's really key to writing something good because if you don't know where it's going, that means the audience doesn't know where it's going either. You have to be clever enough to take it to a wonderful authentic place by just letting the characters tell you where they need to go.

JB: When you start, do you know the general subject matter?

Henley: Usually, but in the play I'm writing now, as well as in *Exposed*, it wasn't that clear. It became clear in *Exposed* that this is all taking place in a winter solstice, the darkest night of the year. The play I'm working on now I call "The Men's Play" because all I knew was I wanted to write a play about men because I don't understand men anyhow.

JB: When you write a play, do you have a specific message you want your reader to get from it? What do you want people to get from *Crimes of the Heart*?

Henley: When I write a play, I don't—since I have no idea what the play's going to be—have a message in mind. But in looking at *Crimes of the Heart*, I can say that my impression as a theatergoer would be that it is a play about these three sisters coming to grips with a lot that happened in their past that left them stunted in different ways and going on from there in the final moment of the play. That's pretty bad, but that's why I'm not a theater critic!

JB: Talk a little bit about the role of Barnette in that play. If you were there while an actor was doing the part, what would you say to him?

Henley: I would say, "Don't err on going too sweet." He's very, very committed to winning this case. He's very fiery and there's also a rage in him. Barnette's often wrongly done as a sweet old southern boy, and it's kind of icky.

JB: How much do you feel like you consciously engage with work from prior literary traditions? You mentioned that *Crimes of the Heart* is based on *Three Sisters*, and I was wondering if you intentionally wrote it that way or not.

Henley: I think I probably did it subliminally with *Crimes of the Heart*. In fact, I know I did since I love *Three Sisters* so much and I'd rehearsed it over and over again, seeking the part of Irina. It was in my subconscious. Although I must admit that more recently, in the play *Impossible Marriage*, I remember deliberately wanting to steal from Oscar Wilde. I went and read everything he wrote and I said, "Give me some of that and some of that. Sprinkle it on me." So I don't know. It's not usually very conscious, but it can be.

JB: What other kinds of dramatic literature influence you?

Henley: This is going to sound so boring, but Shakespeare. I've taken five years of Shakespeare class and . . . the more I just want to know him.

JB: What have you, as a playwright, learned from Shakespeare?

Henley: Shakespeare is one of those people, like Magic Johnson in basketball. You can't learn really because what they do is too superior to what humans can do. You just sit back in awe. Some playwrights you can read and kind of go, "Oh, here's how they do that." But Shakespeare . . . how'd he write that? Oh, it's so humbling.

JB: Are any of your characters based on people you know—or knew?

Henley: Sometimes they evolved from a couple of people I know. A couple of times I've said that person is so appealing to me I'm going to write a character just like them. That's only happened a couple of times. But by the time the character comes out in the play, it's no longer the person at all. People say, "I'm Babe, aren't I?" And I say, "We just met!"

An Interview with Beth Henley

Dan O'Brien / 2011

From *HowlRound Theatre Commons*, September 29, 2011, Emerson College, howlround.com. Reprinted by permission. Dan O'Brien is a playwright, poet, essayist, and librettist. His critically acclaimed plays have been produced in the US and abroad. He is the author of four volumes of poetry and the essay collection *A Story That Happens: On Playwriting, Childhood, & Other Traumas* (2021).

Dan O'Brien: It's the middle of August, the middle of the afternoon, and Beth Henley and I are sitting in a coffee shop in Westwood in Los Angeles. We're a week or so back from teaching together at the Sewanee Writers' Conference in Sewanee, Tennessee, so maybe I'm feeling some withdrawal, from the conference, the cocktails, talking with Beth. But this question of southern writing and southern writers, so-called, has been on my mind. . . . Are you cool talking about what it means to be a southern playwright?

Beth Henley: Yeah, with the caveat of "whatever that means."

Dan: Did you see a lot of theater growing up?

Beth: I probably saw more than the average Mississippian circa 1960. My mom was an actor; she worked in the community theater at New Stage in Jackson, so I read a lot of plays, Samuel French and Dramatists Play Service, because they were short and I liked dialogue. That was something of an anomaly, I think. Most people from Jackson don't become playwrights because it's such a peculiar sort of job. You have to go to New Orleans, or somewhere.

Dan: Or New York. I think it's interesting that you're from the South, but as a playwright so much of your career has had to happen in New York City, and yet you live in L.A., which is sometimes an odd place to be a playwright. When I tell people here that I write plays—not TV or screenplays—it doesn't seem to compute.

Beth: It computes like, "Loser!"

Dan: Yeah . . .

Beth: Is that cake any good?

Dan: I'm just pacing myself. You want some?

Beth: Yeah, I'm starving!

Dan: So have you ever felt like, I don't know, pigeonholed as a southern writer?

Beth: I feel like if they're giving you a job or a prize, they can categorize you any way they want. Like all these prizes are for southern writers? Okay, throw me one! All these prizes are for women? Okay, throw me one!

Dan: Was it ever annoying to be compared to other southern writers?

Beth: I remember that, but it was much to my advantage to say I wrote like Eudora Welty or Flannery O'Connor. It was just ridiculous. Great company. They'd be like shuddering if they heard that. I just give it up to people's desire to categorize. Then they feel like it's something they don't have to read because they already know what category it's in. "Oh, I don't like that category!" Or, "I've already read enough of that category!"

Dan: There's a dark sense of humor in a lot of southern writing. That's what I love about your new play, *The Jacksonian* [set to premiere in January 2012 at the Geffen Playhouse, directed by Robert Falls]. It's a disturbing play, but it's also very human and very funny.

Beth: I guess, but if you read Philip Roth—isn't he dark and funny?

Dan: Sure. But it's different. It reminds me a lot of Irish writing. I think there's a special kind of weirdness in both Irish and southern writing.

Beth: Oh there's a weirdness all right . . . I mean, it's probably less weird if you're born there though. You know? Because you just grew up with it and it wasn't really that weird, and then suddenly you're out in L.A. and go, "Wow, that was weird!"

Dan: So we were talking about weirdness in southern writing.

Beth: Well, there's a lot of alcohol in the South also. It's very much of a drinking culture, particularly when I was growing up. I mean it still is, but not like it used to be, like, "I'll get you a to-go cup for the road! So you can get from the house to the party!" Never a moment of sobriety! And I also think there's something interesting about the notion that the South was defeated, and in the face of defeat, humor is often the best defense for humiliation.

Dan: Do you feel like that's still a big part of being a writer from the South, dealing with that sense of humiliation?

Beth: Less so now because every place has opened up, like, a McDonald's. But I think there's something gripping about being so far behind the rest of the country on so many racial issues. Racism's always referred to somewhere in my plays—well, not always referred to directly, but often, like in *Crimes of the Heart*, Babe is having an affair with a Black gardener.

Dan: With *The Jacksonian* [which takes place in 1964 in Jackson, Mississippi], do you feel like you're dealing with this history of racism in a more head-on way?

Beth: Yeah, more head-on, definitely. It's a really horrifying issue to deal with, and you don't want to do it. I think it's so dark for me to go to that time in my life because I was young then, and I was so confused. Because here was your governor, people you were meant to look up to, teachers, politicians, family members, people that fed you and cared about you—who were virulent racists. And you knew it wasn't right, but you couldn't figure it out when you're really young.

Dan: Did you always have that sense that something was wrong, or was it more like a dawning awareness?

Beth: It always made me sad. And then suddenly I tried to pretend like it didn't make me sad and it was right. Because I must be crazy or something, what's wrong with me to think this isn't right when obviously this is how life is? So I think it's very shattering to grow up in cultural apartheid, for Black and white—more for Blacks obviously.

Dan: What was it like growing up with so much of the rest of the country criticizing the South for its racism?

Beth: There was so much less information that was parsed out, at that time and at that age. I mean you'd come home and you could watch the evening news. Or you'd have the *Clarion-Ledger*, which was the most racist paper in the country, voted so for like twenty years running. And of course there wasn't any education about any African American ever doing anything. The things that were going down, like people sitting at lunch counters and having cigarettes burned into their skin? I wasn't aware of that part of it. It's just that my mother would say, "You're living in historical times." James Meredith was trying to go to Ole Miss, but from the perspective of our neighbor Kathy Stevens who was a freshman and going out for rush and what's this going to do to pledge week . . . ? You know?

Dan: Are you saying you felt insulated from all that?

Beth: I didn't feel insulated at all. I mean you couldn't possibly feel outside of it. They bombed the rabbi's house a few blocks away from our house, and our windows shook.

Dan: A neighbor of yours? Was anyone injured?

Beth: I don't think anyone was injured. But their place was definitely blown up, their house.

Dan: Why specifically were they targeted, other than racism?

Beth: They were Jewish—oh, other than racism?

Dan: Were they activists?

Beth: I don't know, but they also bombed the local synagogue. The KKK or whoever—The White Citizens' Council was meant to be not so vicious but I don't know. Oh, and my sister's fifth-grade teacher was killed. She was working with the KKK and she showed up trying to shoot somebody down, riding behind her boyfriend on a motorcycle wearing, like, mini-shorts, or what do you call those short-shorts?

Dan: Like Daisy Dukes?

Beth: Yeah, and she got blown away. I'm not sure who shot her or why. I remember the newspaper article my little sister had up in her bedroom with a sweet-looking photograph of her teacher.

Dan: I remember last summer you told me you've never written in a nonfiction sense about your childhood.

Beth: Well, I guess I'm not a nonfiction writer.

Dan: But even as a play, you haven't ever written anything that you'd consider strictly autobiographical, right?

Beth: I think it's taken me this long to be able to actually write about that time and that place in my life. Because it was incredibly devastating and incomprehensible and terrifying—and just sad, sad, sad. . . .

Dan: Those are some words I'd use to describe *The Jacksonian*. Even though there's humor, I think the audience will feel this kind of heartbreak and devastation you're talking about.

Beth: The notion of the play is, "If you're living in Jackson, Mississippi, your soul is lost." It's like you're living on top of a swamp of bones and blood and hate. That was the heartbreaking thing for me looking back on Mississippi in that time. I mean there were people who were really extraordinarily brave because they stayed in Mississippi, like Eudora Welty, William Faulkner, and Willie Morris, who came back to Mississippi and lived there and tried to see the place, and write about it. I didn't have the guts to do that. Well, also I'm a playwright so I had to leave.

Dan: Well, thanks for talking to me about all this, Beth.

Beth: Thanks for asking me. Can I finish your cake?

Dan: Absolutely.

Beth: I love sugar.

Ridiculous Fraud and The Jacksonian—Beth Henley's New Plays about the South: An Interview

Verna A. Foster / 2012

From *Southern Quarterly* 50 (Fall 2012): 43–57. Reprinted by permission of Verna A. Foster and *Southern Quarterly*. Verna A. Foster is a professor of English at Loyola University Chicago. She is the author of *The Name and Nature of Tragicomedy* (2004) and the editor of *Dramatic Revisions of Myths, Fairy Tales and Legends: Essays on Recent Plays* (2012).

Beth Henley has been writing distinctive plays in a great variety of styles for over thirty years. Henley was born in Jackson, Mississippi, in 1952 and attended school there. After graduating from Southern Methodist University in 1974 with a degree in theater, she did graduate work in acting at the University of Illinois for a year and then moved to Los Angeles. Henley's plays of the 1980s are set in her native South, in Mississippi or Louisiana. Most of them are, in Henley's words (following Tennessee Williams), "memory plays." They include *Crimes of the Heart*, which won the Pulitzer Prize in 1981, *The Miss Firecracker Contest* (1980), and *The Debutante Ball* (1985). In her plays of the 1990s, Henley moves away from the southern locations and modified realism of the earlier work and experiments with various nonrealistic dramatic styles. These plays include *Abundance* (1991), a revision of the mythic Wild West; *Signature* (1996), set in a futuristic Los Angeles; the expressionistic *Control Freaks* (1992); and *L-Play* (1996), which comprises a number of short plays written in different styles, all on topics beginning with the letter L.

Since the publication of the two volumes of her *Collected Plays* in 2000, Henley has produced *Family Week* (2000), about a psychologically damaged woman and her visiting family in a desert recovery center; *Sisters of the Winter Madrigal* (2001; actually written much earlier), a kind of dark fairy tale; *Exposed* (2003), about five interconnected but isolated people in Los Angeles one Christmas; *Ridiculous Fraud* (2006); and *The Jacksonian* (2012). In these last two plays Henley returns to southern locales.

Ridiculous Fraud was originally produced at the McCarter Theatre Center in Princeton, New Jersey, opening on May 12, 2006, and subsequently by South Coast Repertory in Costa Mesa, California, opening on October 13, 2006. The McCarter production was directed by Lisa Peterson, and the South Coast Repertory production by Sharon Ott. *Ridiculous Fraud* depicts the complicated relations among members of an old New Orleans family: brothers Andrew Clay, a politician; Kap, a duck-hunting guide; and Lafcad, an underemployed philosopher. Their father is in the penitentiary for fraud, their mother dead. Lafcad refuses to marry his rich fiancée and goes off to hide at his Uncle Baites's farmhouse in the backwoods. Andrew's wife, Willow, the daughter of his financial backer, Ed Chrystal, hates her stepmother, Maude, who is dying of cancer. Andrew has an affair with Maude, for which Kap takes the blame, allowing Ed to punish him by cutting his face. Uncle Baites has taken up with Georgia, a "lost girl" with a wooden leg. The play moves from the Clay family's decaying mansion in New Orleans to a backwoods farmhouse to a cabin *"deep in the woods"* to the family tomb in a New Orleans cemetery, and the passing of time is seasonal and cyclical: summer, fall, winter, and finally spring, specifically Easter Sunday. Willow is now pregnant, Georgia is reborn as a silver angel (a street performer in Jackson Square), the family has a picnic, and Lafcad and Georgia dance.

The Jacksonian premiered at the Geffen Playhouse in Los Angeles, running from February 15 to March 25, 2012. It was directed by Robert Falls, Artistic Director of the Goodman Theatre, Chicago, and starred Ed Harris, Amy Madigan, Glenne Headly, Bill Pullman, and Bess Rous. *The Jacksonian* is set in a motel on the outskirts of Jackson, Mississippi, from March to December 1964. The foreground of the play is taken up with the separation and impending divorce of a middle-class couple, Bill, a dentist, and Susan Perch, and its effect on their teenage daughter, Rosy, and secondarily with the relationship between the bartender, Fred, and Eva, "a waitress and motel maid" at the Jacksonian, where Bill is currently living. Eva has given Fred a false alibi in a murder case on the understanding that he will marry her. But in the background lies the virulent racism of 1960s Mississippi. There is a casual allusion to the firebombing of a "Negro" church in Meridian; the local school has only recently accepted some Black students. The man accused of the murder of a woman at a local gas station, actually committed by Fred, is an old Black man with glaucoma, charged simply because of his race, whom Eva would like to see lynched. Bill Perch learns accidentally that his father was a member of the Ku Klux Klan. And the firebomber we hear about early in the play turns out to be one of Bill's patients. On learning of his patient's involvement in the bombing and his plan to dynamite a synagogue, Bill pulled out all of the man's teeth and has consequently lost his license and his ability to provide for Susan. Susan confronts Bill in his motel room with Eva. The play concludes with a conversation between Bill and Rosy.

On July 2, 2012, I interviewed Beth Henley by phone about *Ridiculous Fraud* and *The Jacksonian* and about the South she depicts in these recent works. The telephone interview was followed up by an email exchange in July and August 2012. I would like to thank Jenny Frey for help transcribing the interview.

Loyola University Chicago

Verna A. Foster: Thank you very much for agreeing to this interview for the Jubilee issue of the *Southern Quarterly*. I want to ask you about your recent work and, given the venue of this interview, your representation of the South. Your two most recent plays, *Ridiculous Fraud* and *The Jacksonian*, are, like your early plays such as *Crimes of the Heart* and *The Miss Firecracker Contest*, set in the South. *Ridiculous Fraud* is set in New Orleans and the Louisiana backwoods, and *The Jacksonian* is set in Jackson, Mississippi, where you grew up. After living for so many years in L.A. and writing plays set in a great variety of locations—nineteenth-century Wyoming for your Western, *Abundance*; Wisconsin for *Revelers*; L.A. in 2052 for *Signature*—what made you decide to return to the South for *Ridiculous Fraud* and *The Jacksonian*?

Beth Henley: Well, I got a commission from the McCarter Theatre, and I wanted to write a play with men. The last play I did was *Family Week*, which has four women. I was down in Mississippi, and I was talking to a duck hunter. We were talking about his passion for the beauty of duck hunting. And that inspired me to start thinking about this play.

VAF: And what about *The Jacksonian*?

BH: *The Jacksonian* is the play that has been haunting me for a lot of my life, and it was the first play I've written that is set in the place I was raised. I've written plays that take place in Mississippi towns: Hattiesburg, Hazlehurst, or Brookhaven. But I'd never been able to write a play set in the place I actually grew up in. I had to travel all over the country and back again to get to my hometown. The play takes place in 1964. That was an extremely troubled time in the history of Mississippi, and it was a remarkable place to be coming of age in because there was so much confusion. People you loved could be racist. The governor was racist, and so was the whole society. It was condoned. It's a very terrifying and fascinating thing to think about, to be innocent in that time and wonder when you're young: is this the way of the world?

VAF: Yes, I can see there could be a great deal of ambiguity in trying to figure out what's going on. I'd like to come back to *The Jacksonian* later on, but I want to talk about your earlier play *Ridiculous Fraud* first. Several reviewers of the productions of both *Ridiculous Fraud* and *The Jacksonian* comment on your return to "Southern Gothic." What does that term mean to you? Do you find that designation of your plays set in the South helpful?

BH: It's really not helpful to me, and I don't know really who it's helpful to.

VAF: People writing reviews, I suppose.

BH: *The Jacksonian* is more Southern Gothic, I think, than *Ridiculous Fraud.* Maybe I don't understand the term. It's a bit nebulous.

VAF: Has your view of the South changed since you wrote your earlier plays in the late 1970s and 1980s and you have lived for many years in L.A.?

BH: The South has changed. The country has changed. And I've changed. My views have changed. All of it has changed.

VAF: So altogether, you can't entirely separate them out. *Ridiculous Fraud* is set "Five years before Hurricane Katrina" (that is, 2000), while *Crimes of the Heart* is set "five years after Hurricane Camille" (that would be 1974). Why do you relate the temporal settings of these plays to hurricanes?

BH: I didn't really intend to when I was writing *Ridiculous Fraud.* Hurricane Katrina happened, and it brought such a devastating change to the temperament of the city, and people's lives were very different. The world I was writing about was before Hurricane Katrina.

VAF: So it was to emphasize that the play is set in the past.

BH: Yes.

VAF: *Ridiculous Fraud* seems to be a counterpart to *Crimes of the Heart* in several ways, apart from the relation to hurricanes. In the earlier play there are three sisters, and in *Ridiculous Fraud* there are three brothers because, as you say, you wanted to write for men. Were you conscious of any other parallels?

BH: I think in many ways the personalities of the brothers correlate to the personalities of the sisters. There is also an absence of parents. And all of the characters seem to be dealing with various types of youthful struggles.

VAF: Would Andrew be like Meg? Do you see exact parallels or more in general?

BH: He's the oldest. He's more like Lenny, taking charge. Trying to control the family or trying to put the right face on the family. I would say that Meg is like the second brother, Kap, because they're kind of the rebellious ones, and then Lafcad and Babe are kind of the idiot savants of the family.

VAF: Critics have often compared your plays to Chekhov's. While the tone of *Ridiculous Fraud* is not Chekhovian, there are several striking Chekhovian motifs in *Ridiculous Fraud*, such as a comment someone makes about everyone casually eating at different times (as in *Uncle Vanya*), Georgia shooting off a potato cannon (guns figure in several Chekhov plays), and especially Ed's suggestion that Uncle Baites could make money by cutting down trees (*The Cherry Orchard*). Were you thinking of Chekhov, or is there some other reason your characters are saying these kinds of things?

BH: I am really in awe of Chekhov, so I'm sure, subliminally or even consciously, I steal from him. In *Ridiculous Fraud* the thing that I consciously was stealing from him was working in four acts. How to tell a story in four different parts. Four different seasons, four different times of day.

VAF: I was struck by that as well: your symbolic handling of time and place in *Ridiculous Fraud*. Just as Chekhov uses changes in place and time symbolically in both *Three Sisters* and *The Cherry Orchard*, *Ridiculous Fraud* moves from the Clay family's mansion in New Orleans through the Louisiana backwoods and finally to a cemetery in New Orleans and through the seasons from summer to spring, specifically Easter. Would you say a little bit more about your use of time and place in *Ridiculous Fraud*?

BH: It starts in a city, New Orleans, where social facades are important and moves to Uncle Baites's place out in the country where there's more of a sense of freedom: shooting the potato cannon and passing love notes. And things get even wilder when it gets deeper into the woods. And that's when actual violence and lust erupt. And then it's back in New Orleans, but in a cemetery, an almost heavenly place, a spiritual realm.

VAF: Despite their use of Chekhovian motifs, do you see *Ridiculous Fraud* and *Crimes of the Heart* as different kinds of plays?

BH: Well, when I'm working on them, they're all particular. Thinking about it, I can see similarities between those two plays and many of my other plays that are comedies in a dark sense. And also they're about young people in their exuberant madness and the recklessness of youth. People who have been children and are having difficulties turning into adults. So I think there are scenes that correlate and a tone that correlates. I don't know if that answers the question.

VAF: Of course, you also have characters in your plays who are very unusual, like Georgia, the strange girl with the wooden leg, who finally works as a silver angel mime in Jackson Square. She certainly seems different from anyone in Chekhov or even *Crimes of the Heart*, though she does remind me of other eccentrically honest outsider characters in your plays, such as Mac Sam in *The Miss Firecracker Contest* or Frances in *The Debutante Ball* or also some of the really strange characters in the late plays of Tennessee Williams. Why do you like to incorporate people like Georgia in your plays?

BH: I am very interested in the outsider and how the outsider provides another worldview or perspective. I think I've done that a lot—like Pixrose [in *The Wake of Jamey Foster*] is an outsider. And Popeye is an outsider in *The Miss Firecracker Contest*. Violet in *The Debutante Ball*. And since I do write plays about families, an outsider's view of the family can be illuminating. You see the shenanigans of the family from the outsider's eye.

VAF: I note that in both *Ridiculous Fraud* and *The Jacksonian* you deal with politics somewhat more explicitly than you have done in earlier plays. Andrew Clay in *Ridiculous Fraud* is running for office as and eventually becomes State Auditor. Meanwhile his father is in jail for fraud, and, despite his attempts to present himself as, and I think to be, a man of unimpeachable integrity, it appears that Andrew is in his rich father-in-law's pocket. Are you commenting here on contemporary southern (or indeed national—one thinks of Illinois) state politics?

BH: Obviously it's a statement about corruption and the quality of lies and deception people live with. In my mind, that's one of the themes of the play—what are the frauds that people are presenting and living with and denying or having to face. And the politics is part of that.

VAF: *The Jacksonian*, your most recent play, is also about corruption, but it is a kind of corruption, cultural racism, that the characters are unaware is corruption. *The Jacksonian* had a very successful run in L.A. this last March in a production directed by Robert Falls and with a wonderful cast. I appreciated your sending me a transcript of the play since it has not yet been published. In your description of the setting you say that the titular Jacksonian motel exists "as a haunting memory, a sort of purgatory that was Jackson, Mississippi, circa 1964." Could you elaborate on what you mean by that?

BH: I didn't put that in the program. That was actually a note for myself. It kind of pushed me away from naturalism or realism. I wanted to be allowed to see this piece in a dream-like way, in a nightmarish, *film noir* way, where it doesn't have to be conventionally real.

VAF: Is the play a "memory play," as you describe your early plays set in the South?

BH: I think *Jacksonian* is even an older and a deeper memory play. Further back in time.

VAF: How do your memories of growing up in Jackson seep into the play?

BH: I think they're the crux of the play.

VAF: In terms of the politics or in terms of the family?

BH: Well, I think both.

VAF: Why did you choose to set the play in 1964?

BH: I think one of the reasons is because in 1964 there was something called Freedom of Choice, which let African Americans have the choice to go to white schools. So there were African-American students in the white schools, but not many. This was before the busing, forced busing, that is, in 1969. So things were changing. There had already been the Freedom Riders, and then there was that summer of 1964 when the civil rights workers were murdered in Neshoba County for encouraging voter registration. The KKK was blowing up synagogues. The fear of change, the fear of retribution enhanced the hate. Things become even more violent trying to stop the change. And that was part of that era. Those are some of the practical reasons.

VAF: But none of these things is directly referred to in your play. Why did you decide not to refer to the activists being murdered or the civil rights work that was being done or desegregation—why did you not refer to most of that explicitly in the play?

BH: Well, I think what I was interested in was how evil bleeds into the lives of all people who exist in apartheid. What it does to people who would be maybe good people in other situations. It bleeds into the everyday lives of people who are trying to have an occupation and a family and go to school. The corruption and violence are in the air you breathe.

VAF: Yes, I was struck by that. Serious racial issues emerge in *The Jacksonian* through casual racist allusions by characters—notably Eva—who are usually unconscious of the horror of what they're saying. So the play is very unsettling for what the characters don't say but assume.

BH: They assume it's fine to talk like this.

VAF: Yes, and that's really even more horrifying.

BH: Yes, and it's not only okay; it would not be okay to *not* talk like that.

VAF: Were you concerned at all that some younger audience members outside the South (in L.A., for example) might not recognize the political situation that is subtextually present in the play?

BH: It was interesting because the wonderful actress who was playing Rosy was not aware of a lot of the history and had her mind blown when we started talking about what was actually happening in Mississippi at that time. So, it was a concern, but Amy Levinson [Literary Manager and Dramaturg at the Geffen Playhouse] put a nice piece in the program about the history and some shocking photographs from that time.

VAF: *The Jacksonian* deals with issues of class as well as race? Would you comment on class in the play?

BH: I think that there are big class differences in the eyes of the characters. Fred and Eva are lower class, and the dentist and his wife are more upper-middle class. There's something unsettling about the behavior of people when it comes to class status. The dentist's wife calls the bartender Fred but refers to her husband as Doctor Perch.

VAF: How much do you think Mississippi has changed since the 1960s? How would you envision your play being received in Mississippi today?

BH: I'm not sure. The New Stage Theatre in Jackson asked to see the play. I haven't heard if they are actually interested in doing it. I would be terrified, frankly, because it's kind of a personal play.

VAF: I would think residents of Jackson today would want to see your play.

BH: Well, I hope you're right.

VAF: Are there any plans in the works for future productions of *The Jacksonian*? In New York or Chicago, for example?

BH: I hope. I don't know. I'm trying to get the next production of the play and cobble it together and figure out where and when and how, but I don't have any real facts on that.

VAF: When will *The Jacksonian* be published?

BH: I'm not sure. I was sort of waiting to see if there's going to be another production because sometimes you make little changes in seeing it again for the second time. So I'm not in a huge rush to publish it because it's a peculiar play that still might be evolving.

VAF: Why do you call *The Jacksonian* a peculiar play? And how and why do you see it evolving?

BH: The play is not linear. I'm playing with the effect violence and shock can have on time. That's why it's peculiar. And because part of what I'm exploring is the crossing webs of time, which is a fluid, evolving notion, it seems after only one production this facet may not be set in stone.

VAF: Back in 2009 at the Comparative Drama Conference in Los Angeles you mentioned that you were writing a tragedy. Is *The Jacksonian* that tragedy?

BH: Yes.

VAF: Do you see the play as sharing in any of the classic features of tragedy? Is Bill Perch a tragic protagonist, for example?

BH: Yes. I mean, I think so. He has hubris, and he kind of brings himself down. He tries to control things in a forceful, violent way that is all that he perceives he has available to him, and he ends up being part of the destruction as well.

VAF: Does he have an *anagnorisis*, or recognition?

BH: Linearly, the last thing you see is him at the ice machine with blood on his hands. And, I think, that that could be interpreted as a sort of recognition.

VAF: That he realizes what he has done?

BH: Yes.

VAF: Did you want the play to be cathartic in the Aristotelian sense?

BH: I just wanted it to be alive.

VAF: Do you think there is any possibility for purgation of the audience?

BH: What do you mean? What does that mean—purgation?

VAF: Well, actually, that's the question I'm always having to answer for my students, and I'm never sure if I understand it myself. A feeling of having experienced a lot of horror and somehow being cleansed or freed from it in some way.

BH: Yes, actually I do. It's not turning away from the horror of what human nature is capable of, given the chance. Of how evil can reign and then it begets evil. At the very end, I have a scene at the Coke machine between the father and daughter that suggests that now maybe things can get better, even though it's in the past; maybe the past is the present because I'm dealing with time in the play. Maybe coming home today is literally today.

VAF: One of the things I found most fascinating about *The Jacksonian* is your non-linear use of time. The action takes place at the Jacksonian motel over several months, beginning and repeatedly returning to a night a little before Christmas, December 17, when a murder takes place but ranging back and forth from March to December 1964. Why did you decide to play with time in this way?

BH: To tell you the truth, it just felt that way when I was working on it. Somehow these events had fractured time. And working with Bob [director Robert Falls] on this, I think what we're trying to do—and it's one of those things that nobody gets, probably—is that the whole of the play takes place in a flash of Rosy trying not to realize what's happened: that her mother's dead. She keeps trying to move time back and trying to escape time, but the scenes she remembers keep moving time forward.

VAF: You say in your note to the play: "Rosy's terror and will quake the landscape of time, space and memory."

BH: That's what I mean: she's trying to will that this didn't happen, that her mother isn't murdered if she can just will time. You know, when something terrible happens, you think, "if I just hadn't done this, that could change." In other words, it's hard to accept something really horrific, and the mind can play tricks.

VAF: So it's definitive, then, that the murder has taken place? Because I did wonder if it could also be some precognition and that there was still a possibility that the events could be avoided.

BH: I think that's a great interpretation. And I think that would be Rosy's interpretation—maybe if she gets back to that summer day when they're having sodas and things get better instead of worse—before her father pulled out Phil Boone's teeth and before he's addicted to every drug there is.

VAF: I think that would be fascinating—if there's a possibility that these events actually might not occur.

BH: Part of the idea of the play is that something terrible happens, but if one thing were to change—if Susan doesn't go back to the hotel, if Susan hadn't called, if Bill hadn't had Eva in the room—there are a number of ways that the murder could have been avoided.

VAF: That things could be different. You use Rosy's direct addresses to the audience to help the audience know what month we are in. But also Rosy seems obsessed with the nature of time. She says, for example, that she feels "the skin of time." Could you say something about how time operates in the play and your own understanding of the nature of time?

BH: In Rosy's case, she really has a specific goal and a specific action in mind: to force time back. She feels the skin of time but doesn't know where it touches. She refuses to know where she is in time. Because the present can't be if the present means her father has murdered her mother. My view of time? Time—that's a great mystery. I'm fascinated by time. And it changes as you get older.

VAF: Mid-twentieth-century English dramatist J. B. Priestley in plays such as *Time and the Conways* and *An Inspector Calls* presents characters who have a precognition of events that will occur in the future. He believed such precognitions could enable people to change potential future events. I sensed something almost like this in *The Jacksonian*, that there was this sort of playing with time, that it was ambiguous and rich and you couldn't quite come to a determination of what was going on.

BH: I think that's true. It always interested me. I believe in prescient creativity. When I was working on *Ridiculous Fraud*, I kept seeing, for no reason, that it ended in a cemetery—the above-ground tombs in the cemeteries of New Orleans, and I did research on those cemeteries—and I didn't know who was going to die in the play or why they were going to be there. While I was writing the play, my mother died, and it ended up that the characters were there to see their mother. I can't help but—and that's happened at different times with different plays—sometimes things happen in the plays before they happen in life.

VAF: Could you elaborate on that last point or give an example from another play?

BH: The plays seem to be more attuned to what is going on in and around me than my conscious self. *Abundance* revealed that there would be immense consequences to some choices I made in my life before I was aware I had made any choices at all.

VAF: Rosy in *The Jacksonian* makes us aware of how unforeseen consequences of choices we make can reverberate through time. She seems to be a choric figure.

BH: Right.

VAF: She is also important in her own right. What is the relationship between the political evil in the play's background and the family murder that takes place in the foreground?

BH: I think they're living in an atmosphere of violence. And I think that it infuses, you know, the smells of the air. You can't be living there and not be affected by it. Or you may not feel you're affected by it because you've cut it off so much—you've denied it so much. And I think in many ways that's what some of these characters have done. And when you deny something it can often come back and surround you and have a terrible effect.

VAF: The richness and tension of *The Jacksonian* come from the connections you make between the political and the family and the way you manipulate time, giving the play its edge. Are you working on another play now?

BH: I finished a first draft and now even a second draft of a play called *Laugh*, which takes place in Hollywood in the 1920s and 1930s primarily. It's a slapstick comedy, which I've never done before. I mean, I've done comedy, but I've never done pies in the face. Clearly it was a radical reaction to *The Jacksonian*. I just wanted to make people laugh. Including myself.

VAF: There is quite a lot of laughter in *The Jacksonian* despite its dark and serious qualities, much of it deriving from Bill's occupation as a dentist. Could you say something about the kind of laughter *The Jacksonian* evokes?

BH: The humor in *The Jacksonian* often comes from a tense tone of foreboding. The audience knows something dreadful and violent is going to happen because of how the play begins. All exchanges are ominously heightened. But *Laugh* has a bold physical humor. The play is not ambiguous. These people are good, these people are bad, these people are funny—much more caricature.

VAF: I look forward to seeing *The Jacksonian*, and *Laugh* when it's ready. Thank you again for taking the time to talk to me.

Beth Henley Returns to New York and Her Southern Roots with Gothic Black Comedy *The Jacksonian*

TheaterMania / 2013

From TheaterMania, November 7, 2013, theatermania.com.

There's not a lot of southern comfort to ease the characters of Pulitzer Prize winner and Tony- and Drama Desk-nominated Beth Henley's Gothic black comedy-drama *The Jacksonian*, having its New York premiere courtesy of The New Group at Theatre Row.

Set in Jackson, Mississippi, during the Christmas of 1964, and amid the fiery tensions of racial strife, church bombings, and talk of lynchings, there's a murder and robbery at a gas station near a once-posh motel called The Jacksonian. An elderly Black man has been arrested but swears he's innocent. News of this incident reaches a successful dentist, estranged from his wife and ensconced at the motel, where he receives mysterious visits from the couple's affection-starved, troubled teenage daughter, who's becoming a pawn in the family turmoil.

The holidays are anything but merry when the dentist's wife arrives for a visit that the husband hopes will lead to reconciliation, while a scheming, bigoted hotel maid, desperate to be wed to the very weird hotel restaurant bartender, decides instead to set her sights on the dentist. As the dentist's world falls apart, he engages with the ditzy maid in a drug-addled bacchanal that has tragic consequences.

"I didn't set out to write a black comedy," says Henley, taking a break from rehearsals. "The vision wasn't easy to come by. Ideas just don't pop out or suddenly dawn on me. Not at all. Not this time! The plot evolved gradually. I don't know where the idea came from. Since I teach [at Loyola Marymount University] and have a son in high school, I don't have the luxury of writing every day.

"When I get home," she continues, "like other mothers, other women, I have to do the laundry and fix dinner. Then, when I go to work in my office, there are distractions. I may be tempted to read a book. When I get serious, however, I go off, isolated, and sit until the inspiration hits. This one took a long time to write."

A Mississippi native long known for spot-on southern sensibilities that tend toward Gothic farce with caricatured, dysfunctional families and unhinged, quirky free spirits, Henley is a prodigious writer with a four-decade-long relationship with not-for-profit companies. Sadly, she has been absent from Broadway since 1982 and her short-lived play *The Wake of Jamey Foster* (the follow-up to her 1981 Pulitzer-winning and Tony- and Drama Desk-nominated *Crimes of the Heart*).

The Jacksonian, which received its share of acclaim during its debut in L.A. last year, is her first New York work since the month-long engagement of *Motherhood Out Loud* for Primary Stages in 2011, for which she was a contributing playwright. As sole playwright, her more recent work on a New York stage was the 2010 production of *Family Week* for MCC Theater. A planned Broadway revival of her 1981 play, *The Miss Firecracker Contest*, was announced last year, but never arrived.

With *The Jacksonian*, instead of an outrageous comedy, Henley has written a play noir. "I didn't want it to unfold in a linear way, but in fractured time," she says. "That really worked for creating an emotional through-line as opposed to a storytelling through-line. It was hard. I spent a lot of time attempting to get it right."

She's abetted by Tony-winning director Robert Falls, artistic director of Chicago's Goodman Theatre, and a strong cast: Ed Harris, Juliet Brett, Amy Madigan, Glenne Headly, and Bill Pullman. Harris and Madigan are happily married in real life, which adds a bit of irony to their roles.

Told in flashback by the daughter, the play brims with suspense, dark humor, and the surreal. In *The Jacksonian*, it appears Henley is channeling writers that include the likes of Tracy Letts, and southerners William Faulkner, Tennessee Williams, and Flannery O'Connor. An early tagline for the show also revealed the influence of writer-director David Lynch: "*The Jacksonian*, where you go to bury your secrets, is an unsettling world where the subversive becomes commonplace and the passage of time becomes hauntingly unpredictable."

Though the play uses the signage of the now-razed "highway hotel" called The Jacksonian (Bob Hope, Elvis, Cher, even Roy Rogers and Trigger were among celebrities signing the register), Henley claims that's just a coincidence. "It's also not based on a specific murder and robbery or characters [who] stayed at a motel."

Parts of the play are influenced by major changes in Henley's early life, including her parents' separation (and later divorce) when she was in high school. "That's what we [writers] do," she laughs. "Draw on what we know. Everything I write is an amalgamation. I don't pin any one thing on any one person."

A scene in *The Jacksonian* is modeled after the time she visited her attorney father turned state senator "in his marital exile at a hotel, bringing him a small Christmas tree as a peace offering from mother."

Henley was also drawn to the socio-political landscape of Mississippi in the 1960s. "Growing up then, I was influenced by what was happening and how things were changing. The violence going on in reaction to change affected everyone. I set the play there because I wanted to see how that impacted the personal," she says.

These events forced her to deal with dark places she hadn't previously wanted to explore in her work. "It's taken my whole career to be able to look back at those times with enough distance to be able to write this play. The problem was trying to figure out how to do it, to get raw enough and find the strength to do it."

Director Falls calls *The Jacksonian* "disturbing, very funny, and very much a Beth Henley play. She's no longer the cozy family writer she was once labeled."

The play also had an impact on Headly. In an interview with TheaterMania, she observed, "Obviously Beth felt compelled to write this play. I sensed a lot of anger, pain, and confusion. It would make explosive theater, and I haven't found many new plays to be explosive. It was scary, dark, and oddly very funny."

Henley admits that "the play may never have happened without the push Glenne gave." Headly helped get the play out there, first getting it into the hands of Robert Falls at the Goodman Theatre and later to the contacts at the Geffen Playhouse.

"The play was constantly evolving," Henley explains. "The actors took their characters in directions that enhanced the play. As a writer, I can only see so far, and they seemed able to see beyond the mountain. Any time actors have a question or comment, I listen very carefully."

Henley makes a rare admission. "As it did in L.A., *The Jacksonian* plays differently in front of different audiences. Some find it funny, some don't find it funny at all. The cast is amazed at how varied audience reaction can be, but they just keep playing the truth of the play."

The Long Journey Home: An Interview with the Playwright about Her Play *The Jacksonian*

Robert Falls / 2014

From americantheatre.org, February 1, 2014. Used with permission from Theatre Communications Group. A shorter version of this interview appeared in *American Theatre*, February 2014, pp. 58–59. Robert Falls is the artistic director of the Goodman Theatre in Chicago. From 1977 to 1985 he was the artistic director of Chicago's Wisdom Bridge Theatre. He won the Tony Award for directing the 1999 Broadway revival of *Death of a Salesman* and the Drama Desk Award for directing the 2003 Broadway revival of *Long Day's Journey Into Night*.

Robert Falls: From the beginning of your career, you've been labeled a southern playwright, if not a Southern Gothic playwright. How do you feel about your legacy as a writer and your connection to the South?

Beth Henley: Well, I feel that, as hard as I try, I can't wrench the South out of my bones. It keeps reoccurring in my work. Being the place I grew up it left a deep imprint.

RF: This is the first play of yours, though, that's centered in Jackson, Mississippi, where you grew up.

BH: Yeah. I've never been able to write about that particular town. I've always written about places on the outskirts.

RF: What made you avoid Jackson? Was it conscious or unconscious?

BH: I think it was unconscious. I don't know. I thought it was too close to write about Jackson.

RF: Too close to you? Your family?

BH: To me and my family. And also, the vibe of Jackson is different. This play has a different vibe than that of *Crimes of the Heart*.

RF: What would you say the different vibe is? Is there a particular vibe to this play as opposed to *Miss Firecracker* or certainly *Crimes of the Heart* or *The Wake of Jamey Foster*?

BH: Well, it has a vibe of violence that's not kidding. In *Crimes of the Heart*, a character shoots her husband, but he lives. In *Wake*, a character gets kicked in the head by a cow and dies. But in this, I knew I was going to incorporate murder, and I didn't want to do it in a surreal or theatrical way, like in my play *Control Freaks*—this felt terrible and hard, tragic not ironic.

RF: Was a murder or a death always the centerpiece? Was there an initial image that made you work on this?

BH: I've always wanted to write a play where a young girl brings in a Christmas tree for her father's motel room. The sadness of that image has haunted me for a while. And I knew somebody was going to be murdered, but I wasn't sure who it was when I started writing the play.

RF: I read once that you keep a notebook and record images. Can you talk about your process of building a play over a period of time?

BH: I work from a lot of notebooks. I write down bits of dialogue I hear that may or may not even fit in this play, and I write down tone. Tone is so important; I think that's the soul of the play. If you can get the tone, that's for me the most difficult thing. And I write down character images. I knew, for instance, there was a bridal dress that matched the bone ivory shoes—images like that. I wasn't sure whose dress it was. So it's images. It's dialogue. It's ideas for scenes.

RF: One of the things that's unusual about the play is that it sits on top of a larger social and political background. It's set in 1964. Do you want to talk about your own experience of 1964 Jackson that might have led somewhere into this play?

BH: I was only twelve. It's so incomprehensible—the young civil rights supporters who were working for voter registration, [James] Chaney, [Andrew Goodman] and [Michael] Schwerner, were brutally murdered and people weren't exactly upset about it. It was such a schizophrenic atmosphere of gentility that just kind of accepted racism and ignored murder. It took its toll on everyone who lived there, and I didn't even realize how bizarre it was until I left. I just thought this was normal life, and the national culture was not very enlightened at that particular point in time. It was very twisted to grow up in a culture of apartheid with people you love.

RF: Younger members of our company, and even some not-so-young members of the company, had a little difficulty remembering that sense of what 1964 was like, particularly in Jackson, Mississippi. Could you tell me that story about your sister's teacher and her involvement?

BH: There had been a lot of violence against Jewish leaders and bombings of synagogues in Jackson and Meridian. The Jewish community went to the FBI for help. Through an informer the FBI knew a bomb was going to be planted and they planned a setup around this man's house. My sister's fifth-grade teacher, Kathy Ainsworth, was in the car with the bomber, and she was wearing hot pants. The guy put the bomb in the driveway, and then as he was running back to the car, they shot him, and she ended up getting shot and killed. The man survived though he was shot nineteen times. That was also around the time when the National Guard had to be sent down to get James Meredith into Ole Miss. The Freedom Riders were getting off interstate buses and going directly to Parchman Penitentiary. There were sit-ins at drugstore counters. It was really bizarre just to try to be growing up and living your life and figuring out how to do homework with all of this in the background, because you're trying to put the world together.

RF: Clearly that found its way into the play, and in our productions, we worked really hard on intertwining the personal and the political. That evil is built on top of this swamp of the blood of slaves and of African Americans, and out of that swamp comes a pervasive sense of evil that informs the world of this motel, and some of the characters within it.

BH: That sense was better incorporated in the New York version of the play than at the Geffen. I was just seeing the pattern, and I was able to reinforce it more in the second production.

RF: You also develop your plays in somewhat unusual ways. You've always been very closely aligned with a number of brilliant actors who've been loyal to you over your career. It's almost a Beth Henley rep company. Can you talk about that?

BH: I'm on my third draft before I give a new play to anybody, and then I try to give it to one or two people to read, and then do revisions from that. I ask actors that I know to come to my living room and to read it. I don't give them any direction. It's very safe. The characters just come out of my heart and into the universe when I hear the actors speak the lines. It's exhilarating. If there are big bumps in the play, I generally know it's my fault, because the actors are so good.

RF: What's wonderful is that all these actors—Glenne Headly, Amy Madigan, Bill Pullman, Ed Harris—have worked with you.

BH: I've not worked with Ed before, except on a skit with him. I mean, he's done readings often in my living room.

RF: That's what I was saying—you have this extraordinary cast that obviously ended up deeply committed to the play. And you and I have known each other for many years, although we've never had the opportunity to work together. Do you want to talk about how it came together? It's a little unusual.

BH: It is unusual. Glenne Headly thought you would be great to direct this, and you were doing *The Seagull* and were hard to get a hold of. I was so terrified and thought you would not want to do it, but I wanted to work with you so much. You read it and you called me and I was actually in Mississippi because my uncle had just had a heart attack. You said you wanted to do the play, and I was so happy.

RF: We have a very similar belief in how theater works. For better or worse, you and I studied acting together and had similar experiences with an acting teacher, Edward Kaye-Martin. You write brilliantly for actors, and I do my best work with actors from an acting point of view, having studied it.

BH: We got really lucky that all the actors and you were available. And the Geffen was available.

RF: It just kind of came together. We did it at the Geffen Playhouse, which was a wonderful experience. We were tremendously supported, and the audiences were really terrific, and it was never as if we thought about bringing it to New York. We were just concerned about doing the best production we could. Although once it opened, we thought, "Well, this could be kind of successful in another venue," and there wasn't a lot of enthusiasm out of New York. Then it was just kind of a wonderful memory for all of us, until Scott Elliott and The New Group got a hold of it and said, "Wow, would you guys like to do this in New York at our space?" And once again, it was just amazing synchronicity that all of us were available to jump in and work on it again.

BH: Ian Morgan, the associate artistic director, read the play and sent me this great email letting me know how much the theater wanted to make the production work. It was stunning how all of the pieces fell into place.

RF: Let's talk a little about working with the actors, particularly Amy and Ed, who are married in real life and playing a married couple onstage. Ed and Amy are two of the great American actors. There was just this amazing openness and comfort and safeness that they had as actors to go into the darkest possible places with each other but also to experience love. Love is at the root of these characters' relationship, and something goes terribly wrong in that relationship. It was just terrifying and beautiful and deeply moving to watch them, and I think a lot of it was just because they're brilliant and also because they just trust each other. What was your experience?

BH: They just—the connection could be so terrifyingly deep and there was such an ease. It was a joy to watch great actors work.

RF: It wasn't a collaborative process in terms of the play—you at all times were the author of this work and everything sprung out of you, but there was a sense of family and love. I know that seems like a weird phrase to use in the theater—oft used but often not really meant—but this experience really was sort of driven by love on everybody's part.

BH: Everybody put their heart and soul in it, and they stuck their neck out for me and for this play, and I'll be forever grateful. It was just one of the greatest times of my life.

An Interview with Beth Henley

Karen Carpenter / 2017

Transcribed from mp4 files held at the William Inge Archives, Independence Community College, Independence, Kansas, and edited for length and clarity. Published with the permission of the Independence Community College William Inge Archives. The interview was conducted in late March 2017 in Los Angeles in preparation for the William Inge Theater Festival, which took place on April 19–22, 2017, and at which Henley was the honoree. Karen Carpenter was the Festival's artistic director at that time. Carpenter is also a director and producer with numerous credits Off-Broadway and in regional theaters, as well as the former associate artistic director of The Old Globe in San Diego.

Karen Carpenter: You wrote a play in sixth grade and then you said it was a long time before you wrote another play. Were you writing other things?

Beth Henley: I wrote, you know, little stories, but I remember reading one in class—maybe it was junior high school—and because the story was not doing what I wanted it to do and I could tell it sounded sentimental or dumb and I felt so bad for the character because I loved her so much and she was so full of loneliness and I was unable to portray it, I left the class crying. It was one of those times when you can't help something. But then I was wondering, why aren't I in big, big trouble for this? Because I threw down the story and ran to the restroom and cried, and I didn't get in trouble for it. That always amazed me [*laughs*]. In those days, you could get in trouble for anything!

KC: You wanted to do her justice.

BH: Yeah. I really cared about her. I shouldn't have been reading the story at that point in the writing of it, but there you go.

KC: I'm very enamored of your lost girls.

BH: She wasn't really a girl. It was called "The Christmas Corsage" and I think she worked at a dime store and had to buy herself a corsage at Christmas, and I felt more sorry for her because she was what I thought was ancient—like thirty [*laughs*].

KC: When did you write your next play?

BH: I went to SMU for college and I took a playwriting class. That's where I wrote *Am I Blue*.

KC: What motivated you to take a playwriting class?

BH: I got an idea. My boyfriend and I had gone to New Orleans and stayed in the French Quarter, and it was the first time I'd heard the song "Am I Blue?" I kept saying, "Play it again." I loved that song and begged them to play it even when they were leaving. I kind of had this energy of the French Quarter as it was at that time—it's not remotely like that now—so it was a place I felt compelled to write about. So I had an idea and I took the playwriting class and the one great assignment was to write a one-act play by the end of the semester. So I did and I don't think it was very good, but you had to turn it in. They did a production of it at SMU and I think I did revisions. But I was still so mortified that I had it under a pseudonym, Amy Peach. And that just drove my mother and father crazy when they went all the way up to see it and they couldn't bring the program back with my name on it because it was "by Amy Peach," and they told all their friends I'd written this play. But I was very unsure about it.

KC: What was the experience of seeing it? Did you have a different experience seeing it? Did you want to own it?

BH: No. It was very much like any production. You see it first and it's just horrible, and you're so disappointed because it's nothing like what you'd hoped, but then by the end, as they perform it more and more it gets better. And I really loved the people who were cast as the leads, so I got to where I liked it very much. But the odd thing was it was done on the same bill as Frederick Bailey's play *The Bridgehead*, which was this Vietnam play. Mine was about two virgins, one in high school and one in the first semester of college—played up against this very violent, very topical, very important play. So . . . I don't know [*laughs*].

KC: *Am I Blue* may have suffered in the contrast. One thing I love about *Am I Blue* is all these denizens of New Orleans that you have throughout it. It's so *of* that city.

BH: I love that city.

KC: So this really was your first play. And your first play became known because, after SMU, it was done again. Right?

BH: Yes, I think it was after *Crimes of the Heart* was done. Stuart White was the director and he read it and he did it [at Circle Rep in 1982]. A beautiful production.

KC: There are some acting programs that just sort of strip you of everything and then they try to remake you in some mold they think is a successful mold. Whereas, actually, what makes a career is your uniqueness, is being who you are. Was college a good thing for you?

BH: College was a great thing for me because, besides having some excellent teachers, the students that were working there at the time were some of the most gifted and invested artists I've ever known; and the bar was so high with what people were trying to accomplish that I thought the rest of the world was going to be like this. And I *needed* help. I took a movement class. I was all hunched over when I came. It was Jim Hancock's class, and to pass the class you had to be able to stand on your head for five minutes. I thought for sure I would flunk, but I learned to do it. The voice thing was the Lessac voice system. [*She demonstrates, very deep-voiced:*] "Thoose oold booats doon't flooat," trying to get rid of our southern accents. And the inverted megaphone [*she demonstrates, again deep-voiced:*] "Hellooo, Hellooo." I don't know if it helped or not—anything would have helped me [*laughing*] coming from public school in Mississippi. And the [SMU] teachers were very committed.

KC: You grew up in Jackson, right? A university town and the state capital. So from there to Dallas. Was that very different?

BH: Dallas seemed so different because it had this *huge* sky, this *endless* sky. And you'd go to these little bars that were in churches and order Black Russians. I just was terrified, but I learned so much. So I really thought Dallas was kind of like Paris from my perspective.

KC: Did you go to Paris as a young person?

BH: I did. I went when I graduated from college. I went to Paris with my boyfriend, and we were just like rubes abroad [*laughs*]. It was beautiful but stressful.

KC: Did you see theater in Europe?

BH: Yeah.

KC: What theater do you remember seeing?

BH: I remember we went to see *Figaro*, and they had a place for us to get the tickets that were *sans vision*. So we had to stand up there; we could hear it, but we couldn't really see it. [*Laughing*] These balconies that were *so* high.

KC: Did you see great art in Europe that affected you?

BH: Yes.

KC: Do you remember anything in particular?

BH: I know we got to see the *Mona Lisa*. I was troubled by the disappointment factor [*laughs*]. This long line and "what's it gonna do?" but I didn't have the eye to really see the difference between the *Mona Lisa* in the Louvre and the *Mona Lisa* print [*laughs*]. So I don't know. I had a lot to learn. . . . We didn't want to be on a tour. That was beneath us, so we went over there on our own—[*rolls her eyes*] idiotically.

KC: Did you only go to Paris?

BH: We went to London as well.

KC: Did you see any great performances in London?

BH: I'm trying to think what we saw in London. I've been to London so many times since. I'm not really sure what we saw then.

KC: Let's talk about *Crimes of the Heart*. After you wrote *Am I Blue*, had the bug bit you? Were you like, "I want to keep doing this"?

BH: Well, I wasn't confident, that's for sure, and I still had the same fears that I didn't really have enough talent or insight or intellect or experience to be a writer—even though I was writing in notebooks, things, I don't even know what they were. It took me a while to get up the courage to commit to writing something.

KC: And how did that occur?

BH: I was at the University of Illinois for one year.

KC: What were you studying?

BH: Theater. I was meant to be getting a Master's. And so I had to teach, which was a catastrophe. [*Laughing*] I actually had to teach Lessac Voice for the Stage, which I'd only taken one semester of in my freshman year. So I had all these freshmen; I was going [*she demonstrates the technique, deep-voiced and laughing:*] "Hellooo! Thoose oold booats doon't flooat. Everyone!" Oh, it was horrible. *Horrible.* This one kid—I said, "All you have to do is do one speech." And he didn't learn it, and I said, "Do you know 'The Lord's Prayer'?" "Do you know 'Happy Birthday'?" [*Laughs*] "Come on. Say *anything* because I want to pass you." I felt so bad.

KC: You were rooting for him.

BH: I was rooting for them. At the same time, it made me have a bad taste in my mouth. If this school can actually have *me* teaching this class, how good can it *be*? But it was money and sort of a free Master's degree—that I never finished. But there I met Claudia Riley and she was writing plays and she encouraged me to write plays, so I'm grateful for her.

KC: How was *Crimes of the Heart* born?

BH: I was living out in Los Angeles.

KC: How did you get from the University of Illinois to L.A.?

BH: I drove [*both laugh*]. I went down to Mississippi. I'd gotten this old disaster of a car in Texas that was a huge Oldsmobile. Gold and just a really embarrassing sort of car, but it was cheap and it kinda worked. So when I got here, Fred Bailey, who had done *The Bridgehead*, was producing his own plays at La MaMa [Hollywood] for like five hundred bucks or something. And so I had written a screenplay that, of course, wasn't getting anywhere. And I thought, I'll write a play; we could do it here. I was thinking very practically: it needs to be a small cast, one setting that we could afford. A kitchen. And I remember thinking, what can you do to make a kitchen different? And I thought, put a cot in it because that'll give people different places to sit. And I thought, okay, the birthday cake at the end—well, we can't afford a cake every night, so the lights will just have to go out as they head toward cutting the cake [*laughs*]. I was always pretty practical— in playwriting. So I wrote it and I had a reading of it and Frederick Bailey gave it to the Actors Theatre of Louisville. He'd won the year before. Then a friend of mine, Sharon Ullrick, gave the script to her agent, who gave it to Gilbert Parker, who became my agent, and he just read it and called me up and said, "Do you want me to represent you?"

KC: So Fred sent it to Actors Theatre of Louisville?

BH: But Gilbert Parker, who was a very well-esteemed agent, I think he called up and kind of probably encouraged them to do it as well.

KC: So he [Parker] was immediately taken with your writing.

BH: Right.

KC: Wow. Did that surprise you?

BH: I was very surprised. And I remember I was with Steve, my boy-friend, and we were coming back from Thursday night at the fights because it was only two dollars to get in to the boxing and I'd had so much fun 'cause I went with all the guys and I had a hat on and was way dressed down. And then I came in and I got the call and I remember feeling: I don't want anything to change. I liked writing in private and even though it was great news, it was terrifying news—that call from Gilbert, saying he wanted to represent me.

KC: And so what was the call like that told you you'd co-won the [American play competition at Actors Theatre of Louisville]?

BH: I'm not sure who gave me that. I think Jon Jory may have. And I was speechless to the point where I think he thought I was mentally ill— 'cause . . . [*she says flatly:*] "Oh. Okay." I wasn't excited; I wasn't curious. I was just terrified.

KC: Maybe in shock.

BH: In shock, yeah. So Jon Jory calls and invites me to come to Louisville to meet with him. I don't know if we were going to work on the script. But I was staying at their house, which I found very nerve-racking. In those days, you always stayed at somebody's house, and the main thing I remember is wearing the wrong clothes. I had on a skirt that was too wintry for the weather; I thought it was going to be cooler. And it had a tight waist and my stomach started blowing up from nerves and I just remember I was so uncomfortable [*laughs*]. That's the main thing I remember.

KC: Is it all *your* experiences that inform those characters? Is it an homage to Chekhov's *Three Sisters*? Is it *your* sisters? Or did it just come to you?

BH: It's probably all of those in a certain way. I was in love with Chekhov's *Three Sisters*. I wanted to be in it in college and was not picked and was devastated. And I think—I'm not sure, it was either subliminal, or maybe it was purposeful—you could do those plays in rep: Irina could be Babe; Masha could be Meg; Lenny could be Olga; and Chick could be Natasha; Vershinin could be Doc [*laughing*]; and Tuzenbach could be Barnette. It was strange how that lined up, but also I grew up with sisters and I guess this is true not necessarily of just sisters, but families, how when somebody's out of the room you get with the other person and then when they leave—you're always talking about somebody else's problems when they're gone, with the other person. So these strange alliances that are formed and then when they're revealed, everyone's mad. Because "I didn't know you were going to say that to her. Why'd you. . . ." You know, those sort of dynamics of loving each other but judging each other were kind of at the forefront.

KC: There are some really hard truths in that play that you found humor in. It's the most dire things that you find a way to make funny. How did you develop your sense of humor, and how do you find humor in these things that are so harrowing?

BH: I think it's possibly my worldview that everything seems to have two sides. Nothing is quite really, really funny without pain, and nothing is really, really tragic—with a few exceptions, or maybe more than a few—without something at least ironic or *so* perplexing. When I wrote *Crimes of the Heart*, I didn't realize it was as funny as it was, and neither did Jon Jory. In rehearsal they were saying, "Is this a comedy or a drama?" and we turned to the first page, and it says, "*Crimes of the Heart*: A Play" [*winces and laughs*]. I think of things kind of logically. They come to me with a truthful logic, like when I wrote the line "Why did Mother kill herself? Because she had a bad day." I was very sincere in that thought; that can happen to you on a bad day. There are many days you just barely scrape by without killing yourself. And some, you miss the mark. But then that was very, very funny in the context of a line onstage because it was understatement, I suppose. But it took me a while to be able to realize what lines would work as comedy.

KC: So you discovered in that play comedy that you didn't realize might be inherent in it?

BH: I knew some things were funny, but I wasn't clear—'cause to me I was dead serious about all of these characters—and loved them and didn't think of them as wacky.

KC: Do you love all your characters?

BH: Let me think. I love most of them. [*Pauses*] I'm trying to think of the very worst ones. Yeah, I do. I love all of them—because of their weaknesses.

KC: Are you able to sit in the audience when your plays debut?

BH: Oh yeah. I think it's crucial to be there in previews. You learn so much. That's where I make some really good changes.

KC: What kind of changes?

BH: Things that I had a question about and the director or the actor wanted to give it a try. And then if it doesn't work—or if it *does* work, it becomes very clear—at that time we're ready to throw it out because "oh, wow, that was boring." Sometimes I overwrite, and things need to be thrown out. But sometimes you want to give it a chance, like maybe it will be the best part of the play. In previews you just learn so much about the rhythm.

KC: So you're sitting in the audience for *Crimes of the Heart* [at Actors Theatre of Louisville]—your first real, big production. What were you feeling?

BH: Terror. I remember my mother was there, and my cousin Lucy had decided to give a dinner party before the play. She was my mother's first cousin. So all of these relatives were there and the food didn't come and the food didn't come, and there were problems in the kitchen; and I had to leave without dinner. In the car running over there, my mother and I had Pepto-Bismol, chugging Pepto-Bismol—"Here, you want some?" "Yeah, I'll have some."—'cause [*laughing*] we were so sick to our stomachs.

And I just sat there frozen, just frozen, but I loosened up. I had some of the greatest—Kathy Bates was in it, Susan Kingsley; it was extraordinary. They gutsed it out, and they figured out what the play was about. So I felt this sort of relief, but I was so overwrought with nerves and neuroses, it didn't really settle until the play was over and several drinks into the after-party [*laughs*]. Then I could feel okay.

KC: Meanwhile, people are telling you how much they've enjoyed it, right? So you start to learn from an audience?

BH: I don't learn from them telling me. I learn from listening to them listen and respond in the audience. Because unless it's somebody you really know—even if you really know them, if they're seeing the play after it's opened, they need to lie because it's too late. You just don't go back and tell somebody how bad their play is. You never do that with actors, *for sure*, and you may as well not do it with a playwright. You know, just kindness: "congratulations," "well done" [*laughs*]. In previews, you're there taking notes, figuring out how to fix this and that. But I sit in the front row [at the] opening, so I won't know what's happening behind me. And I just look at the actors and just breathe up their kindness for actually showing up onstage and knowing the lines and giving it their all.

KC: You have a tribe of actors that have worked with you repeatedly. When you work on a play, you have some actors who know your work and have worked with you often—can you explain that process a little bit?

BH: Yes. After I finish a play—and if I finish a play, it's like its eighth draft and I've given it to some people to read and then gone back and revised it—but when I've got it as good as *I* can get it, I just invite people over to my living room, invite some friends, especially people whose eye I trust or who are just supportive or interested, but no professional agents, nobody that could possibly do the play, and I have my friends read it. It's really a relief because those characters are now out in the world, spoken by somebody else and they're floated away from your psyche in ways you didn't really think they might be. And if you're working with really good actors, if something is amiss, they can sometimes make it *not* seem amiss, so you have to be [*laughing*] a bit careful. But I don't care at that point; I just want it to work as best it can.

KC: Hearing it is a part of your process.

BH: Very much. It's always been true.

KC: Tell me about the life of *Crimes of the Heart*. How did it win the Pulitzer Prize?

BH: A miracle of odd circumstance. It was done at Louisville, and then it was kind of done around the country. It was done in Palo Alto, J. Ranelli directed it; in St. Louis, Stuart White; and J. Ranelli also did a production in Baltimore. And Melvin Bernhardt wanted to do it at the Manhattan Theatre Club, and so they did it there. And—talk about timing—it was the very first year they said a Pulitzer Prize could go to a play that wasn't on Broadway. If it had been done a year earlier, it wouldn't have had that opportunity. And because it won the Pulitzer Prize, that gave it enough motion to get it to Broadway. It was not moving to Broadway; the reviews had been good but not overall entirely great. So I was very lucky.

KC: How did you find out that you won a Pulitzer? How did that information come to you?

BH: On the phone. I was at my house, a house I was renting with my boyfriend. And it's so seventies—we had one of those French telephones, those really campy-looking ones that you talk on and can't move around. My agent called me and he said, "I have some news for you." And I said, "What?" And then we got cut off somehow. So then I picked up the phone and it was the newspaper: "Did you know you won the Pulitzer Prize?" I was like, "No!" And then I—I don't know—I talked to my agent. We called some people. We went out to this Russian restaurant and just drank. And then we came back to my house and people were coming in that we knew, and got a pizza and drank some more.

KC: So you found out from the newspaper guy?

BH: I think so.

KC: Somebody from the Pulitzer calls you or something? We have the telegram that William Inge received when he won for *Picnic*.

BH: He got a telegram? I don't think I got a telegram.

KC: You were not yet thirty. Is [winning a Pulitzer] a daunting thing? Is that somehow a burden, too?

BH: I didn't really even know what a Pulitzer Prize was. I couldn't have told you who won a Pulitzer Prize. I just knew that this made me a hotshot. It also meant maybe I could be a writer. If they are giving me this Pulitzer Prize, that means I probably can be a writer, and that was the greatest thing because I had no real confidence that I could make a living as a writer or have a life as a writer. It was very terrifying and very—to get a lot of attention is so daunting to me sometimes. To suddenly go up and you've got this national award—I didn't handle it as well as one would hope. I did do a lot of stupid things, but fun things. Those were the eighties and you could go, "Let's get a limousine!" [*Laughing*] "Let's get some Champagne!" My grandmother—bless her heart—she sent me a corsage. That was her response to me getting a Pulitzer Prize. So I was wearing this corsage [*laughs*].

KC: How wonderful though! And then *Crimes of the Heart* had its Broadway production.

BH: Yes. With the same cast that had done it at the Manhattan Theatre Club. So it was virtually the same production.

KC: And there you were on Broadway. Was it like "Pinch me. I'm in a dream"?

BH: I don't know. I just knew the most important thing was to keep writing. I was already working on another play. Before I have a play produced, I always want to be working on another one, which hasn't always been the case, but I knew to keep my eye on the ball of working.

KC: After Louisville, you started writing another play?

BH: I was writing another play when I was in Louisville. I was working on *The Miss Firecracker Contest*.

KC: How did the idea for *Miss Firecracker* come to you?

BH: Well, my boyfriend at the time, Stephen [Tobolowsky], grew up in Dallas, and he said there was a Miss Firecracker Contest. And I said, "A beauty contest?" I'd never heard of a beauty contest on the Fourth of July. And that was just so intriguing to me. Because it seemed there was a raunchiness about it that interested me. I've always been interested in the idea of beauty. And what is beautiful and what is not is in the eye of the beholder. Because when I grew up, beauty was such the thing. It very much reminds me of William Inge, how you've got these four years of beauty and then it's over for a woman because of course you can't have a job or anything. And some of the lines were from what my mother told me her mother said, which was: "You've had your spoonful of gravy, now go out and get a rich husband." That was kind of what it was like for women. And I found that so troubling because I realized that once you had to rely on someone for your income, there is no end to the amount of grief you will have to put up with just to survive. So I like the character Popeye; she's going about taking care of herself with her sewing. Also the idea of Carnelle, of someone who is trying to reform, is trying to change. I'm interested in that theme of *can we change?*

KC: Redemption?

BH: Is there redemption or enlightenment of any kind? And madness—the brother had been in the madhouse. And who *is* the mad person? And—who told me?—there was this story about this woman who actually did have pituitary glands put in her, and she did become monkey-like. I'd read that somewhere or somebody told me that story. And I was so intrigued that somebody who is kind of monstrous becomes physically monstrous.

KC: When Carnelle picks up that flag, having been devastated, having come in last—you've already made it clear earlier in the play that the person who comes in last follows the float—when she picks up that flag, it feels like a moment of triumph. Carnelle commits to something and she sees it through. Where does that come from?

BH: It's kind of the energy of life. I respect people who care enough to throw their hat in the ring—'cause many times I don't have the interest, I don't have the energy, I don't have the concern. Sometimes it amazes me that anybody wants to do anything in this world. So when people really want to do something wholeheartedly and they put themselves into it, I find that compelling. And then the many ways that it can come out—successfully, a huge failure, it can hook you into something you didn't know it would hook you into and then you become addicted to this sort of safety or this sort of adventure—but *action*. What is the Greek word for "to do"? People that *do* stuff, I like to write about.

KC: Let's talk about *The Wake of Jamey Foster*. So you had written *Miss Firecracker*, but it wasn't in production yet.

BH: Actually, *Miss Firecracker* was produced in L.A. in a small theater with Belita [Moreno] and Cheryl Anderson, who I knew from SMU, and Mary McCusker and Steve Tobolowsky and Jonathan Banks. Directed by Maria Gobetti. So it had been done. But *The Wake* we did in Hartford, Connecticut, with almost the same cast [as would be on Broadway later that same year, 1982], except for Amanda Plummer, who had to go do the one about the nuns [*Agnes of God*]. That was the part we had to replace and that's where we found Holly [Hunter].

But that [production of *The Wake of Jamey Foster*] was a study in a playwright going from "Oh, you're wonderful" to "Oh, your play's going to close in ten minutes." And that was kind of exhilarating and of course devastating because on Broadway they wanted to run the play for twenty-one days. If it were ever to be made into a movie, it had to have run for at least twenty-one days to get the film rights. So after it got *horrible* reviews, devastating reviews, it was kind of on life-support for twenty-one days. And you're watching all these people, like the people who do the wigs, the women in the restroom handing out towels—they're all going to lose their jobs. It was so crushing. *And* Holly's father died during *The Wake*; she had to go back to Georgia. So it was all, kind of, fraught with death. And it was opening around Halloween, the day of the dead. [*Laughs*] There's a picture of me sitting in the gutter with a bottle of whiskey after the reviews came out, and Gilbert Parker sat down beside me in the gutter, on the curb; we're sitting there, and my other—my Hollywood—agent is standing up smoking a cigarette. And Belita, in the photograph, is down there talking to me, telling me it's all going to be okay: "Didn't we say that just to be here is enough?" And I was going: "We *lied*. We *lied*." [*Laughing*] You want it to be successful. . . . So that was heart-wrenching, but I just thought, well, this is how life is, isn't it. It kind of just sets you up for how life is.

KC: So those were the days when you got the reviews at the party?

BH: [*Nods*] *Very* glamorous; you're at the party and then suddenly everyone is gone [*laughs*].

KC: And you want the play to have a life, so you suddenly think the whole thing is sunk.

BH: Which it is.

KC: Did the play go on to have a life?

BH: It's rare. It's produced occasionally.

KC: I love its outrageous theatricality. . . . Let's go on to *The Debutante Ball*. Where does an idea come to you like that particular one, which I think is profoundly about a mother and a daughter?

BH: In an odd way, this is one of the few plays that was in some respects based on an event. There was in Jackson—I'm not even sure if the daughter was a debutante or not—but the mother shot the father and killed him, and she was in jail and the rumor around town was that the daughter had really done it. Because it was an abusive relationship, I think the mother finally got out. But I found that idea very compelling: taking the blame so it wouldn't be on your daughter. But the cost that would be to the daughter.

KC: You had a bathroom onstage.

BH: Gilbert, my agent, was kind of unhinged by the bathroom onstage, but I just know if you're getting ready to go to a ball or out, you're *in* the bathroom, you're putting on the makeup, you're shaving your legs, you're doing your hair; and I wanted the image of the mother being in the bathtub with the psoriasis, just the vulnerability and how exposed she is. I just had some images that were in the bathroom, so I just put it in there. If you're a woman, so much of the interesting stuff is happening in the bathroom. You're trying to get ready, and other women are trying to get ready.

KC: Isn't there a rape in the elevator in that play?

BH: I'm thinking what it is is that Teddy, the debutante, whose mother has gone to jail for her, feels so guilty and I believe she insults this man who's disfigured and then out of guilt is compelled to have sex with him. Because that's how guilt can work, when you think you're not worth anything, so any sin you make you must try to repair.

KC: By "sin," do you mean religious . . . ?

BH: No, I don't think I mean religious.

KC: Just against another person.

BH: Yeah.

KC: Let's talk about *The Lucky Spot*. What a beautiful play this is. Again, there's a young girl. Why the young girls?

BH: I think there's something that intrigues me about innocence and inexperience and the yearning and the fraught emotions—but they somehow lack a bitterness that comes with age and still have a wonder at the world. She's so happy that they bring a tree into a room for the Christmas tree; [she] had never seen that because she's very back-country.

KC: Where did you first do *The Lucky Spot*?

BH: At Williamstown. And then it was done at Manhattan Theatre Club.

KC: Same cast?

BH: Different cast.

KC: Did Christine Lahti play Sue Jack at Williamstown?

BH: Yes, and Carol [Kane] played Lacey. That's where I met Carol—in Williamstown.

KC: And who played the girl?

BH: Holly did—when we did it at Williamstown.

KC: Into the play comes this character Sue Jack, who seems to me a force of nature. Where did the character Sue Jack come from? How did she come to you?

BH: I really wanted to write a part for Susan Kingsley, so I wrote that part with her in mind. Her range was just phenomenal; she was one of the greatest actresses I've ever known or worked with. I don't often do that, but I wanted her to play the role. . . . I don't know if I'd finished it by the time she died. She was very young.

KC: But she lives in that role.

BH: [*Nods*] I dedicated the play to her kids, Roxanne and Gar.

KC: Is Pigeon, Louisiana, a real place?

BH: Actually, yes. I was looking at the map, "Oh my God, Pigeon. Yeah, right!" And it's kind of in the part of the state I wanted it to be in, the southern.

KC: The music in *Lucky Spot* . . .

BH: Oh, I love the music.

KC: You have a whole list of music in that play, everything from Bessie Smith and Louis Armstrong . . . some gorgeous music, right?

BH: Yeah, I love the music of that era. I listened to every song in the background very, very carefully with the dialogue and how to play it, and which worked and which *version* of "Sweet Sue" to use, and I had to have them shoot up the jukebox so I could go to the race records that were in the attic by the guy who lived here before. So I had to plot out all these things so I could use the music I wanted to because none of that music would have been on a jukebox.

KC: So you wanted the tone to change at a certain point?

BH: Yeah, when they start the dance club.

KC: So that the underscoring is a completely different kind of sound.

BH: Yeah.

KC: Marvelous aspect of it. So music is a part of your writing always? Do you play music while you're writing?

BH: I play, I don't know, the sound of the ocean or something when I'm writing [*laughs*]. I get too into music. A lot of people write to music just blasting; I don't do that.

KC: I feel like your writing voice changed in *Abundance*. Obviously you weren't in the South; you were in Wyoming Territory, and is it St. Louis at the end?

BH: Yeah.

KC: How did the idea of writing about that period, of pioneering, of womanhood out West—how did this come to you?

BH: I think there are two things. Once, I was out on a boat and I saw a boat named *Abundance*, and it occurred to me: When do you have an abundance? When do we stop wanting more? When is it just like not only do we have enough, we have too much? This *never* seems to occur in the human psyche. "I have so much, let's give it away." Kind of a Christian idea that hasn't really taken. But also, I had been given this book, *Wisconsin Death Trip*. It's an incredible book with photographs and newspaper articles from an era. It's so full of violence, and it's so full of pictures of baby corpses, odd, horrible accidents, and people going insane. And it's like "Oh, so this is how it *really* was to be in the West." Not exactly like . . . *Bonanza* [*laughs*]. It got me very interested in studying that period. And then I wanted to write something—I liked the idea of two women, one whose dream was to be in love, and the other whose dream was to have adventure and excitement and break all the rules, and how the situation reversed their dreams. So in a way, they each got the dream they didn't want, that was the other's. But kind of in the end they are each other's dreams because they have a real connection and have really experienced things together. They've hurt each other but they understand each other. And they've loved each other very much, more than they've loved anyone else.

KC: I think this is the amazing thing about this play: the relationship between the women and how it's challenged to the utmost, in the most profound ways imaginable, and yet they still do love each other.

BH: But I think that's getting older and living life—and you're ground down and there are so few people you can look in the eye and actually feel connection with and love in that deep, profound, vibrant way.

KC: What was the process of that play like? Michael Roth told us yesterday a little bit about the first production [1988–89 season] at South Coast Rep. Martin Benson also—I was so glad they did it again [in 2015 at South Coast Rep]—that he wanted to direct it . . .

BH: That was *fantastic*!

KC: With a *big sky*. He said, "It didn't have a big sky! It needed a big sky!"

BH: I know!

KC: But Michael also said that it was done in New York [Manhattan Theatre Club, 1990], and it really did not deliver the way it had at South Coast Rep.

BH: No. It was one of those fraught experiences when an actress came and she was very tired from doing a film and came a few days late and then dropped out after a week or ten days. We had to get Tess Harper, who's brilliant and wonderful, but it was kind of like she was dropped in with all these lines to learn and two weeks to rehearse. It was kind of like the spirit of the play couldn't emerge under these circumstances.

KC: And yet you can't stop the train. . . . [Michael] said there's something so powerful about your voice in this play and in some ways it's somewhat post-modern, and he wanted you to have that triumph in New York that you had had at South Coast Rep.

BH: Oh, it's the vagaries of theater.

KC: But it didn't devastate you?

BH: Of course I was devastated. I'm endlessly devastated. To the point it's boring [*laughs*]. I get so sick of it. I get so sick of coming back and being heartbroken and not being able to work and thinking I'm going to get over it and not getting over it. You know, it's just—I don't know. It *is* boring.

KC: It's a terrible place to be. Inge never wrote another play after two of those.

BH: I feel heartbreak for Inge because he—you can't care that much. You have to love your work more than you love your success, or you're really going to be in a bad trap. I really do love my work. I mean, I hate when things fail and you're publicly humiliated and what you love is trampled on, but I'd rather be doing what I love. I feel so excited that I get to have a life where I get to do what I love. I appreciate that. And that may come from being a woman; I was never expected to be a big success, so the fact that critics don't like me—I'm like "Oh yeah, that was like my dad" [*laughs*]; "Yeah, I didn't do that well in school." I think it works in my favor to have people expect nothing [*laughing*].

KC: Let's talk about *Signature*. Wow, the sheer inventiveness of *Signature*! This future that you invent! How was it born?

BH: I think in a certain way, you're always writing in response to your last play. And after the kind of trauma of *Abundance*, or whatever it was, I kept wondering: What is your signature? What is the importance of having a signature? John Keats wrote: "Here lies one whose name was writ on water." And I kept thinking: Why is it so important to leave a signature?

Boswell is obsessed with leaving a signature. How that boxes you in if that's what you're fighting for. And also, just how love *can* kill you. Do not take it lightly; it *can* kill you. And the idea that you need to die for love to prove that you love. If the pain of losing love leaves you, that means you were not really in love. He's going to be put in a capsule and die for love, and it's so stupid, but it's so understandable.

KC: Is *Revelers* reminiscent of your own theater history?

BH: There's a small storefront theater called Center Theater [Chicago], which I worked at, and I know some of the people from when I went to the University of Illinois. They were very generous in doing my plays, so it's a little bit of an ode to them but also to an acting teacher I had, who was absolutely brutal about the truth; he would say, "Go up onstage and just live in the truth," and it would be in an environment that would make no sense. It wasn't a living room; it wasn't a kitchen; it was just a big mess, and [*intones deeply:*] "Go live in the void and be true in the void." And I never knew what he was talking about. And I always went up there and wasn't living the truth in the void [*laughs*]. But I learned more from him than I learned from most teachers because it was so important to make things alive, to be in the moment, not to be canned, not to have it all figured out. But it was painful, and the guy didn't have a gentle personality.

KC: Sheer inventiveness on your part [in *Revelers*]! Caroleena, the Jill-of-all-trades, this idea of her channeling the dead director, doing the high-wire act and all of this? Again, what led you to certain things?

BH: I felt like I'd gotten myself into something that I didn't know what to do with. And I'm not sure this play works very well, but [*laughing*] it's an attempt.

KC: I will say I recognize many people in it.

BH: Well, it's very much a sort of homage or . . . I don't know . . . of theater people, people who are doing theater in a small way and haven't made it to the top.

KC: Now, you directed *Control Freaks*.

BH: I directed it in Chicago at that little theater, Center Theater, first. Then I directed it at the Met Theatre, where I was part of the company in Los Angeles. And I was so mystified by the play, I didn't know who to even *ask* to direct it.

KC: You say you were mystified by it. It came out of you, but you didn't really . . . ?

BH: It was almost like I was embarrassed to ask somebody to direct it because it was so brutal. But I'm a terrible director. It was really painful. I had to just give so much love to the actors, who hung in there, and through their courage and will, the play evolved into something kind of spectacular.

KC: The brutality in that play, did that surprise you as you were writing it?

BH: Yeah. You're writing and you're kind of like "Don't censor yourself—keep writing—this is—I can't believe. . . . " You write it in kind of a white blaze of not knowing what you're writing.

KC: And then you see what's there and you're like—whoa!

BH: [*Makes an affirmative noise along with a sort of amused grimace.*]

KC: And Holly Hunter played this part? Did she play it in Chicago also?

BH: No. It was a whole different cast in Chicago.

KC: So this character of Sister with these multiple beings in her—was Sister always someone who had these multiple personalities?

BH: Yes, and that's why it's very hard to explain to somebody when they're reading it, like, "*What* are you *talking* about? I can't even understand this. This is Pinkie? This is Spaghetti? This is Sister?" Her psyche is shattered, and it works once you kind of unravel it; but when you just hand it to somebody to read, it's not necessarily clear.

KC: The most horrible things happen in this play *and* there's also this kind of hilarity, too. Is that important to you to be able to laugh at . . . to *not let* the horror triumph? She transcends; she flies away.

BH: It's not a realistic, naturalistic play. There's absurdist, expressionistic—I don't know what you want to call it. But from the very beginning, they're eating tea out of these little tea cups; it's all about control and then it unravels and becomes more and more out of control because they're trying so much to keep it controlled. And the control freaks collide and it becomes total hellacious chaos—which is something I think works, and I did a lot of it instinctually.

KC: When you directed it at the Met here in L.A., this was a cast who knew you?

BH: They knew me, and I was asking them to go to such deep, dark, brutal places, and I wasn't a big enough net to hold them up. I wasn't a safety net. Because it's hard to be a director. As a playwright you can just go up to the director and you can be nice to all the actors and encouraging. To direct you have to have a real eye. I was missing so many skills to be a director. I felt bad that I put these actors—asking them to be first-rate when I was far from first-rate as a director.

KC: Did they need a safety net because of the brutality of the play?

BH: Yeah.

KC: Have you seen it done to good effect since then by another director?

BH: Yeah, they did a production in London that was really good. It wasn't as good as the one at the Met Theatre, but it was well done.

KC: There's so much joy in *Impossible Marriage*. Were you pregnant when you wrote *Impossible Marriage*?

BH: Holly was getting married and I was her maid of honor and I *was* pregnant, so that image interested me, but I wasn't pregnant when I wrote the play. But I was grappling with this idea of an impossible marriage, meaning me as a writer being a mother, having a child, how impossible that marriage is and how will it ever work.

KC: It's a beautiful play. . . . Tell me about the genesis of *L-Play*.

BH: I started a number of things. And I was trying to experiment with different styles, and I thought why not write a play and all the scenes start with L, like "Loser," "Lost," "Learner," "Lunatic," "Leaving," and they're all in different styles and they're all actually plays. "The Lunatic" has three scenes and "The Learner" has three different monologues, but that's kind of the only unifying element. It's kind of like it's searching for connections [*laughs*]. The thing I use *L-Play* for now is in my class. I'll have them do four different L plays, so they'll get a sense of four different theatrical styles. So when they start writing their plays, they'll know—like in one play, a shoe is a character; one play is with masks; one play's kind of German expressionistic. But as a *play*, I would say [*L-Play*] fails.

KC: Were you writing it because you were looking to expand stylistically? Or challenging yourself? What drove that?

BH: The very first scene in it, the lead character gets shot and killed. That happened when I was writing it, and then I thought, "Well, the play's over. What're you gonna do?" But I like the ominous quality of the piece, and then I just got into the fun of it. It seemed so ridiculous it was fun.

KC: To write in different ways, right?

BH: Yeah.

KC: You referred to a period of time when it was hard to write.

BH: That would be my whole life.

KC: Really!? So it's a struggle? [*Henley nods.*] All the time? [*Henley nods.*] But you love it?

BH: Whatever.—I do love it, but it's also a lot of disappointment.

KC: I like what you said earlier about having to love your work more than you care about the outcome—you have to love it for its own sake. . . . Let's turn to the later plays. *Ridiculous Fraud* seems, even though it's more than ten years ago you wrote it, a very timely play.

BH: Yeah. A friend of mine wants me to make it into a screenplay, so I'm trying to see if I can do that. . . . I had just done a play—Carol [Kane] was in this play—*Family Week*, and that's four women. And I was thinking, "What's wrong with me? Let me write about men. Let me write three young, handsome men" [*laughs*]. It was kind of a slight nod to *Crimes of the Heart*—three brothers versus three sisters. I wanted to see if I could write male characters and write them well. That was part of it.

KC: And the political aspect of it? Was that something that was troubling you at the time?

BH: I'm trying to think with *Ridiculous Fraud* how much I thought about the politics. My father had been in politics and I was very cynical about politics, particularly in the South, particularly in Louisiana, and I wasn't sure how much that was going to be a part of the play. But I was in Princeton at a writers' retreat and I really didn't have much at the end of the ten days. I was driven back to the airport by this intern and he told me about his father being put in jail for fraud. Then I was kind of transfixed with that idea. What if you have to deal with the shame of that? And it's your father and you're a man. How are you going to repair that? Or how are you going to retreat from that? So that was kind of a linchpin to figure out how to do the rest of the play.

KC: And the duck hunting in *Ridiculous Fraud*? Not being able to kill the deer—this is Kap—because of the doe looking with those eyes, but being able to shoot the ducks. [*Both laugh.*] Where did that come from?

BH: A friend of mine in Mississippi was dating a duck hunter, and he was telling me about just how beautiful it is to see all the ducks light down in the water, sort of the magic of it, the kind of mystical feeling—and then, blown away by your own gun. That sort of contrast was fascinating to me. How do you blow up something that you find so beautiful? And he listens to his duck calls, and it's usually a female who's leading the flock of birds, that you try to imitate her voice to get the others to come to you. So how much do we trick each other in life? And why, really?

KC: To what end? And then Ed carries the blue mallards in, and they just gut them. Oof. . . . The woman who's dying of cancer . . .

BH: Maude.

KC: Maude. . . . But she's having affairs as she's dying!

BH: Just one.

KC: But Kap takes the retribution. Kap takes the scar for Andrew, right?

BH: Right.

KC: So that Andrew can carry on.

BH: I guess you can't say it's for one reason. I mean, it's out of solidarity, but at the same time it has a vengeance to it and a cruelty—"You can't take your own cuts; I'm taking the cuts for you."

KC: Do you know the ending of a play when you begin to write the play?

BH: No.

KC: What was the first piece of *The Jacksonian* that occurred to you?

BH: I think it was an image I'd had of a daughter bringing in a Christmas tree to her father, who was living in a motel, to try to cheer it up, which kind of has the opposite effect.

KC: And then what was the next thing that might have occurred to you?

BH: I do remember early on thinking that she had shoes to match her dress, for the wedding dress. And how important that was to her.

KC: When did the murder of the woman in the gas station come into the play?

BH: Early on, it was a woman in a restaurant, but that got too confusing, so it had to be a woman in a gas station. But I knew somebody was going to get murdered in the play; I knew it was about murder, but I didn't know who was going to get murdered onstage.

KC: Did you know it was going to be about race, too?

BH: Oh yeah. Because of the era it's set in.

KC: Tell me about the manger scene in the play when the daughter keeps playing with the baby Jesus.

BH: It's just so odd to me that in Mississippi, particularly at that time, manger scenes were everywhere. It didn't matter that it was a bar. Just the juxtaposition of the baby Jesus and the bar with the bottles back here and the Christmas lights. There used to be nativity scenes all over everywhere when I was growing up in Mississippi. I liked the idea of her being able to pick up the baby Jesus. And the waitress says, "*Put* that baby Jesus back in that manger where it belongs!" And she doesn't; she just throws the baby Jesus. I thought that was a way to show rebellion in a teenager that would really get under the skin of the waitress.

KC: It's sacred to Eva, the waitress, even though Eva is profane. You have in the beginning of scenes one line in italics, saying, for example, *Eva inadvertently reveals Fred's guilt.* Was it your intent that those be like title cards—literally conveyed to an audience—or not?

BH: No. I thought when I wrote it I didn't understand how confusing this was going to be. And maybe they would be title cards, but in the end they weren't. But I thought to help the reader—because it's a struggle to read.

KC: Because the chronology goes back and forth . . .

BH: Back and forth . . .

KC: Did you know a hotel like The Jacksonian in Jackson, Mississippi? Was there a seedy hotel there?

BH: A lot of it is in my mind. I mean I've been in seedy hotels, but I think this one just took on a life of its own.

KC: Did you write it linearly and then . . . ?

BH: No. I kind of wrote it just scenes and then I'd figure out—I wanted it to be, in a way, from Rosy's, the daughter's, point of view after she's seen her mother dead, basically trying to psychically hold time back, to change it. So all of these scenes are in many ways going through . . . could we stop time. It's how time slows down when you're in shock, and time spins, and time quakes. So I wanted to deal with what would be her madly going back trying to review the time and when could it have been stopped.

KC: As if she could change the outcome.

BH: Yeah.

KC: Wow. . . . And it's a drama; there is *not* the kind of humor in it that is prevalent in many of your works. There is some, but it's a real drama. And it's manipulative. As the bartender is unmasked, you start to think he's going to commit another murder. For some of the play you think he is going to kill Rosy. Why did you do that?

BH: I didn't know who was going to get killed. Sometimes I thought Eva was going to kill Fred, or the husband would be killed by his wife because she attacks him so brutally. So I wasn't sure, but I knew there was a murder.

KC: And he almost kills Eva, too, when he has her try the chloroform and he ends up knocking her out and stuffing her in the bathroom to hide her from the wife.

BH: And she kind of loses it after that.

KC: So the play surprised you too?

BH: [*Nods*]

KC: Were you surprised that you let humor go? Or was it the era that informed that?

BH: I didn't think about it being funny or not funny; I was just telling a story.

KC: *Laugh* is such a departure from *The Jacksonian*! Did you *need* to write *Laugh*?

BH: Yes. After writing *The Jacksonian*, I just went in the total other direction to write *Laugh*. I wasn't even sure I was going to write another play. I thought, "Well, maybe that's it 'cause I'm feeling really burnt out." So I spent a lot of time watching Mabel Normand and Fatty Arbuckle and Charlie Chaplin and really early, early silent films 'cause I love that era. And Buster Keaton is my favorite, ever. I started thinking, "Well, why don't you write something?" It's so hard to write a slapstick comedy that's like: *This is a comedy.* Yeah, *Crimes of the Heart* is a comedy, but just to *try* to write something that's a comedy is *so* hard. I don't think I succeeded, but it was interesting to try. I think *Laugh* has a lot of nice qualities, but it doesn't really succeed. It was *so* difficult to *try* to write funny [*laughs*]. I just saw a production in Dallas, and it was well done. Maybe if I could work on it in three more productions, I could get it right.

KC: Do you continue to work on plays?

BH: Not generally after they're published in Dramatists [Play Service].

KC: But through productions before publication, you keep working?

BH: Absolutely.

KC: And what are you working on when you continue to tinker?

BH: I think it's like anything: When you're cleaning a desk, you have to get this dirt away before you can see that dirt, or *that* could be shinier; and there's something you've always kind of not liked but ignored it because there were bigger things to deal with, and when those are settled down you can go, "Yes, that was always making me cringe! And now I can fix it." You can't always fix things, but those things that have been bugging you, you can make better.

KC: And do you do this all the way through the rehearsal process?

BH: Yes.

KC: Have you ever done major rewrites—like cut scenes, reorder things . . . ?

BH: Oh, definitely cut scenes and reordered things.

KC: I think this gives hope to young writers.

BH: The thing I will say to young writers is I work very, very hard for the draft I give to people not to be half-baked. You know, "I'm finished and I feel so good." *No.* Go back. Please, go back.

KC: Are you honing language, phrasing, musicality . . . ?

BH: Absolutely.

KC: Rhythm?

BH: Yeah. And you have to read it over and over again to get the sense of how the rhythm is actually playing from the beginning of the play to the end of the play.

KC: Do you read it aloud?

BH: No. I don't torture myself like that [*laughs*]. They talk in my head.

KC: Tell me about the Tennessee Williams *Desire* project [2015]. I'm curious about how you came to write *The Resemblance Between a Violin Case and a Coffin*.

BH: Tennessee Williams is an enormous hero of mine and has influenced me more than anybody. I wasn't *that* familiar with his short stories, and it seemed like an interesting project. I'm not even sure it was a great idea, but I did it.

KC: Was it a commission?

BH: It was a commission.

KC: Did you get to choose the story?

BH: No, they gave me the story. I was sort of grateful because I don't think I could have ever chosen a story. There are so many.

KC: And does that story have that title?

BH: Yes, "The Resemblance Between a Violin Case and a Coffin." I wanted to work with Michael [Wilson] because I knew he was kind of a Tennessee Williams aficionado, so that was exciting. I was privileged to work with the other writers. But in the end I felt like it wasn't that successful because you should just go read his story; it's a lot better than the play. If he didn't make it into a play, as he did with many of his short stories, that's probably because it wasn't meant to be a play. So it was more like a failed exercise.

KC: I've seen it beautifully done, and I wouldn't say that it failed. I found it beautiful. It stayed with me.

BH: Wow.

KC: You've just finished a draft of a new play? Do you want to share what you're doing right now?

BH: I don't know. I haven't had a reading of it, even in my living room, so I'm a little nervous to even speak about it because I may just chuck it [*laughs*].

KC: Can you talk a little bit about teaching?

BH: I teach at Loyola Marymount in Los Angeles, and I'm really lucky because I teach one class and I have twelve students. Even though it's taken me ten years, I'm finally feeling like I'm a better teacher. It's so hard to teach. As a playwright, I'm very associative—you're not really a leader, you're just kind of a collaborator—and to teach, you have to take responsibility. Originally, I was much too, like, "Do you think we should have an exam?" "How long do you think the break should be?" "Just come back whenever you want" [*laughs*]. I wasn't keyed into how to energize and focus and encourage. And these are undergraduates, so you really have to be helpful. It's a small class, so I really get to talk to them one-on-one, and I love that. I love people discovering how to be creative. And they all help each other; they read each other's plays and offer comments. They're really good-hearted.

KC: Has it helped you in your writing to be teaching writing?

BH: By teaching, I'm afforded the opportunity not to have to go off and try to get third-rate movie jobs or television jobs that are never going to get made anyway. And you've got to deal with many people to decide what to do. It's got a lot of input that makes things a bit bland. So I much prefer teaching because you get to go read a lot of plays—I'm reading more new plays; I'm rereading plays I love. I really enjoy that.

KC: Did you work on *Laugh* with a comedy class at LMU? Did I read that?

BH: Yeah. I was working with a professor, Ron Marasco, who's willing to take any insane chance, and he said, "Well, let's just work on it in class." The students were really game. There were days when we were throwing pies; we were like, how do you build a pie-throwing? It was really fun but a little unnerving for me because I'd never done that before, and I felt too exposed because the play wasn't in great shape. But I did actually take out a lot of really bad stuff from having them do it.

KC: So they were working with your text but improvising the physicality of it?

BH: Well, working on the physicality, and then they went off and did other things, too. Like there was a TV scene with Lucille Ball where she gets a pie in the face, and they had to stage that precisely, using the dialogue and every move so they could see how it built: What's the wait-for-me moment? And what's the reversal?

KC: Were they improvising at all or just improvising physically?

BH: In this exercise, they were trying to precisely replicate.

KC: But with your play?

BH: With mine, they were improvising.

KC: And you'd never worked with improvisation as a tool for writing before?

BH: No.

KC: Was it helpful, ultimately?

BH: I think it was, but I think Lucille Ball was probably much more helpful. Because when you're doing physical comedy, you need some sort of precision, and when you're developing a play, it's far too liquid. It was a successful class in that it was unique, but I don't know if it would be better not to have been working on my play and just to be working on the physical comedy.

KC: I'm sure you feel talked out, but this was hugely helpful.

In Conversation with Theresa Rebeck and Beth Henley

Theresa Rebeck / 2019

From Alley Theatre, March 2019, alleytheatre.org. Reprinted by permission of the Alley Theatre. Theresa Rebeck is a playwright and director, whose more than fifty one-act and full-length plays have been produced on Broadway, Off-Broadway, and at theaters throughout the US and abroad. She is the creator of the television series *Smash* (2012) as well as the author of three novels.

Prior to the start of rehearsals, Literary Manager Lily Wolff had the privilege of reconnecting *Crimes of the Heart* playwright Beth Henley and director Theresa Rebeck, two luminaries of the American theater and both award-winning playwrights. We are thrilled to share this excerpt of their fond phone call.

Theresa Rebeck: Hi Beth, this is Theresa Rebeck. Do you remember me?

Beth Henley: Of course I do!

TR: Oh, okay! We met so long ago. Carol [Kane] introduced us, we had dinner. Oh God, it was like in 1990, I think. '91?

BH: It was, it was. Oh man. . . . That was a while ago. I'm so happy you're directing this play. I'm flabbergasted. What were you thinking?!

TR: [*Laughs*] I'm thinking it's a terrific play! I'm thrilled! Maybe I can explain to you the things I've been thinking about and then you can tell me if I'm out of my mind.

BH: [*Laughs*] I would love that.

TR: So, here's what we did—because we felt like the play has achieved a kind of mythic or iconic status—it's a slightly abstracted version of the set with slashes of red in places, like the door, the stairs. . . . It's like a perverse valentine image, sort of violent, but it's a beautiful red. One of the things that we've been thinking about is that the play is very, very funny, but it's also very dark. I think I've seen versions of it that don't quite plumb the depths of how dark some of your choices actually are.

BH: Yeah, people like to lean into the funny stuff.

TR: Yes. And we'd like to lean into both. Because it's post-MeToo, there's a new consciousness about some of the darker aspects of the play. The window has been opened so you can really look at the grief and horror that surrounds those choices and actions. I always think that you have to leave blood on the floor anyway if you want to get a really good laugh. And by really acknowledging the darkness in your play, we can use that as a springboard towards the comedy. And that there's room in Meg and in Lenny for a more contemporary awareness of this stuff, so that we can see the rise of knowledge in them. There's a real shrewdness, especially in Meg. She knows a lot. She's on her way to becoming somebody truly wise. Babe is Babe. But Meg and Lenny are on their way to survival and, further than that, to life. I might—I was thinkin' of havin' that door on hinges and letting it open and close on its own. I'm a little curious about the possibility that the house is a little haunted—

BH: Oh, I love that, yeah!

TR: —by their inability to move on.

BH: I'm way on board with that. It's in retrospect that I realized what a rage I was in when I wrote that play.

TR: Oh great! That's great to know!

BH: Just an incredible rage. I mean it was kind of sublimated. . . . There's something about growing up with misogyny, not to mention bigotry. . . . How limited your knowledge could be in the sixties and seventies, if you're not a brainy person, like Babe, you're just in the fishbowl of Hazlehurst [Mississippi, the setting of *Crimes of the Heart*], you don't have a view of the world.

TR: Yes, that might be why I thought that door might need to be swingin' open on 'em. I think the universe has got to start saying to them, "Get out of the house. Get outta here." And Alexander's set is hot rather than warm. It's not a cozy little house, it's a little more disturbing than that.

BH: I'm so glad you're directing. I love it.

TR: I like it too. Grateful for the opportunity. Obviously I'm still one of those people, I'm just glad to be telling stories. Have you directed yourself?

BH: I directed one of my own plays, *Control Freaks*, and I basically had a nervous breakdown [*laughs*]. It was really challenging. Maybe if I were directing someone else's play it wouldn't have been as traumatizing. When did you start directing?

TR: Four years ago. And I started directing actually in film. I'd always wanted to do it. And I finally thought, I'm going to have to create my own opportunity because no one's going to help me. And my aunt, who I adored, left me a little bit of money and I decided, I'm going to use that money to make a movie. I had a play that I adapted that was a bit like *Crimes of the Heart* in a way; it was four people in a house—it was good! It came out like a Cassavetes movie, sort of . . .

BH: Oh, I love Cassavetes . . .

TR: Me too. So I'm really proud of it.

BH: What is the name of it? I want to see it!

TR: You can get it online! You should watch it! It's called *Poor Behavior*. It costs, like, six dollars. I always thought that was a great deal [*laughs*]. And then I directed *All My Sons* at the Alley with their company and it was a really beautiful experience for me. They have such great resources and wonderful actors. And then after that, I directed a play by a friend of mine [Neena Beber] called *A Foreign Body*, about Roman Polanski getting a lifetime achievement award and then the woman that he assaulted shows up. Most of it's set in a hotel room, and her younger self sort of emerges from the furniture and the scenes from his movies sort of emerge, too. So, now, I really want to make that into a movie and I think it's really a great time for it. People are really thinking about how they feel about work by artists who have done reprehensible things. And then, I directed one of my own plays, which really went fine. But you're right it's much more overwhelming. Like, when you're writing a play it's just you in your head and your typewriter or your computer and that's quite enough! But sometimes I got too lonely. I did, I got too lonely.

BH: Yeah, that's what I found.

TR: I did it for a long time and now I just need to be around people more. That's why I like directing. And I love your play. I feel like it's really fascinating and human. That's the other thing I feel—like there's such room to go into the surreal . . . I don't know how surreal I'm gonna go yet, I want to see what you can do with this set. Sometimes I don't quite know until I'm walkin' around it. But I really enjoy it and I'm glad to be doing this.

BH: Oh well I'm thrilled you are! I love it that it's kind of morphing out of naturalism. Because it's kind of like a dream play at this point, it's so old! [*Laughs*] It was written right when the feminist movement was starting. That's a really crucial element. That's why it wasn't quite right when they set the film in the eighties, because it wasn't on the cusp of the feminist movement like it's meant to be in '74. When people were just finding out that maybe this isn't the way things should be.

Lily Wolff: Theresa, I'm curious, do you have an early memory of experiencing *Crimes of the Heart* for the first time?

TR: It was one of those moments in which it became clear to me that women could write plays. Because I grew up in Cincinnati and I'd go to see plays at Cincinnati Playhouse in the Park. Student matinees. Playwrights were like gods to me.

BH: Yeah . . .

TR: Tennessee Williams. And Arthur Miller. And Molière. Shakespeare. They were like gods, really, so it never even occurred to me that I could do that. And then I started seeing a few plays by women. And that was like a bolt to my heart. And so I remember that. Thinking, oh my God, maybe I could do that. Women can do this. I said to my mother, "I would like to be a playwright." And she went white. Gray. It was the craziest thing she'd ever heard. And I thought, is this a crazy thing? Because now women are writing plays. So, *Crimes of the Heart* was very much in my consciousness after that. As were Wendy Wasserstein and Tina Howe and Marsha [Norman].

BH: Marsha!

TR: And at the time we really thought, wow, these great women who have come before us have opened the door for us!

BH: Oh man . . . good luck!

TR: Yeah, but you guys were, at that moment, our leaders. Just the coolest of the cool. I remember seeing you once after I got out of college and I was just a wannabe playwright. You were working on something at New York Stage and Film. And I did, I had that kind of like "Wow . . . there's Beth Henley" moment.

BH: Knock it off . . .

TR: And we really thought that things were moving. I was absolutely unprepared for the backlash. I think we all were. So I had a great opening of innocence around *Crimes of the Heart* and Beth Henley and the idea of being a female playwright. It really was significant to me. Little did we know that they were going to start hitting us on the head . . .

BH: I just weep when I see these young women designers and directors. When *Crimes* was first done there was no question of having a woman direct it. There weren't any. I mean, Emily Mann was around, but that was it.

TR: Well, things are moving. They are. But, boy, it's hard. The other thing that's happened in the theater, especially in New York, is there's a kind of bottleneck. There's a handful of directors that are considered to be the ones you have to have. And I finally thought, I don't want to be disempowered anymore. I don't want to hear that for a play to move ahead you have to have one of these ten directors. That's not coherent, you know. So, I started directing myself.

BH: I think I'm too lazy to direct now [*laughs*].

TR: It's a lot of work.

BH: It just took everything I had. You know. So I love directors. I love when you see a director that keeps working full-tilt, that hasn't gotten into that—just another job, you know . . .

LW: Would you both tell us about something you're working on right now?

BH: I'm working on *Lightning*, which the Alley is going to be doing a reading of.

LW: On the 29th of April! And where are you in the process of developing that play?

BH: It's about the hundredth draft. Four thousandth draft [*laughs*]. New York Stage and Film did a reading of it. And then at the O'Neill I had three or four days to work on it and it got a staged reading. And I got to learn a lot from that, because theater is in three dimensions. But I'm still really exploring how to make it work. And this piece is so dynamic, it will be great to work on it again.

TR: I'm working on *Crimes of the Heart* . . . [*laughs*], and then after that I'm directing a new play by my friend Rob Ackerman. It's called *Dropping Gumballs on Luke Wilson* and it's about the great documentarian Errol Morris. He made *The Thin Blue Line* and the one he's really known for is *The Fog of War*.

BH: *The Fog of War*, oh, I love that one.

TR: It's a documentary about a documentarian! And to support his work as a documentarian, he makes commercials sometimes. And it's about this moment when he was making an AT&T commercial and the props person, who was my friend Rob, who's a really wonderful playwright and supports himself by doing props for movies, had to drop gumballs (which represented connectivity) on this movie star. On Luke Wilson. And he hits him with one of them! So, that turns into Luke Wilson giving him the finger.

BH: Well, that's what they're paying Luke Wilson for, I guess!

TR: Right. And so, then Errol Morris decides that he kind of likes what happens when the actor gets hit by the gumball. It gets a reaction out of him that he thinks is really interesting. And it just kind of goes from there . . . and it's very, very funny and perverse and philosophical about morals in the workplace. And the morality of storytelling with live creatures, which is what we are. And it's very fascinating and really funny and I get to direct it!

BH: Wow. That sounds brilliant. Where are you doing it?

TR: At the Working Theater in New York. I love those guys. It's a bunch of working-class people who are union members and stuff. And they don't always do a full season. They're a fascinating theater and I'm really pleased to be doing it with them. And then after that I'm doing one of my own plays called *Dig* and I'm directing it up at the Dorset Theatre Festival.

BH: You're like so inspiring, man.

TR: [*Laughs*] Just listening to you I was like, WOW, this is beautiful. I'm having a time-travel experience. It's so great to look back and go, oh yeah, man, you were like a guiding light. You still are. But to think back on how much that changed me . . .

BH: That just means so much to me.

KP Live ABCs: Beth Henley!!!!!!!!

Samantha Barrios and Sam Gianfala / 2020

Transcribed from a Zoom interview conducted on November 19, 2020, as part of the Kentwood Players, Los Angeles, web series *KP Live*, on youtube.com/c/kentwoodplayers. Published with the permission of Samantha Barrios and Sam Gianfala. Samantha Barrios is an actor and director in Los Angeles; Sam Gianfala is an actor, screenwriter, and director in Los Angeles.

Sam Gianfala: She is a professor of mine at LMU [Loyola Marymount University], where she teaches playwriting. You might know her from plays such as *Crimes of the Heart*, for which she won the Pulitzer Prize. She also wrote *Control Freaks* and *L-Play* and *Revelers* and so many other things. It is my pleasure to welcome Beth Henley! I'm so glad you could make it tonight.

Beth Henley: I'm thrilled. It's so great to meet you via . . . whatever [video-conferencing app] we are.

Samantha Barrios: Thank you so much for joining us!

Henley: I'm honored.

Samantha: When Sam told me his playwriting teacher was Beth Henley, I said, "I'm coming over to sit off-camera and watch your class." And he said, "You can totally do that."

Henley: You can totally do that; it's Zoom.

Samantha: Zoom is magical. I have so many questions. For starters, will you tell us a little bit about how you got involved in theater?

Henley: My home state is Mississippi, and I grew up in a very segregated and harsh society. My mother was an actress and she was a beautiful actress, and she started this theater, the New Stage. I just loved watching her in plays. When I first went to the theater—we didn't get to see the show because it was too adult—they had this set and they started tearing it down and my mother was crying 'cause she said, "That's my kitchen"—it was *Hatful of Rain*—and I was just so struck by this phenomenal idea that you could love something so much, give it to people, and then destroy it and go on.

Samantha: Yeah, the most heartbreaking for me still to this day is the strike. So that's how you got introduced to theater, and you're an actress as well.

Henley: I acted some in college because I was in a theater program. I think acting is really great for a writer because even if you have a small part—like I was in Molière's *The Imaginary Invalid*, and I had one scene but got to hear the whole play over and over again and the rhythm of it and how the audience responded. Also, if you're memorizing Shakespeare, that's some intense knowledge about language. But I have never—I think I can say this truthfully—gotten paid to act—oh, except for outdoor theater in the Salem State Park in 1976, but such a little amount.

Samantha: But you had the experience. At what point did you go, "I can write this"? "I can write stories that change people's lives." At what point did you make that decision or discover it?

Henley: This is going to sound pathetic, but after I won the Pulitzer Prize [for *Crimes of the Heart*].

Samantha: Let's talk about *Crimes of the Heart* for a minute. . . . What inspired you to put this to paper, this story?

Henley: Well, I really didn't know if I was a writer. I'd written a play in college, *Am I Blue*, that they produced, but I used a fake name, Amy Peach, 'cause I was so embarrassed by it. Then I came out to L.A., and my grandfather, who was from Hattiesburg, Mississippi, was lost in the woods. He was in his seventies and he always went hunting and riding, and his horse came back without him. So there was this big event where everybody, from all over the state really, came in and walked, you know, six feet apart, trying to find him. Finally, he showed up at this small shack, and they said, "You're Mr. Henley; everybody is looking for you. Do you know where you are?" He said, "I'm in Copiah County." He was fine, but I just liked that there was all this drama about everybody coming back to look for him. My mother and father were divorced, and she was coming from a party and she was wearing an evening gown. This weird thing of people coming back in a crisis, so that was what sparked it.

Samantha: Of course that's exactly what happens. There's a crisis and the families come together. But it's also interesting to me because you—obviously, being from Mississippi—have such an understanding of the South, that duality of the South. . . . We're *all* from the South . . .

Sam: I don't know if you knew this, Beth, but I'm from Louisiana.

Henley: I knew that. I don't know how I knew that. . . . Oh, I know when you mentioned it! You said, "I fear going back to Louisiana." [*Laughter*]

Samantha: Don't we all. But there's that duality of the South that I think is misunderstood in that people don't maybe understand that complexity and the reasoning behind why we smush the drama and we put on that happy face.

Henley: Where are you from, Samantha?

Samantha: Oklahoma and Tennessee. The play also has that feeling of "*I* can talk about my family. *I* can say that they're crazy, but *you* cannot."

Sam: I feel like that family dynamic is definitely a southern family dynamic: Nobody else can talk about my family except for me.

Henley: It might be a part of human nature. I think a lot of people like to complain about their wives or husbands or children, but not so much if *you* do.

Samantha: Talk to me a little bit about the timing. How is it received? It's essentially your first play.

Henley: I had this incredible luck of a friend of mine—this is how you get places: miracles—gave it to an agent of hers and a big agent from New York was at his place in L.A. and he got the script and he read it on the plane, and he called me up and said, "I want to be your agent." I was like, "What?" He submitted it to the Actors Theatre of Louisville, which was doing—I think they still are doing—a new play series, and it co-won the prize. So it was produced in Louisville, and then people were interested in producing it in New York, but they wanted me to change the ending so that everything was perfect and Barnette saved the day. I was luckily so young—and didn't care if I was poor—I just said no.

Samantha: Oh, thank you! That's so interesting because it's not neat; it doesn't wrap in a—it's heartwarming but . . .

Henley: Still, bad things are coming for some of these people.

Samantha: Yeah, exactly, and there's not the knight in shining armor that comes in and everything is going to be fine. How was it received?

Henley: I had a beautiful, beautiful cast. Susan Kingsley and Kathy Bates were in the original cast. Susan Kingsley—I don't know if you know who she is—was just one of the greatest actresses on the planet. It was received very well in Louisville, but I remember standing outside the theater. It was snowing, and I was like "People are paying to go see something I wrote? Are they crazy? I'm such a fraud. Look, they got babysitters. Oh my God." I was really taking Pepto-Bismol [*gestures gulping from a bottle*].

Samantha: Wow. It's always fun for me to hear successful people talk about their nerves or their questioning because I always think that's unique to me [*laughs*].

Henley: I was nervous about tonight. I'm serious.

Samantha: Oh, that's so funny; I wouldn't have thought that.

Sam: Was there a point either when you were writing it or during the actual production or after it that you realized that this play might have been something special?

Henley: I remember after I wrote it, I was working in the parts department at TRW for, like, $2.20 an hour, and part of my brain was going, "What are you doing here? You've written a *brilliant* play!" And the other part was going, "You are so full of it; you've just got to try to get a ten-cent raise so you can pay the rent." So, I was very torn between "Oh that's a really good play. I know it is!" and "Then why are you workin' at TRW?"

Samantha: I want to talk a little bit more about your process and the other shows that you've written, but I feel like what you're bringing up is a bit of a problem that we have with how we view the arts, which is that you write something that is educational, that is moving, inspirational, and people will pay to get entertained, but it's still not given the kind of value that a person can live off of.

Henley: Yeah. I've been around a long time, and this country does not support the arts. And the arts need to be supported very, very badly. A lot of really stunning, original playwrights have to go off and write TV series to make a living. They end up having a child; they end up wanting to pay their rent. I've written plays as well as screenplays, and the screenplays I've primarily written for money. The thing is—I wanted to tell your listeners—when you write a play you maintain the copyright. That means if you, Samantha, write a play about your first love and it's a big success and the movies buy it from you, they give you a bunch of money but you no longer have control over the property as a film. They can fire you. They can rewrite you. You don't have anything to say in casting. Whereas, if you are with the Dramatists Guild and they do your play, you have casting approval. They can't change a line unless you say it. The bad thing is you get zero money, basically, live like a pauper. But you should definitely join the Dramatists Guild if you're a writer. Some students wrote really personal screenplays and then they got bought and they got $50,000, and then this great story is sitting on the shelf because of a billion reasons impossible to describe.

Samantha: Right, sometimes we don't think about the nasty side of this business.

Henley: I think one of the worst stories is my friend Craig Bolotin—he's a screenwriter—he'd written an original screenplay and it was done by Marty Ritt, the director, and they were into filming and he had a heart attack and had to go to the hospital and because of insurance and everything else they cut off the production and they owned the script and that was it. And ten years later, it was made with the same title, totally rewritten. It can be rough sledding.

Samantha: Right. It sounds to me that you have a stronger connection with theater than . . .

Henley: No question.

Samantha: Do you find the impact from theater is stronger or do you feel like there's more of an impact in the storytelling or do you feel like they may be equal or is it just apples and oranges?

Henley: I have been in a theater and crying so much that I couldn't get up and leave the theater. I've also seen films that blow my mind and have changed my life. Theater is what I grew up with and I love the aliveness of people being there performing for you and the audience is breathing and you're breathing and the audience laughs and you change the performance a little. Or the audience gets bored, and you change. Just the reality of that fascinates me. But I grew up with theater so for me personally that's what I love, but film, I can't say enough about the beauty of film for sure. And now television.

Sam: All three of us here are people who have passion for both theater and film. For the two people [viewing this] that don't know, I go to LMU and [Beth] is my teacher. My major is film production but my minor is theater. It's completely different storytelling. In our playwriting class, I felt like the way that I had to write is way different from the way I have to write in my screenwriting classes, not just technically but also just the kinds of stories I'm telling. What inspired you to want to start teaching playwriting and teaching it at the college level?

Henley: Money. Regular money. A salary. I'd never had a salary in my life. I'd always been an independent contractor, having to get a job. And you spend two years on a play and it ditches. The idea that you can teach one class—and I love the students and they inspire me. Especially during the pandemic, I have never been so grateful for my classes, but I'm always grateful for them. I meet terrific people at a very interesting time in their lives. I was a terrible teacher when I started; I was just awful. I'm not even a good teacher now, but I'm not a bad teacher.

Sam: You're a *wonderful* teacher! I'm about to gush about you for ten minutes . . .

Henley: It's hard to go from being professional to academic. There's a big, big difference. I have to learn things by osmosis a lot of times and that was one of them.

Sam: For me—just to gush about you for a few seconds here—I feel like, as I've been taking your class, you have helped me understand *what* I want to write about. I feel like in a lot of the screenwriting classes I've taken, they handle a lot of the technical stuff . . . but I feel like you really made me realize the kinds of stories I want to tell. We did an exercise in class; you made us write a whole scene in five minutes, and at the end of the five minutes, we had to change to a completely different scene. Mine was absolute word-vomit. Then we did a different exercise where you were like, "Okay, write for four hours with no distractions." I sat down and started writing; I wrote ten pages—and an hour and a half had passed! It just came out of me! So doing those kinds of exercises really helped me understand the kinds of things I wanted to tell and the characters I wanted to create.

Henley: I feel like my main reason is to teach people to try to hear their own voice and to try to ask questions about it and not look at failure as failure—look at failure as information. You figure out what's not working and move forward.

Sam: I really appreciate that you created that atmosphere in the class: it's okay to do something that you're not happy with or that you think is bizarre or weird or bad; it's okay because that's how you learn. So I really thank you for that.

Henley: Thank you, Sam.

Samantha: There is a monologue that I saw a girl do, and I always wanted to work on it. It's from *Miss Firecracker*. I also relate to that 'cause I did pageants—not to win, just for the scholarship money!

Henley: Fantastic! I'm writing, actually, a screenplay ["Miss Macy"] based on a podcast by a woman who was winning these contests in Anniston, Alabama, and she came from a very poor, very ignorant background, and this woman who had a charm school really mentored her and got her to the Waldorf Astoria in a modeling contest and kind of changed her life. But what did you win—or not win?

Samantha: In the pageants? There was—not Miss Congeniality, they had another word for it.

Henley: I love that word: Miss Congeniality.

Samantha: They also had a special award for talent. They also got a dentist to give a scholarship for a really great smile [*laughing*]. For the talent—every girl (back whenever I was in pageants in the nineties) sang *Phantom of the Opera* or some medley from *Phantom of the Opera* and it was like "Oh my gosh, if I hear this one more time . . ."—so what did I do? I came out in a giant square-dancing outfit with a big old huge bow in my big old curly hair and sang "I Cain't Say No" from *Oklahoma!* and it doesn't matter whether or not I'm good . . .

Henley: I love that! Have you seen the new [2019] *Oklahoma!* or heard it? Not *that* new. That song, the lyrics in that song, the story of that song is so feminist for when it was written—the whole way you can view a woman that's completely fun.

Samantha: I still sing it and we're looking through post-MeToo eyes and, exactly what you say, it was so scandalous, those girls saying that, and *now* I'm looking at it going, "Why am I apologizing?"

Henley: The way she [Ali Stroker] sings the song is: "I can't say no" is kind of a triumph.

Sam: Not to get back on track, but . . . what is the thing that keeps you coming back to theater and what do you think is the power and the importance of theater and why is it something that you've been so passionate about—for your whole life?

Henley: To me, one of the happiest things is when I write a play and then I do a reading in my living room just with people I know, actors I know, and the characters are released into the room and I hear them for the first time. I don't give any notes or tell anybody how to act it or not act it. That is such a heroin high. It's irresistible. And starting rehearsal, a heroin high. Then there's torture along the way certainly, but it's just such a beautiful experience and everyone is trying to tell a story together and they're trying to tell it with complexity and nuance and flair, and that attracts me very much.

Sam: I swear every guest has said it's about the community and it's about all of these different people coming together to tell the same story.

Henley: A mini-version of life because these people come together; they create something; they give it out to people, and then it—poofs. But anybody you've been in a good production with, you always feel close to them in a deep way.

Samantha: What's your process when you start to work on a piece? Are you always writing and then just something unfolds, or how do you get these ideas and then what do you do when you get them?

Henley: It's sort of different. Right now, I'm writing a screenplay based on a podcast, so that's very solid. The podcast has a beginning, middle, and end—although it's ten minutes, and so you have to make it two hours or whatever. But for plays I like to keep notebooks and write every day, even if it's just three pages or something. And I end up finding what I need to write about a lot of times. Sometimes it comes to me—once or twice that's happened—but generally it's a search.

Sam: You had assigned to us to write a ten-minute play and so I was like "Gosh, I don't know what I'm going to write about." So I just sat down and just started spitballing ideas, and then at some point I thought, "I can't get this out of my head." So I was like "Oh good, that *is* how you're supposed to do it."

Henley: There's no "how you're supposed to do it." That's the way *I* do it. There are a million different, better ways to do it, clearer ways to do it, stupider ways to do it; you just gotta do it. That's what my motto for my class is: Show up, just show up. And I particularly meant that on Zoom, and my class really does show up for everybody else that's there, even never having seen them face to face. And that's kind of extraordinary.

Sam: Especially reading each other's work, I think, has really brought us together as a group and keeps us so engaged in class. I love seeing what other people have written and being able to read it out loud, and then when other people read aloud mine, it was an amazing experience.

Henley: It's only nine people but they're a very talented nine people, and I think the acting has been kind of extraordinary, or at least people just dipping into reading things cold.

Samantha: You've touched on two things that I think are great: one, that you do this regularly, and I think that gets a little bit of the fear out, right? If you're doing it all the time, you don't have time to sit down and . . .

Henley: I would be lying, Samantha, if I said that I was doing it all the time. There are days and days and *days* and days and days and days and *days* I do nothing.

Samantha: [*Laughing*] Of course. . . . When you've got your idea, you've written it, you've fleshed it out, you've done however many drafts, and you're now releasing it for production, how involved do you like to be in the production of a play?

Henley: Well, if it is the first production, very involved. Like I mentioned, you have power as a dramatist at the Dramatists Guild. You can approve the director, approve the cast. They can't change it. But you hope to get a director who is in your groove and can really help you shape your play and make it better and actors that can make it better. I mean that's the beautiful thing about theater—if my level is here, with all the help of designers and actors and directors, it can go up here; on the other hand, it can go down there, which is a bummer.

Samantha: When you're producing for the first time and you have that influence from the designers and actors and everybody, do you find that you make changes?

Henley: Absolutely.

Samantha: Large changes? Or just different words here and there?

Henley: Some scenes go. If you have good actors, they can make bad things work 'cause they're so good; so you really have to be vigilant and say, "Is that just working because this genius actor's doing it or is that really helping with the rhythm and story and the character?" "Have I already said that about the character and don't need it?" Having a production, my favorite part is when you're having previews, and that means you do a performance at night with an audience—excruciating—and then the next day you go and work on revisions. That's when you figure out just so much, so much that you can't figure out in a rehearsal room.

Samantha: Do you find, though, that sometimes you get varied feedback, or one night audiences are behaving in a certain way and then the next night maybe all the laughter in . . .

Henley: A lot of that depends on the size of the theater. That's very true in smaller theaters, but if you're in a big Broadway theater, which I'm generally not in, there does become . . . the things that get the laughs. It's a percentage thing; there are so many people that *will* find that funny. Whereas, if you've got a hundred people, they might find *nothing* funny or *everything* funny.

Samantha: In the process of building it, how do you filter that out?

Henley: Well, you don't. You want the audience response. They're a huge part of creating. I mean they're in there too, telling you . . . and maybe they're laughing *too* much and you want them to be more serious.

Samantha: I hear a lot from writers that you can constantly be working, constantly be changing little nuances, and constantly be fixing something or be affected by what you're hearing from the audience. Do you feel that same way too? Do you find that at some point you just have to force yourself to think, "Okay, this is it. We're done. No more changes."

Henley: Well, definitely, if, say, I was doing a play, after previews for the actors you set it; that's it. You don't want to mess the actors up anymore; they're already flustered by the idea of previews and changing things in the day and doing it at night. Definitely, after opening, there are no changes. Not that if I'm publishing it I wouldn't make little changes here and there, but for the company, lighting designers, everybody's got to know this is pretty much set.

Samantha: It's such an interesting thing to say, "Here's my baby; it's yours now."

Henley: It's always so sad because you see your connection and your company; they don't need you anymore. But they're going on to maybe the best part for *them*: performing in front of an audience. But I wouldn't trade it for anything.

Samantha: That's part of our journey as artists. There are going to be those moments that are sad. There are going to be those moments that are terrifying, and then there's that bliss and joy that are irreplaceable. Before we get on to our silly questions, do you have an endgame? Do you have an objective when you're writing your pieces that you want the audience to walk away with?

Henley: No, never, never, because everybody's different. Everybody's at a different place in their life, and somebody may see something in a love story that will make them weep, and somebody may see something that will make them cringe. I just want them to be involved and be a little bit concerned. That's what I hope for, not for a lesson. I don't want to teach a lesson. I don't know anything, so basically it's impossible for me to teach a lesson because I really don't know anything.

Samantha: I'm hearing you say that, and I'm like "I'm gonna beg to differ 'cause I've got the works, the fruits of your labor. . . ."

Henley: What do I know? I mean, look at the world; it's unknowable. This is the most unknowable creation, the world.

Samantha: I love that you say, "I just want them to be involved."

Henley: Sometimes they're not, believe me. They're sleeping.

Sam: It's also so interesting to think of the audience as part of this creative process, too, especially when you're going through the previews. They are very much involved in the creative process. If they're not engaged and they don't care, it's like, well, why not?

Samantha: We always ask our fun theater questions. Do you have a favorite experience or piece that you really love, or maybe a production that has stood out to you?

Henley: Some of the greatest experiences are in my living room when I'm hearing it for the first time; my actor friends and a few other friends that I know will give me some slack. But I really loved the production of *The Jacksonian* that was directed by Robert Falls. We did it in Los Angeles and we did it in New York, and it kept growing. It was a difficult play—it was out of time—and I was very proud of that. A lot of times you feel like you missed the mark, but I thought we got pretty close.

Sam: This is my favorite question: Have you ever had any debacles that have happened in a production? Funny stories or crazy stories? You don't have to name names if you don't want to.

Henley: Endless, endless, every production! Okay, I was doing my second play [*The Wake of Jamey Foster*] on Broadway, and it had been done in Hartford, Connecticut, and was beautiful, but it didn't work on the Broadway stage. We're at the after-party and people start leaving. This is how long ago it was: you're waiting for the *New York Times*, you're waiting for the reviews. Suddenly, they say you're over, and I was literally on a street corner, sitting in the gutter with a bottle of whiskey, crying; and my best friend, Belita [Moreno], who was in the play, came up and said, "But we said it didn't matter. We're here. It's just about doing the show." And I was like, "We *lied*. We *lied*" [*laughs*]. And it closed in twenty-one days. Yeah, that was grim.

Sam: But look where you are now!

Samantha: I think it's kind of wrapping it to where we started, which is we don't value creativity and art in this country.

Henley: [*Nodding*] Right.

Samantha: We have an expectation for it, and we put this expectation on writers, directors, and actors—creators—which is "Entertain me. Move me. Educate me." And I don't think that's the purpose of our art. I think the purpose of our art is to share and just be involved.

Henley: That's beautiful.

Samantha: Thank you. And I feel like that's why you can sit in your living room with your friends reading a piece you wrote and say this is one of my favorite experiences in my life because it's about that journey, and I feel like that's what we need to be celebrating.

Henley: It's such a life worth living: to be in tune with the creative process and to grow that in other people.

Samantha: And then, in the same hand, I'm with you in the gutter with a bottle of whiskey going "We *lied*!" because it does mean something. [*All laughing*]

Henley: Two things; you can feel both ways. I was so gutter-bound. My family was there. They were very mixed about what this play was about. Luckily, one of the actresses who was in it, Pat Richardson, said, "Okay, if the reviews are bad, we meet at my apartment on Riverside Drive." We all ended up on Riverside Drive. I also had another terrible failure; I was the last one at that party and everyone was gone. That one was Off-Broadway; it can be *brutal*. And that show [*Family Week* in 2000] closed in a week. It's rough sledding.

Samantha: I can only dream.

Henley: I hear you. I've been very, very blessed. Miraculously blessed.

Samantha: Thank you so much for taking the time to meet with us and let us ask you all these questions.

Henley: Thank you, Sam. And it's great to meet you, Samantha. Sorry I wasn't here for your birthday.

Samantha: That's okay! This is such a treat, and it is such an honor to meet you and speak with you; and thank you for your work.

Henley: That's very heartwarming. Thank you for your work in theater and keeping it alive! Bye, guys. Thank you so much.

Index

Abdul, Rosa, 68
Academy Awards, xiii, 66, 81, 84, 96
Actors' Equity, 18, 31, 72, 79, 116
Actors Theatre of Louisville, xii, 8, 11, 23, 28, 31, 33, 77, 83, 85–86, 93, 114, 141–42, 179–80, 181, 207
Agnes Scott College, 29
Ahart, John, xii
Ainsworth, Kathy, 172
Allen, Woody, 133
Alliance Theatre (Atlanta), 29
Anthony, Joseph, 139
Arbuckle, Fatty, 196
Armstrong, Louis, 187
Arquette, Rosanna, 49, 50, 52
Art (Reza), 134
Auntie Mame (Lawrence, Lee, and Dennis), 120
Austen, Jane, 100

Badlands. See *The Bridgehead*
Bailey, Frederick, 5, 6, 11, 38, 86, 93, 124, 140, 141, 176, 178, 179
Bailey Junior High School, 4
Ball, Lucille, 26, 198
Barrios, Samantha, 205–16
Bates, Kathy, 77, 86, 141, 142, 181, 207
Beardsley, Aubrey, 104, 119
Beckett, Samuel, 67, 78, 97, 106, 109
Benson, Martin, 188
Beresford, Bruce, 46, 52, 81, 146
Bergman, Ingmar, 140, 147

Bernhardt, Melvin, 182
Betsko, Kathleen, 33–44
Blumenthal Performing Arts Center (Charlotte, NC), 94
Bolotin, Craig, 208
Bowie, David, 27
Brett, Juliet, 168
Bridgehead, The (Bailey), 5, 93, 124, 140, 141, 176, 178
Broadway, 3, 14, 17, 18, 24, 28, 31, 36, 45, 66, 72, 93, 114, 115, 120, 168, 182, 183, 185, 213, 215
Brookhaven, MS, xi, 4, 13, 46, 63, 84, 157
Bryer, Jackson R., 136–50
Bukowski, Charles, 13
Byrne, David, 50, 51, 55, 84

Calandra, Dale, 80
Caldwell, Elizabeth ("Lydy") Becker Henley (BH's mother), xi, xv, 3, 4, 10, 21–22, 24, 27, 31, 36, 37, 42, 46, 55, 56, 57, 59, 63, 85, 97–98, 103, 107, 112–13, 119, 123–24, 136–37, 151, 153, 165, 176, 181, 184, 205, 206
Canton, MS, 46, 63, 84
Carpenter, Karen, 175–98
Carter, Billy, 36
Cassavetes, John, 201
Cather, Willa, 78, 107
Center Theater (Chicago), 79, 80, 95, 127, 190
Center Theatre Group (Los Angeles), 116

Chagall, Marc, 104, 119
Chaikin, Joseph, 139
Chairs, The (Ionesco), 115
Champ, Clark, 80
Chaplin, Charlie, 196
Charlotte Repertory Theatre, 94, 95, 127
Chekhov, Anton, 12, 26, 28, 73, 78, 90,
    96, 98–99, 104, 139, 149, 159–60,
    173, 180
Cher, 168
Cherry Orchard, The (Chekhov), 73, 98,
    139, 159
Children of a Lesser God (Medoff), 122
Circle Repertory Company (New York),
    176
Civil War (American), xii, 49, 81
Clarice Smith Performing Arts Center
    (University of Maryland), 136
Clarion-Ledger (Jackson, MS), 153
Cleevely, Gretchen, 112
Clinton, Bill, 117
Columbia University, 100–101
Confederacy of Dunces, A (Toole), 69, 92
Copiah County (Mississippi), 8–9, 206
Cronkite, Walter, 9, 102

Dallas, TX, xi, 4, 7, 8, 15, 23, 31, 35, 50,
    137, 138, 177, 184, 196
Degas, Edgar, 39, 133
De Laurentiis, Dino, 45, 47
Dellasega, Mary, 83–92
Demme, Jonathan, 50, 55, 114, 146
DeVries, Hilary, 26–28
Dickinson, Emily, 100
*Dirty Ugly People and Their Stupid
    Meaningless Lives* (Bailey), 140
Disney, Walt, 133
Dorset Theatre Festival (Vermont), 204
Dostoyevsky, Fyodor, 78
Drama Desk Awards, 167, 168
Dramatists Guild, 208, 212
Dramatists Play Service, 123, 151, 196

DuBois, Marlene, 80
Duchess of Malfi, The (Webster), 120
Duling Elementary School, 4

Eliot, T. S., 78
Elliott, Scott, 173
Eugene O'Neill Theater Center
    (Waterford, CT), 203
Eugene O'Neill Theatre (New York), 42

Falls, Robert, 152, 156, 160, 163, 168, 169,
    170–74, 214
Faulkner, William, 125, 154, 168
Fawcett, Farrah, 36
Fog of War, The (documentary film), 203
Fonda, Jane, 27, 34
Foote, Horton, 139
Ford, Richard, 78, 102
Foster, Gloria, 73, 139
Foster, Verna A., 155–66
Frelich, Phyllis, 122

Gaskill, William, 139
Geffen Playhouse (Los Angeles), 116,
    152, 156, 162, 169, 172, 173
Geno, C. C. (BH's sister), 4, 8, 10, 19, 36
Gianfala, Sam, 205–16
Gilbert, Lewis, 69
Glass Menagerie, The (Williams), xi, 85,
    107
Golden Theatre (New York), 115
Goodman Theatre (Chicago), 156, 168,
    169
Gorky, Maxim, 78
Greene, Alexis, 118–35
Gringo Planet (Bailey), 141
Grosbard, Ulu, 93
Gussow, Mel, 26

Hamlet (Shakespeare), 63, 106
Hancock, Jim, 177
Hannah, Barry, 102

Harper, Tess, 189

Harris, Ed, 114, 156, 168, 172, 173

Hartford Stage, 35, 37, 185, 215

Hatful of Rain, A (Gazzo), 205

Hattiesburg, MS, 46, 63, 84, 157, 206

Hazlehurst, MS, xi, 4, 8, 13, 46, 63, 84, 118, 157, 200

Headly, Glenne, 156, 168, 169, 172, 173

Hedda Gabler (Ibsen), 78

Hellman, Lillian, 78

Henley, Beth: on comedy/humor, 12–13, 24, 26, 38, 72–73, 81, 94, 106, 111, 120, 139–40, 152, 154, 166, 180–81, 195–96, 199–200, 213; on connection between her playwriting and her acting experience, 12, 63–64, 67, 81, 95, 206; on critics, 14, 35, 41, 53, 66, 78, 124–25, 134, 189; on directing, 17–18, 34–35, 71–72, 82, 92, 95, 127, 139, 142, 144, 190–92, 200, 202–3; on feminism (including position of women playwrights/writers), 28, 40–41, 43, 76, 90, 99–100, 103, 123, 133–34, 135, 140, 201, 211; on Los Angeles/L.A., 6, 7, 13, 18, 23, 33–34, 58, 68, 69, 102, 117, 125, 129, 130, 145; on New York City, 16, 17, 24, 58, 65, 113, 117, 119, 129, 134, 145, 173; on politics, 43, 55, 56, 160, 161–62, 165, 169, 171–72, 193; on process (playwriting), xvi, 27, 34, 57–58, 60–63, 66–67, 67–68, 94, 101–2, 106, 108–9, 129, 132, 133, 148–49, 171, 172, 182, 196, 203, 211–12, 213; on process (rehearsal), 34–35, 59–60, 142, 181, 196, 212–13; on racism, xv, 56, 140, 152–54, 157–58, 160–62, 171–72; on stage writing vs. screenwriting, 7, 44, 47, 50, 68–70, 82, 104–6, 108, 117, 129, 132, 145–46, 147, 208–9; on teaching, 100–101, 178, 192, 197–98, 209–10, 212

Works: *Abundance*, xiii, xvi, 30, 61, 62, 65–66, 79, 81–82, 84, 88–89, 90, 94, 107–8, 114, 116, 125, 126, 130–31, 132, 145, 157, 165, 188–89; *Am I Blue*, xi, 5–6, 28, 35, 64, 81, 83, 102–3, 124, 138, 140, 147, 176, 178, 206; "Barbette" (screenplay; film in development), xxiv; *Control Freaks*, 61, 62, 67, 68, 70–71, 72, 73, 77, 79–80, 82, 91–92, 94, 95, 99, 108, 111, 114, 115, 125, 127–29, 132, 143–44, 145, 171, 190–92, 200; *Crimes of the Heart*, xi, xii, 3, 4, 6, 7–9, 10, 11–12, 14, 17, 18, 23–24, 26–27, 28, 29, 33, 36, 39, 40, 41, 50, 51, 56–57, 58, 60, 67, 72, 74–77, 79, 83–84, 85–86, 89, 93, 95, 97, 98, 102, 110, 111, 118, 123, 124, 125, 131–32, 134, 139, 140, 141–42, 143, 148–49, 153, 155, 158–60, 170–71, 178–83, 196, 199–200, 201–2, 206–8; *Crimes of the Heart* (screenplay), xiii, 37, 45–46, 47, 49, 52, 69–70, 81, 84, 96, 108, 129, 133, 146; *The Debutante Ball*, 37, 38, 39, 40, 46, 57, 60, 61, 65, 73–74, 84, 87–88, 89, 99, 102, 121–23, 129–30, 132, 160, 186; *Downstairs Neighbor*, xiii; *Exposed*, xxii, xxiv, 148–49, 156; *A Family Tree* (episode of PBS series *Trying Times*), xiii, xxi; *Family Week*, 128, 132, 155, 157, 168, 193, 215; *Give Me Fever*, xiii; *Hymn in the Attic*, xx; *Impossible Marriage*, 96, 103–4, 108, 110–11, 112–13, 114, 115–16, 119–21, 128, 132, 134, 149, 192; *It Must Be Love* (screenplay), xiii, xxii; *The Jacksonian*, xv, 152–54, 156–57, 157–58, 160–66,

167–69, 170–74, 194–95, 214; *Laugh*, 165–66, 195–96, 198; *Lightning (or The Unbuttoning)*, 203; *L-Play*, 95, 147, 192; *The Lucky Spot*, 52, 53, 55, 60–61, 62, 69, 72, 79, 84, 88, 90, 94, 107, 120, 125, 126, 144, 186–87; *The Lucky Spot* (unproduced screenplay of), 69, 81; *The Miss Firecracker Contest*, xi, 4, 9, 15, 17, 27, 30, 39, 40, 41, 46, 60, 61, 71, 72, 79, 84, 88, 93, 108, 114, 129–30, 132, 142, 160, 168, 171, 184–85, 210; *Miss Firecracker* (screenplay), 69–70, 81, 84, 86–87, 108, 129; "Miss Macy" (screenplay; film in development), xxiv, 210; "The Moonwatcher" (screenplay; became the screenplay *Nobody's Fool*), 7, 21, 28, 30, 46, 49–50, 53, 141; *Nobody's Fool* (screenplay; earlier title "The Moonwatcher"), 49–50, 51, 52, 53, 54, 57, 141; *Parade* (book for a musical), xii, 6, 36, 124; *Report on Motherhood* (part of the multi-playwright *Motherhood Out Loud*), xxiii, 168; *The Resemblance Between a Violin Case and a Coffin*, 197; *Revelers*, 85, 91–92, 157, 190; *Ridiculous Fraud*, 156, 157, 158–60, 165, 192–94; *Signature*, 61, 65, 67, 69, 71, 82, 90, 94, 95, 107, 120, 125–27, 133, 189–90; *Sisters of the Winter Madrigal*, 140–41, 155; "The Stopwatch Gang" (unproduced screen adaptation of the book), 95, 104; "Strawberry" (unproduced screenplay), 46, 53; "Swing High, Swing Low," 21–22, 60, 138; *True Stories* (screenplay, written with Stephen Tobolowsky and David Byrne), 50, 51, 84; *The Wake of*

Jamey Foster, xii, 10–11, 27, 28, 30, 37, 38, 39–40, 42–43, 46, 50, 56–57, 60, 61, 75–76, 93, 104, 111, 120, 132, 134, 143, 160, 171, 185–86, 215

Henley, Charles (BH's father), 4, 8, 10, 31, 36, 43, 55–56, 63, 81, 124, 133, 169, 176, 189, 193

Henley, Elizabeth ("Lydy") Becker. *See* Caldwell, Elizabeth ("Lydy") Becker Henley

Henley, Patrick (BH's son), 111, 116, 118–19

Hoffman, Abbie, 106

Hollywood, 27, 29, 30, 44, 49, 69, 145, 147

Hope, Bob, 168

Howe, Tina, 202

Hunter, Holly, 72, 81, 84, 90–91, 93, 104, 111, 112, 114, 120, 128, 143–44, 185, 187, 191–92

Hurricane Camille, 158

Hurricane Katrina, 158

Hurt, Mary Beth, 111, 143

Ibsen, Henrik, 78

"I Cain't Say No" (Rodgers and Hammerstein), 211

Iggy Pop, 16

I Love Lucy, 26

Imaginary Invalid, The (Molière), 206

Inge, William, 183, 184, 189

Inspector Calls, An (Priestley), 164

Ionesco, Eugène, 115, 147

Jackson, MS, xi, 3–4, 13, 20–21, 24, 27, 31, 45–46, 52, 59, 63, 81, 83, 112, 118, 121, 123, 136, 151, 153–54, 155, 161, 162, 167, 170, 171–72, 177, 186, 195

Jackson Little Theatre, xi, 85

Johnson, Denis, 78

Johnson, Magic, 149

Jones, James Earl, 73, 98, 139

Jones, John Griffin, 3–19

Jones, Paula, 117
Jory, Jon, 11, 28, 86, 179, 180

Kane, Carol, 187, 193, 199
Kaye-Martin, Edward, 173
Keaton, Buster, 196
Keaton, Diane, 49, 52, 81, 84
Keats, John, 189
Kingsley, Susan, 77, 86, 141–42, 181,
    187, 207

Lahti, Christine, 187
La MaMa (Hollywood), 141, 179
La Morte, Dan, 80
Lange, Jessica, 49, 52, 81, 84, 107
L.A. Slugs, 16
Laurel Canyon, 27
Leight, Warren, 115
Lend Me a Tenor (Ludwig), 85
Lessac (voice training method), 177, 178
Letts, Tracy, 168
Levinson, Amy, 162
Lincoln Center (New York), 82
London, England, 35, 69, 77, 78, 115, 146,
    178, 192
Long and Happy Life, A (Price), 69
Loretta Theatre (Santa Monica, CA),
    114, 116–17
Los Angeles Theatre Center, 68
Loyola Marymount University, xi, 167,
    197–98, 205, 209
Lynch, David, 168
Lyons, Bonnie, 96–109

Macbeth (Shakespeare), 137
Madigan, Amy, 156, 168, 172, 173
Mamet, David, 78, 101
Manhattan Theatre Club, 14, 18, 29, 53,
    55, 83, 93, 182, 183, 187, 189
Mann, Emily, 202
Marasco, Ron, 198
Mark Taper Forum, 145

Marriage of Figaro, The (Mozart), 177
Marx Brothers, 139
Maxwell, John, 4
McCarter Theatre Center (Princeton,
    NJ), 156, 157
MCC Theater (New York), 168
McCullers, Carson, 26, 78, 106
Medoff, Mark, 11
Member of the Wedding, The (McCullers),
    78
Mencken, H. L., 66
Meredith, James, 153, 172
Met Theatre (Los Angeles), 95, 114, 127,
    143, 190, 192
Midsummer Night's Dream, A
    (Shakespeare), 64, 92
Mississippi Department of Archives and
    History, 3
Mona Lisa (da Vinci), 177
Moreno, Belita, 34, 185, 215
Morgan, Ian, 173
Morris, Willie, 102, 154
Mullener, Elizabeth, 20–25
Murrah High School, 4
Myers, Leslie R., 45–48

Nausea (Sartre), 106
New Group, The (New York), 167, 173
New Orleans, LA, 64, 103, 151, 156, 157,
    159, 165, 176
New Salem State Park (Illinois), xii, 206
New Stage Theatre (Jackson, MS), 15,
    85, 151, 162
New York Drama Critics' Circle Award,
    xi, 27, 33, 59, 83, 96, 114, 136
New York Stage and Film (Poughkeepsie,
    NY), 65, 95, 115, 126–27, 202, 203
New York Times, 26, 57, 117, 134, 215
'night, Mother (Norman), 29–30
Norman, Marsha, 29–30, 202
Normand, Mabel, 196
No Scratch (Bailey), 17

O'Brien, Dan, 151–54

O'Connor, Flannery, 12, 78, 84, 125, 152, 168

Off-Broadway, 3, 14, 29, 46, 72, 114, 115

Oklahoma! (Rodgers, Hammerstein, and Logan), 211

O'Neill, Eugene, 78

Ott, Sharon, 156

Paris, France, 177–78

Parker, Gilbert, 11, 23–24, 179, 185, 186

Pasadena Playhouse, 116

Passage Theatre (Trenton, NJ), 127

Peach, Amy, 35, 176, 206

Peters, Jill, 5–6

Peterson, Lisa, 156

Picnic (Inge), 183

Pigeon, LA, 84, 187

Polanski, Roman, 201

Poughkeepsie. *See* New York Stage and Film

Powerhouse Theater (Vassar College). *See* New York Stage and Film

Presley, Elvis, 168

Price, Reynolds, 69, 78

Prichard, JoAnne, 88

Priestley, J. B., 164

Primary Stages (New York), 168

Pulitzer Prize, xi, xii, 23–24, 29–30, 31, 36–37, 53, 57, 81, 93, 98, 134–35, 182–83, 206

Pullman, Bill, 156, 168, 172

Purcell, Evelyn, 50

Ranelli, J., 182

Rebeck, Theresa, 199–204

Renner, Pamela, 110–13

Rich, Frank, 83–84

Richardson, Patricia, 215

Riley, Claudia, 178

Ritt, Martin, 208–9

Robbins, Tim, 114

Roberts, Eric, 49

Rochlin, Margy, 51–54

Rogers, Roy, 168

Rogers, V. Cullum, 93–95

Root, Lynn Green, 88

Roth, Michael, 188–89

Roth, Philip, 152

Roundabout Theatre (New York), 96, 103, 110, 111, 114, 120

Rous, Bess, 156

Sade, Marquis de, 133

Samuel French (publisher), xi, 85, 151

Sand, George, 100

Sartre, Jean-Paul, 106

Savannah, GA, 103, 113

Scambiatterra, Kathy, 79

Schlamme, Thomas, 86

Seagull, The (Chekhov), 173

Sessums, Kevin, 55–58

Sewanee Writers' Conference, 151

Shakespeare, William, 12, 64, 78, 95, 100, 101, 106, 125, 137, 139, 149, 202, 206

Shaw, George Bernard, 78

Shepard, Sam, 70, 101, 105

Sherbert, Linda, 29–32

Shirley, Don, 114–17

Shubert Theatre (Boston), 27

Side Man (Leight), 115

Silver, Nicky, 101

Simon, John, 14

Smith, Bessie, 187

Smith, Lois, 112

South, the (American), xiv, 9, 12–13, 24, 33–34, 38, 39, 40–41, 43, 49, 53, 56, 57, 63, 71, 73, 81, 84, 87, 102, 103, 140, 144, 152–53, 157–58, 160–62, 170, 171–72, 193, 206–7

South Coast Repertory (Costa Mesa, CA), 114, 116, 122, 156

Southern Gothic, 12–13, 28, 29, 40, 124–25, 158, 170

Southern Methodist University (SMU), xi, xiii, 4, 5, 6, 7, 23, 28, 31, 33, 50, 53, 81, 83, 93, 95, 96, 97–98, 137, 138, 139, 140, 155, 176–77, 185

Spacek, Sissy, 30, 46, 49, 52, 53, 81, 84, 141

St. Andrew's Day School, 4

Stardust Ballroom (Los Angeles), 16

Steal This Book (Hoffman), 106

Stop the World—I Want to Get Off (Bricusse and Newley), 4

Stopwatch Gang, The (Weston), 95, 104, 111

Streetcar Named Desire, A (Williams), xi, 85, 107, 137

Stroker, Ali, 211

Styron, William, 78

Sugarman, Burt, 30

Summer and Smoke (Williams), 4

Survival Guide/Survival Guide to Civilization (early title of PBS series *Trying Times*), 31, 46, 50

Taste of Honey, A (Delaney), 78

Theatre Row (New York), 167

Theatre/Theater (Los Angeles), 31

This Property Is Condemned (Williams), 137

Three Sisters (Chekhov), 73, 90, 98, 139, 149, 159, 180

Threlkeld, Budge, 50

Time and the Conways (Priestley), 164

Titus Andronicus (Shakespeare), 101

Tobolowsky, Stephen, xii, 16, 18, 46, 47, 48, 50, 51, 84, 179, 184, 185

Tomorrow (Foote, screenplay), 139

Tony Awards, 66, 96, 167, 168

Toole, John Kennedy, 69, 78, 92

Tootsie (film), 31

Trying Times (PBS series), xxi, 55

Two Idiots in Hollywood (Tobolowsky), 31

Ullrick, Sharon, 179

Umberger, Steve, 94

United Artists, 47

University of Illinois Urbana-Champaign, xii, 4, 23, 80, 138, 178, 190

Vann, Marc, 80

Victory Theatre (Burbank, CA), 15, 114

Wadsworth, Stephen, 104, 111

Waiting for Godot (Beckett), 67, 106, 109

Walker, Beverly, 49–50

Wasserstein, Wendy, 202

Wayne, John, 134

Weiss, Hedy, 79–82

Welty, Eudora, 18, 31, 84, 102, 125, 152, 154

West, Mae, 128

White, Stuart, 176, 182

Wild Duck, The (Ibsen), 78

Wilde, Oscar, 104, 119, 149

Williams, Tennessee, xi, 4, 12, 78, 85, 102, 107, 125, 137, 155, 160, 168, 197, 202

Williamstown Theatre Festival (Williamstown, MA), 53, 72, 187

Wilson, Chrissy, 4, 16–18

Wilson, Edmund, 78

Wilson, Luke, 203

Wilson, Michael, 197

Wimmer-Moul, Cynthia, 59–78

Winter, William, 24

Wisconsin Death Trip, 41, 88, 107, 188

Witt, Robin, 79, 80

Wolff, Lily, 202–3

Woodard, Alfre, 86

Working Theater (New York), 204

Zindel, Paul, 11

About the Editors

Jackson R. Bryer is professor emeritus of English at the University of Maryland, College Park. He is the editor of *Conversations with Lillian Hellman* (1986) and *Conversations with Thornton Wilder* (1992), as well as the coeditor of *Conversations with Sam Shepard* (2021), *Conversations with August Wilson* (2006), and *Conversations with Neil Simon* (2019), in the University Press of Mississippi's Literary Conversations Series.

Mary C. Hartig is coeditor of *Conversations with Sam Shepard* (2021), *Conversations with August Wilson* (2006), and *William Inge: Essays and Reminiscences on the Plays and the Man* (2014). She is also coauthor/coeditor of the *Facts on File Companion to American Drama* (two editions, 2004 and 2010).

www.ingramcontent.com/pod-product-compliance
Lightning Source LLC
Chambersburg PA
CBHW020104030726
47498CB00006B/1936